MYSTERY ANIMALS
of Britain and Ireland

MYSTERY ANIMALS of Britain and Ireland

by

Graham J. McEwan

ROBERT HALE · LONDON

First published in Great Britain 1986

Robert Hale Limited
Clerkenwell House
Clerkenwell Green
London EC1R OHT

British Library Cataloguing in Publication Data

McEwan, Graham J.
Mystery animals of Britain and Ireland.
1. Zoology – Great Britain 2. Animals – Folklore
I. Title
001.9'4 QL89

ISBN 0-7090-2801-6

Set in Ehrhardt by Rowland Phototypesetting Limited
Printed in Great Britain by St Edmundsbury Press Limited,
Bury St Edmunds, Suffolk and bound by
WBC Bookbinders Limited

Contents

List of Illustrations

PLATES

FIGURES

PICTURE CREDITS

The following photographs have been reproduced by kind permission of: David Clarke, 9; Fortean Picture Library, 6, 7, 14, 15, 27, 28, 30, 31, 33, 36, 39, 40, 41, 43; Mike Hilton, 37; Professor F. Hodson, 44; Ivor Newby, 14, 15, 30, 31; Mrs M. M. Smith, 29; University of London Library, 45; Nicholas Witchell, 25, 26.

Acknowledgements

I should like to thank the following for permission to use copyright material: Trevor Beer, for an extract from his book *The Beast of Exmoor*; Janet and Colin Bord, for extracts from *Alien Animals*; David Clarke, for an extract from his article 'The Myth and Mystery of Morgawr, the Helford Monster', published in *Cornish Life* magazine; *Daily Telegraph*; Timothy K. Dinsdale, for extracts from *The Leviathans*; *Falmouth Packet*; W. Foulsham & Co. Ltd., for extracts from *Great Ghost Stories* by Elliott O'Donnell; Robert Hale Ltd., for extracts from *The Haunted South* by Joan Forman and *Portrait of Suffolk* by Allen Jobson; *The Orcadian*; Anthony Nichol Shiels, for extracts from his articles in *Fortean Times*; W. W. Norton & Company, Inc., New York, for extracts from *The Dragon and the Disc* by F. W. Holiday; Colin Smythe Ltd., for extracts from *The Middle Kingdom* by Dermot MacManus; Neville Spearman for extracts from *The Undiscovered Country* by Stephen Jenkins and *To Anger the Devil* by Marc Alexander; *Surrey Advertiser*; The University of London Library, for extracts from *The Most Haunted House in England* by Harry Price; Nicholas Witchell, for extracts from *the Loch Ness Story*.

My grateful thanks go to the following for providing general assistance and information: Bob Bird, photographer; Sheila Bird, writer; Janette Bell; David Clarke, editor of *Cornish Life* magazine; Mrs I. Christie; Dr W. H. Dearman of Newcastle University; Mr N. Dean of the Mid-Southern Water Company; Ronald Hagley, MBE; Chris Hall; Mrs E. Hall; Ian Cook; Brian Liversidge; Guy Liversidge; Tommy Joyce; Stephen Coyne; Thomas Welsh; Professor F. Hodson of Southampton University; Mr J. M. Jenkins; Janet Knox; Mrs E. Lennie; Mrs K. S. McKinnon; Bridget Mackenzie; A. L. Manser, photographer, and Tony Manser; Ted Noble; Dorothy Pickard; Bob Rickard, editor of *Fortean Times**; Anthony Nichol Shiels; Bob

* *Fortean Times*, 96 Mansfield Road, London, NW3 2HX; *Fortean Picture Library*, Melangell House, Princess Street, Montgomery, Powys, SY15 6PY

Skinner; the Surrey Constabulary; Mrs A. Sutherland; Mr Tomlinson and the many witnesses of mystery cats in Scotland, Hampshire and Surrey who have written to me describing their sightings.

I should like to express my special thanks to Janet and Colin Bord; to Mr and Mrs A. Hall, for kindness and hospitality and to Chris Hall, with whom I have spent many happy hours exploring 'Surrey Puma' country.

I have attempted to obtain permission for the use of all quotations, but in a few cases I have been unsuccessful in contacting the copyright holders. Any omissions notified to the author will be rectified in future editions.

Introduction

If Sir Arthur Conan Doyle had written no other book than *The Hound of the Baskervilles* this work alone would have assured him a permanent place in the history of English literature. It touches upon a deep, primeval fear – that of being out alone at night on some deserted country road or desolate moor, where some dreaded animal is lying in wait.

British folklore is rich in legends of supernatural beasts which prey on lonely travellers, which is perhaps not surprising when we remember that our ancestors, from pre-history almost until the lifetime of our grandparents, lived in isolated communities in a landscape of moorland, mountain and forest where, in earlier centuries wolves, bears and wild boars roamed. Every region had its own tradition of supernatural animals. The Scottish Highlands were haunted by huge phantom cats – the Cait Sith – while the Fens were patrolled by Black Shuck, the enormous, fiery-eyed ghost hound. Loathsome monsters – Water Bulls and Horse-eels – dwelt in the lakes of Scotland and Ireland, emerging from time to time to drag some lonely wayfarer beneath the waters, while the seas around Cornwall were the home of Morgawr – the Sea Giant.

This could all be dismissed as superstition, except that mysterious creatures are still encountered here in the British Isles. They are now seen not by the ignorant peasants or superstitious fisher-folk of former centuries, but by the people who make up a modern society, such as bankers, building-site workers, policemen, coastguards, lorry-drivers, farmers, schoolteachers and, in one case, a coastal geomorphologist!

This book is an attempt to present and assess the accumulated evidence for the inexplicable animals in Britain and Ireland. Wherever possible, I have contacted witnesses and visited the locations where sightings have occurred, and corresponded with other researchers and also those in authority, such as police officers, investigating reports of mysterious animals.

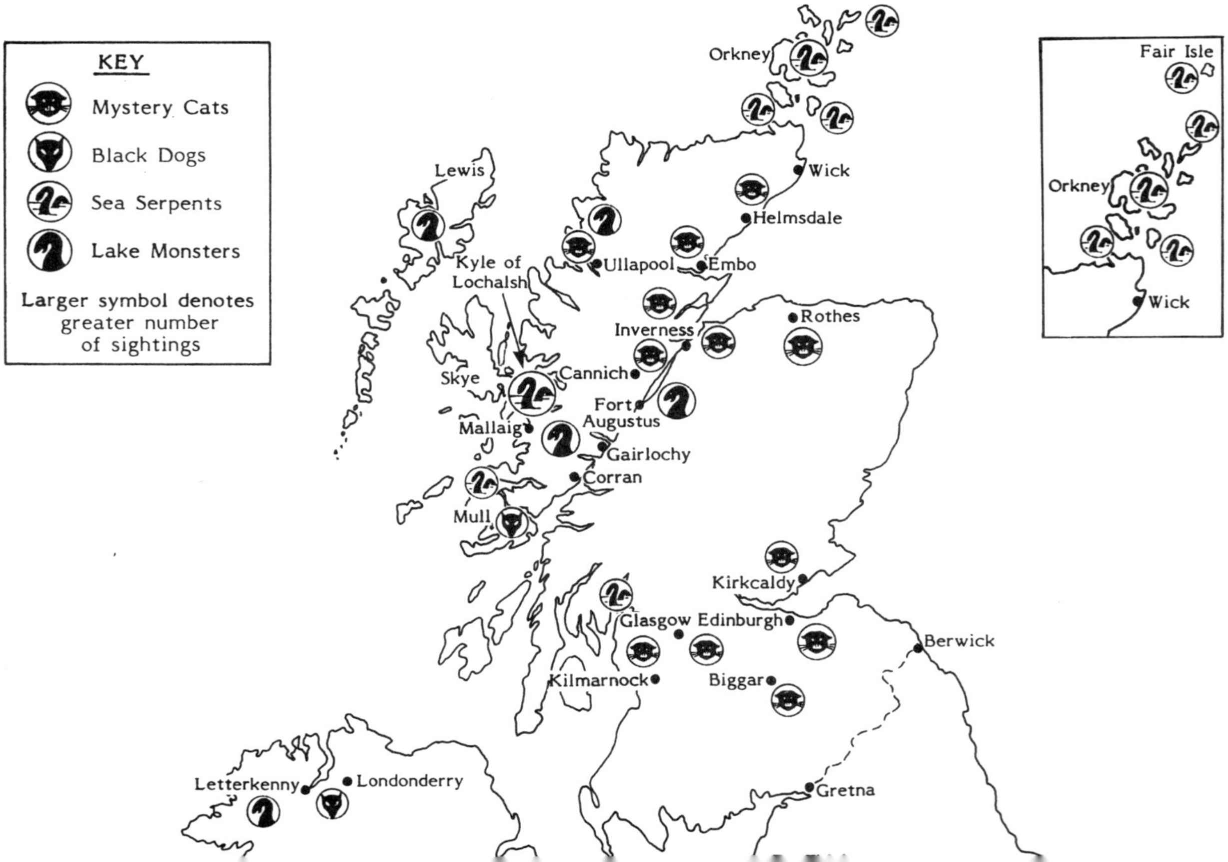
KEY
Mystery Cats
Black Dogs
Sea Serpents
Lake Monsters
Larger symbol denotes greater number of sightings
Orkney
Wick
Helmsdale
Lewis
Ullapool
Embo
Kyle of Lochalsh
Inverness
Rothes
Skye
Cannich
Fort Augustus
Mallaig
Gairlochy
Corran
Mull
Kirkcaldy
Glasgow
Edinburgh
Berwick
Kilmarnock
Biggar
Letterkenny
Londonderry
Gretna
Fair Isle
Orkney
Wick

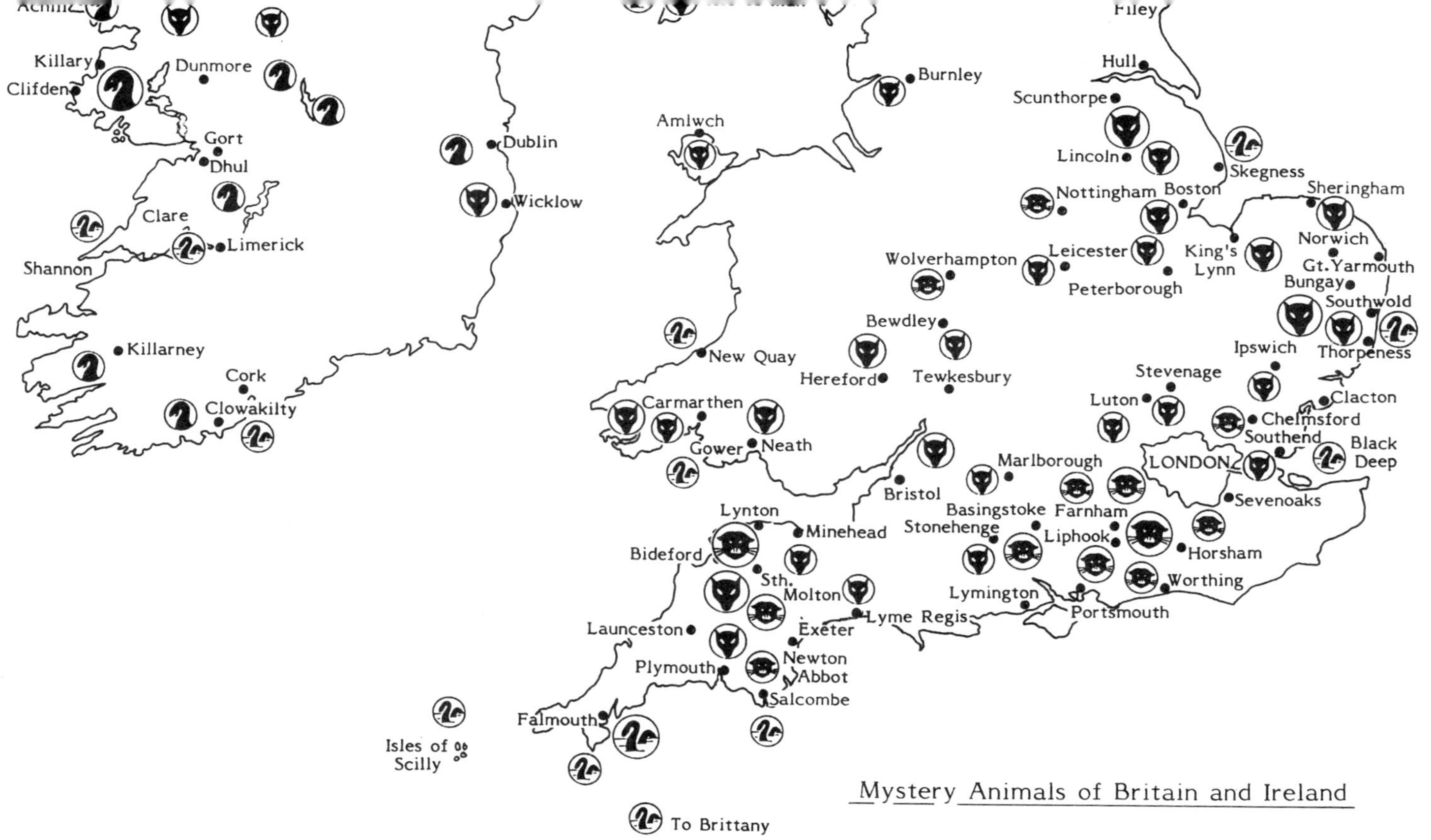

Mystery Animals of Britain and Ireland

CHAPTER ONE

Mysterious Big Cats

There is now no official doubt that the animal is a puma.
Statement issued by the Surrey Constabulary on 1 October 1964.

The Surrey Puma

In the autumn and winter of 1964 a blaze of publicity surrounded reports of a mysterious cat-like beast in southern England. The animal was soon dubbed the 'Surrey Puma' a name which, for a brief period, was seldom out of the newspapers. As the name suggests, most reports of the animal were from Surrey, though there were also accounts from the neighbouring counties of Sussex and Hampshire. The witnesses comprised a varied cross-section of the community, many being life-long country-dwellers who, familiar with rural sights and sounds, were quite convinced that a strange animal was at large. Not surprisingly, the subject was often treated in a very light-hearted manner by the media, but two groups of people took it more seriously – the farming community and the police. In addition to the eye-witness reports, there were several attacks on farm animals, apparently by some large predatory beast, and the farmers wanted to be sure that, whatever the marauder was, it was captured or killed. For the police (several of whom themselves reported seeing the animal) it was a matter of public safety. The authorities thought it possible that a big-cat had escaped from a zoo or circus, or had been released by a private collector who had tired of the responsibility of looking after an exotic pet. Checks were made of various animal collections, but drew a blank, and searches of the fields and woods failed to flush out the animal. These abortive investigations reinforced the sceptics' view that the witnesses had merely misidentified an ordinary country animal. Arguments raged furiously in newspapers and magazines, and several experts were called upon to provide their opinions, but the mystery was never solved.

Before looking at some of the numerous eye-witness accounts of the Surrey Puma we should look briefly at the physical characteristics of the typical puma. This animal, *Felis concolor*, is indigenous only to the New World and found throughout North, South and Central America. It is often referred to as the panther, cougar or mountain lion. Pumas may attain a length, including tail, of eight feet six inches, a height at shoulder of two feet six inches, and a weight of 270 pounds. Most, however, are much smaller. An average sized puma would perhaps be six feet long overall, with a shoulder height of about two feet. The basic colour is a tawny brown but this may be tinged with other colours such as red, silvery grey and slate colour. Puma cubs have spots, but these disappear with maturity. There is no reason why a puma could not survive in England. The adaptability of the big cats is illustrated by the case of the clouded leopard which escaped from Howlett's Zoo near Canterbury in August 1975. The animal was shot eight months later by a farmer whose lambs it had been killing. The zoo's owner, Mr John Aspinall, had presumed the animal to be dead. Pumas are extremely adaptable, both in diet and habitat, and would have no difficulty surviving in the country-side of Surrey and Hampshire.

Although the Surrey Puma first attracted widespread attention in 1964, there are earlier reports of strange cat-like beasts in southern England. In 1959, Mr A. Burningham was driving along a lane near Preston Candover in Hampshire when, as he recalls:

> I was amazed to see an enormous great cat padding across the road and into trees on the other side. It did not look like any domestic cat or dog, but was rather like a cross between the two. It had a cat's head and a short neck and was the size and colour of a yellow labrador. Its tail was fairly long and its coat roughish-looking.

Mr Burningham reversed his car and saw the animal sitting under some trees at the edge of a field, watching some lambs. As his car was blocking the road, Mr Burningham drove off. He later realized that the animal was like a young puma he had seen in a zoo. In the same year an Aldershot taxi-driver, Mr Kilham, saw what he described as a huge lion spring over a hedge beside Tweezledown Racecourse. Earlier, in 1955, a woman walking with her dog near Abinger Hammer in Surrey came across the half-eaten remains of a calf and saw an animal resembling a puma skulking away.

At about 7.45a.m. on 16 July 1962, Mr Ernest Jellett, an employee of the Mid-Wessex Water Board, was cycling down a wooded track leading to Heathy Park Reservoir. About half-way down the track Mr Jellett saw a rabbit, and, beyond that:

> Something like a big-cat was crouching and edging forward. It had a sort of round, flat face, like a big-cat's and its tail was long and thin, not bushy. It had big paws.

The strange animal pounced at the rabbit, missed, and then bounded up the track towards Mr Jellett, coming right up to the front wheel of his bicycle. The frightened Mr Jellett shouted and scared the creature away.

Ernest Jellett was certain that he had not seen a fox or a dog. He described the animal as '. . . not unlike a young lion cub, a light sandy colour, a flat face, very large paws and about eighteen inches to two feet high'. It has been suggested that the animal was a feral cat (a domestic cat turned wild). After several generations in the wild they often grow to a large size and, unlike domestic cats, have disproportionately large paws. The animal that Mr Jellett saw, however, would seem to be too large even for a feral cat.

A few days after this incident Edward Blanks, the manager of Bushylease Farm, Crondall, Hampshire had trouble with his herd of Aberdeen Angus cattle:

> They were making a terrible noise, milling about in the middle of the field. They wouldn't move and took no notice of me. Cattle get disturbed for various reasons but these have never taken so long to quieten down. I usually only have to walk among them and they're okay.

The cattle seemed frightened by something in the nearby woods, so Mr Blanks drove his landrover over to the trees. He saw nothing but believed that the lights of the vehicle frightened something away, for the cattle quietened down.

The December 1962 issue of the Mid-Wessex Water Board Magazine reported that another water board official had seen a mysterious animal:

The strange animal seen at Heathy Park and reported in the last issue has been seen again – this time by L. Noble, Station Superintendent for the Southern Area.

The next sighting of a big-cat was in summer 1963. A long-distance lorry-driver, David Back, stopped his vehicle on the A207 at Shooter's Hill in south-east London to help what he thought was an injured dog. As he walked towards the animal though, it got up and bounded into the woods. The startled Mr Back realized that the creature was not a dog, but a big-cat, somewhat resembling a leopard. Mr Back reported his encounter at Shooter's Hill Police Station and a patrol car and four officers were sent to investigate. Shortly after, the officers reported that a 'large golden animal' had sprung over the bonnet of their car. At dawn the following day, 18 July a search was organized involving 126 police officers, twenty-one tracker dogs and thirty soldiers from Woolwich Barracks, but the hunt was unsuccessful.

Over the following year there were some rather vague reports of an animal resembling a big-cat in Surrey and Hampshire, as well as reports of bloodcurdling howls at night. Things became more interesting in August 1964, when attention was again focused on Bushylease Farm. On 15 August the remains of a calf were found. The carcass had been dragged over several fields from a neighbouring farm, and shortly after its discovery it mysteriously disappeared, farm workers denying having moved it. It weighed between thirty and forty pounds, so the killer must have been a fairly large animal.

On the night of 18 August, Farmer Blanks's cattle broke out of their field, and when rounded up it was found that a four-hundredweight steer was missing. It was discovered in nearby woods, bitten and mauled about the flanks, shoulders and legs, in a pool of blood. A vet was called in, and he made the interesting comment that, in his opinion, the injuries could not have been caused by 'any animal found in this country'.

After the attack on the steer Mr Blanks made several statements to the Press, describing the various incidents that had occurred around his farm since 1962. He had seen a 'puma' clearly on four occasions, and in the distance several times. It was about the size of an Alsatian dog, a light, sandy colour, with a cat's head and a long tail. The creature made unnerving 'yowling' cries and brought with it a smell like ammonia, so strong it was almost suffocating. Other indications of the animal's presence were the killing of wild animals in the vicinity; deep claw marks in the bark of trees (pumas, like domestic cats, sharpen their claws on trees), and foxes in the area continually being frightened out of cover onto open ground. Mr Blanks unleashed his dogs when the animal was around, but they seemed terrified of it, and would not even attempt to follow its scent.

Reports of the mystery beast continued. A reporter for the *Farnham Herald*, driving near Froyle one night, heard a loud screech and, a few moments later, saw a large, sandy-coloured beast with a cat-like head, long tail and laid-back ears, scramble up the bank at the roadside as he coasted past. Animals described as 'big-cat', 'puma' and 'lioness' were seen at Hale Common, at Ewshot and even crossing Farnham by-pass on a Saturday lunchtime. Soon, however, a feeling of anticlimax seemed to have set in. The Press began to make a joke of the subject, and reports fell off. However, if the affair of the 'Crondall Cougar' as it had come to be known, was over, the story of the Surrey Puma was only just beginning.

At 7.50p.m. on 7 September 1964 P.C. Bill Cooper, on duty at Godalming Police Station, received a telephone call from Mr Roy Pettit, a trainer at Stileman's Racing Stables, who had found a trail of unusual paw-prints. P.C. Cooper investigated and found that the prints, each about five and a half inches across, were impressed into a stretch of smooth, compacted sand used for galloping horses. Their depth suggested that they had been made by a large and heavy animal. The trail continued for about half a mile and ended about two yards from a five-foot six-inch chain-link fence. On the other side of the fence was thick undergrowth in which the trail was lost.

Several experts were shown photographs and casts of the paw-prints. Officials at London Zoo said that the prints had been made by a puma, as did Mr Percy Mountrey, a local taxidermist who specialized in big-cats. Others, including the well-known naturalist Dr Maurice Burton, disagreed, saying that the prints had been made by a large dog. In fact, the most one can say about the prints is only that they *could* have been made by a puma.

After the discovery of the paw-prints the police made further inquiries and found that a man picking blackberries near the water tower at Munstead on 3 September had seen a very large, cat-like animal on the other side of the bushes. The animal spat at him and he fled. The witness, Mr George Wisdom, later said that the animal was about five feet long excluding the tail, three feet high, with short stocky legs and large paws. It was a dirty brownish-gold colour, with a dark stripe down its back and tail. The head seemed small in relation to the body. Mr Wisdom had given a remarkably accurate description of a puma.

The two incidents together suggested that a large, possibly dangerous, wild animal was at large, causing the police to issue a public warning to this effect. So began the involvement of the Surrey Police in the hunt for the Surrey Puma, which was to last for the next three years. During this period the police received literally hundreds of reports of the puma. All were investigated and several large-scale searches undertaken. The officer in charge of inquiries was Superintendent Ronald Hagley. Details of all reports were recorded in a ledger, often referred to as the 'puma book' by the Press.

One of the first incidents to be entered in the puma book was the attack on a heifer in a field at High Pitfold Farm at Hindhead, during the night of 22/23 September. The animal was still alive when found, but had deep scratches on its left flank, and gouges in its belly and left hind leg. Tawny hairs were removed from around the wounds. The vet who treated the animal said that, in his opinion, 'the marks were those of a big-cat'. The police echoed this, saying, 'Its injuries were consistent with its having been attacked by a puma or similar wild animal.'

On the afternoon of 23 September, two building workers saw a big tawny animal lying in the sun on a grassy slope behind Hascombe village hall. It was some 300 yards away, and could not be identified, even with binoculars. Two police officers were able to edge their way up the hill and saw, from a distance of about 100 yards, a very large, cat-like animal lying with its legs thrust out and moving its head. The animal sensed them and made off into the woods, leaving the remains of a freshly killed rabbit. Later that afternoon cattle broke out of a field at Ridinghurst Farm near Cranleigh, as if something had frightened them. At 7.20p.m. a farm worker saw an animal resembling a puma walking across a field near the Leather Bottle public house, not far from Cranleigh.

At lunchtime the next day, a man out walking near Hascombe heard a strange screeching cry. Police and an expert from the Zoological Society of London searched and found a dead roe deer, badly clawed and with a broken neck. The latter feature is interesting, for a puma usually jumps onto the back of its prey and attempts to kill by breaking the neck. A big-cat was reported about two hours later at High Loxley Farm, Dunsfold. Police rushed to the area with nets and cordoned off a square mile of farmland and woods, but there was no trace of the animal.

Reports were now coming in thick and fast. Of particular interest was one from a schoolmaster who, on 29 September, saw a very large animal resembling a puma jumping up into a tree at Barrow Hill School. A Zoological Society expert examined the tree shortly after and found claw marks. Pumas often seek refuge in trees when tired or frightened, but such behaviour would be most unusual for a large dog, as some sceptics maintained the mystery animal to be.

On 1 October, the Surrey Police made the following statement to the Press: 'There is now no official doubt that the animal is a puma.'

The sightings continued. On 3 October, two women walking along a bridleway in the Shackleford area at about 4.30p.m. came almost face to face with a puma-like animal which fled, leaping over a hedge about eight feet high. Pumas are noted for prodigious leaps, and such behaviour has been reported by several witnesses in Surrey.

During the winter of 1964 there were several attacks on farm animals of which the police stated: 'The injuries were consistent with the animals having been attacked by a puma or similar wild animal.' However, the possibility that dogs were the attackers cannot be entirely ruled out. Dogs can inflict terrible injuries on farm animals, as anyone who has seen the results can testify.

Sightings continued through 1965. On 27 January Mr Robert Ware, a forest ranger, saw the puma at a distance of only fifteen yards in his car headlights, as he was driving through the vast and thickly wooded Hurtwood Common. He noted that its coat was the colour of winter bracken, which would make it well-camouflaged. Mr Ware was a witness who was well-acquainted with the local wildlife.

At 5.15p.m. on Saturday, 16 October 1965 the Honourable Philippa Thesiger, daughter of Viscount Chelmsford, went to feed her horses in a field near the family home of Chiddingfold Court. She found one of them at the gate, shaking with fear, and another hiding in a corner of the field. Both had been injured.

Then she saw a puma crouching in the grass only twenty feet away. They stared at each other for a few moments until the girl made a noise and the animal ran off. The following night Lady Philippa entered one of the sheds where bales of hay were stacked: the puma launched itself from the hay, went right over her head, as she ducked, and dashed off into the night.

In August the following year the first photograph was obtained. Since late July an ex-police photographer, Ian Pert, working freelance in association with the *Surrey and Hants News*, had been mounting a dawn vigil with an assistant near Worplesdon after a sighting there. Ten days later their patience was rewarded, as Mr Pert described:

> It was between 5.45 and 6.00 in the morning. I was about thirty-five yards away from the animal, which was sandy-coloured, about three feet long plus tail and about two feet high. It seemed to have a small head in proportion to the rest of its body. It was muscular, with a thick and very hefty tail and very sleek. Its face was very cat-like. As soon as the camera clicked the animal was away in a flash.

The picture was published in *The People* on 14 August. The experts were divided. A mammalogist at London Zoo thought the animal was a domestic cat, though he admitted his judgement was based on a photograph taken at a distance. Three experts at the Natural History Museum in London were not so definite. They said the animal was certainly of the cat family but seemed too large to be a domestic cat. They stated:

> We cannot rule out the fact that this could be a puma. A lot depends on the exact size of the animal, which one cannot determine from these pictures.

Dr Edward Orbell, head keeper at Chessington Zoo, stated: 'From thirty-five yards this animal is too big to be an ordinary cat. Its size is more that of a female puma.'

The men who took the photograph were certain that the animal was not a domestic cat, though all one can conclude from the picture alone is that the animal could have been a puma.

There were numerous sightings in August and September 1966. Particularly interesting are two which occurred at the Farnham end of the eight-mile ridge known as the Hog's Back. In

The Shooter's Hill big-cat hunt, 18 July 1963.

Cast of one of the paw-prints found at Munstead on 7 September 1964; the print is about five and a half inches across.

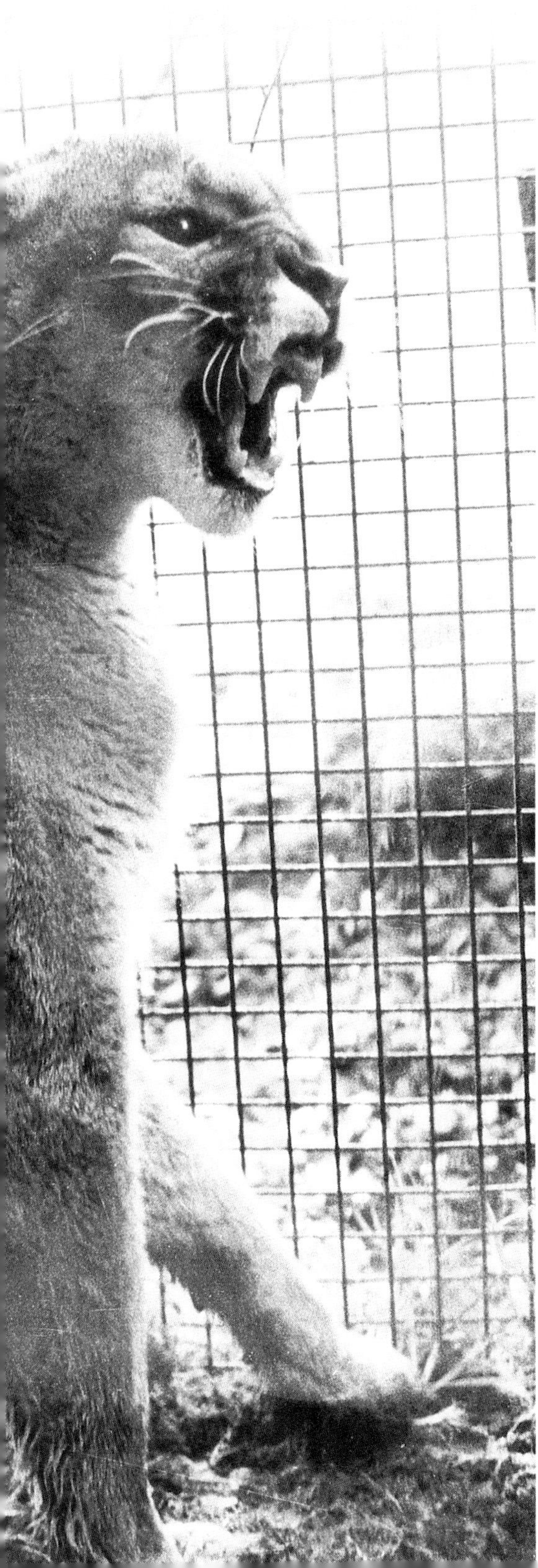

Female puma captured by Farmer Ted Noble in Glen Cannich Inverness-shire, on 28 October 1980.

Farmer Ted Noble at Cannich, Inverness-shire.

Animal photographed at Worplesdon by Mr Ian Pert.

the police record both reports are described with the words, in capitals, 'GOOD SIGHTING'.

At about 7.15p.m. on 23 September, a farmer at Whiteways Corner, Runfold, noticed six of his cattle huddled together in a field staring at an animal which was playing about in a 'kittenish manner'. The farmer approached to within fifteen or twenty yards of the creature before it saw him and bounded away. The animal's description fitted that of a puma.

About nine hours later, at 4.00a.m., two police officers were driving along the Hog's Back towards Guildford. As they approached the Lounge Restaurant their headlights illuminated an animal beside a five-bar gate. P.C. Charles Jenkins, who had been in the force for eighteen years, says:

> I slowed down and swung across the road so that the full beam of the headlights was on the animal. It appeared to cross the road in three or four leaps and bounds, yet was not unduly hurried. . . . Whatever I saw was not a dog, fox, deer or badger. I have seen all sorts of things on night patrols, but never anything like this.

The officers turned the car round and saw the animal go through a hedge twelve to fifteen feet away. They later described it as being as tall as a Great Dane, smooth-coated, and sandy in colour. Its chest and shoulders were very muscular and its long tail just touched the ground with a curl at the end. The face seemed small in comparison with the body.

The last entry in the police 'puma book' is for 17 August 1967. A motorcyclist travelling along a road at Chiddingfold saw a very large animal resembling a puma on the grass verge. A search was conducted by the police but without results.

At this point the police decided to end their investigations into the mystery. The amount of time spent in following up reports and organizing searches had grown out of hand, and if a puma was at large it did not seem to be posing any great threat to the public. Curiously, at the same time as the puma officially 'died' the reports ceased, at least for a while. One possible reason for this is that the puma was actually killed. I have heard from several sources in Hampshire and Surrey that a puma was shot by a farmer some time during the latter half of the 1960s. The carcass, so the story goes, was buried on farmland, and the matter never reported as the farmer had no licence for his gun.

The reports did not cease for long. After a gap of about a year they began again, and this time came from a much wider area.

Cats Across the Country

The puma was seen again near Rectory Road, Farnborough in November 1968, and sightings continued through the 1970s. Several sightings were described in letters from witnesses after I appealed for information in various Hampshire and Surrey newspapers. One account came from Mrs Pickard of Guildford who, with her family, saw an unusual animal in the summer of 1970. She writes:

> My husband, daughter Miriam and myself were on our way to an excavation site at Rapsley House near Ewhurst, Surrey one Saturday. We took a short cut on the edge of the woods when we all stood spellbound seeing the puma, back paws on the ground near the end of a small track, fore-paws on a fence overlooking a large enclosed chicken yard, ears not too long, tail fairly large, and I said or whispered: 'An animal from the zoo.' My legs felt like jelly and believe it or not I had my camera on my wrist but was too dumbfounded to use it. It disappeared so quickly and we all got sticks and made noises as we passed the area – about twenty yards away it was.

Mrs Pickard seems to have been affected by that strange paralysis which is so often reported by those who have encountered something whose existence is hotly disputed. People who have seen the Loch Ness Monster, Bigfoot, UFOs etc, have later reported that they had cameras, even cine-cameras, but were too overcome by amazement to think of using them.

Another letter came from Mrs Anne Stanette, describing an encounter which took place in East Surrey in 1978:

> While I was out riding in Grangers Woods, Woldingham, in May 1978, I saw what I believe was a lion rush across the road in front of me. It ran from the Oxted side into thick bushes on the opposite side. It was about ten to twelve yards from me. It was a beige/light brown colour and had a small head in comparison with the rest of its body. (It had no shaggy mane). Its back legs seemed more muscly than the front. I saw it sideways on. It did not move as a dog does.
>
> At first I could hardly believe my own eyes and just sat transfixed as

> my horse plodded slowly on. He hadn't seen it and didn't sense anything through me, but as we got to the fallen tree where I judged the animal to have come from, Prince started snorting and prancing about and wanted to gallop off. This is not normally the case as he is very sluggish. Needless to say we didn't hang about and went off as quickly as we could. I still had difficulty in believing my own eyes and kept saying to myself 'You can't have' but I did.

Although Mrs Stanette describes the animal as a lion (she must mean lioness as it had no mane), the description is more like that of a puma, particularly with regard to the small head, a feature commented on by other witnesses. Of all the big-cats this feature seems particularly marked in the puma.

The story of mystery cats in England grew ever stranger during the 1970s. Reports started to come in from all over the country often from heavily populated and built-up areas, and the creatures encountered were not limited to pumas. There was, for example, the appearance of the Nottingham Lion in the summer of 1976. At about 6.00a.m. on 29 July, two milkmen, David Bentley and David Crowther, saw the creature near the entrance to Nottingham Airport in Tollerton Lane. Mr Crowther stated:

> We both saw together what certainly to us was a lion. It was fifty yards away, had its head down and its long tail had a bushy end. It was walking away from us but only very slowly.

Mr Bentley added:

> If I had been on my own I don't think I would have told anyone, because they wouldn't have believed it. But it was there and we both saw it together.

The men watched as the animal walked around the edge of a field and then called the police. The police treated the report seriously, and drove around the area, issuing warnings to the public through loud-hailers to stay indoors and keep their doors and windows shut. Over the next eight days the police received some sixty-five reports of a lion in the area. They were able to dismiss some as misidentifications of domestic animals (the 'lion' on one occasion turned out to be a Great Dane) but others were harder to account for. The police said that they were 'ninety-eight per cent certain that there was an animal in the area' and searches with armed men, mounted police, tracker dogs and a helicopter were organized. The public joined in the hunt too: the police were horrified when they went to investigate a sighting and found some fifty people, including children, in a field, looking for the lion. The police stated that there was a real danger, and that people should avoid areas where the animal had been sighted. On the sixth day, as reports continued, Chief Inspector John Smith said: 'We are almost totally convinced it is there.' The lion, however, could not be tracked down, and on 6 August the searches were called off, the police stating that it was no longer officially believed that a lion was loose in the Nottingham area. There were in fact three more reports before the sightings ceased.

An impressive series of puma sightings occurred in the rather unlikely setting of Wolverhampton in the summer, 1980. In July a school-teacher was walking near a disused railway line between Compton and Aldersley when he saw a large animal walk out onto the grass beside the line. He had a good view of it for five minutes from a distance of about fifty yards and described it as being the size of a large dog, brown in colour, with a round cat-like head, pricked ears, short thick legs, and a heavy tail held low. The witness said that, as a keen amateur naturalist, he was quite familiar with the local wildlife, and was absolutely certain that this creature was a puma. He described his encounter to Michael Williams, a superintendent at Dudley Zoo, who was called out to investigate after further sightings and an incident in which a 'large brown animal' attacked a dog which was being walked by a child. With the senior cat-keeper of Dudley Zoo, Mr Williams searched the area around the disused railway line. They were about two miles from the location of the teacher's sighting when they saw an animal watching them from about 200 yards away. Mr Williams continues:

> It disappeared, and then we heard birds mobbing something in the thick cover and an animal emerged onto the track about 300 yards in front. It was a large animal which had a round head, was level across the back, had a heavy tail held low, and when it turned to look at us was very narrow. Everything about it was cat-like, but we couldn't get nearer than about 300 yards. . . . If we could find proof that a puma had escaped within a reasonable area of Wolverhampton then I would have said that we had seen it.

Mr Williams immediately notified the police and a search was organized. The animal, however, had disappeared without trace, and was not reported again in the area.

Another strange feature of mystery cat sightings in the 1970s and 1980s is the increasing number of reports of black big-cats. Between March 1972 and January 1973 there were several reports of a 'black panther' from the New Forest area of Hampshire. One witness was Mr John McPherson who, on 23 January 1973, was driving along the A35 near Lyndhurst when he saw the animal run across the road:

> If it was a cat it was the largest cat I have ever seen in my life. It was large, black and low slung, rather longer than a labrador but about the same height. It had a short head. It was cat-like, but much too big to be one and was definitely not a fox or a badger.

In the summer 1979, a similar creature was seen in the neighbouring county of Sussex. Colin Carter was walking along the South Downs in the Belle Tout area at about 9.00p.m. on either Saturday 30 June or Sunday 1 July, when a large, black cat-like animal crossed the path about ten yards ahead of him. He said that it was 'the size of a small pony'. The creature was seen again on 10 September by John and Frances Clark who were strolling through Tilgate Forest. Seventy to a hundred yards ahead they saw a large, black cat-like creature which they watched for between ten and fifteen seconds before it bounded into the undergrowth. It was between two and two and a half feet tall, with a small head and a long tail. The Clarks described their encounter in the local public house that night and found that other residents had seen the creature.

As pointed out earlier, sightings of big-cats often occur in quite densely populated areas. This is true of the following case, that of the Cuffley lioness.

At 6.00a.m. on 16 May 1983, David Messling was breakfasting in the kitchen of his home in Sutherland Way, on the outskirts of Cuffley, Hertfordshire. Looking out into his garden, Mr Messling saw a large animal leap over the hedge from his neighbour's garden. It was sandy-coloured, with short fur, approximately two feet six inches tall and about four feet long between the front and rear legs. He saw the animal from a distance of thirty yards and was certain it was a lioness. He watched it trot across his garden to the opposite hedge and then follow the line of the hedge down into a small copse, which formed the boundary of his property. Mr Messling fetched his camera and ran down the garden hoping to photograph the creature, but by then there was no sign of it and he was reluctant to follow it into the copse. He left for work, but reported the incident to Potters Bar police station at 7.20a.m.

At 7.30a.m. two police cars arrived at the Messling home, and one of the officers began to search the garden. Looking over the hedge into the garden of 3 Sutherland Way, he saw what he was convinced was a lioness leaping over the hedge on the far side, about fifty feet away. He summoned his colleagues and spoke to Gwen Shipman, the house's owner, who by then had appeared on the scene. She was advised to go inside as there was a lioness on the loose, and, watching from her bedroom window, she saw the animal's face as it crouched in the long grass in the garden of number four about 150 feet away. She could not see the animal's body, but was certain that the face was that of a big-cat.

An enormous police search was organized, involving a helicopter and some twenty cars; residents were warned by loudspeaker vans to stay indoors. Experts from nearby Broxbourne Zoo were summoned, and the gardens were carefully examined. Some indistinct paw-prints and a flattened area of grass where the animal had lain in the garden of number four were found, but there was nothing more dramatic to prove that a lioness had visited a suburban garden.

The police checked with zoos and animal collectors in the area and established that no animal had escaped. Subsequently the police officially stated that the animal was a Rottweiler dog, but this seems very unlikely. David Messling was certain that the animal he had seen from only thirty yards away was a lioness. The police officer, who saw the animal from even closer range, was equally sure of his identification. Furthermore, the animal had cleared in a single bound a hedge five feet six inches high and three feet thick, an impossible leap for a dog.

We conclude this section with a brief examination of the saga of the 'Beast of Exmoor'. The affair became national news in spring 1983, when the Royal Marines arrived at the north Devon village of South Molton to hunt an animal which had been killing farm livestock. The story, however, had begun several years before.

One summer's day in 1971, Mr and Mrs Cross of Ilfracombe

were driving along the B3226 road when they saw a large, cat-like animal emerge from the Wistlandpound Reservoir Track onto the road. They stopped, and the creature which was about fifty feet away began to walk towards them. It was scared off though, when another car drove up and overtook the Cross's stationary vehicle. The driver of the second car also saw the animal, which had fled down the reservoir track, and stopped his car to walk back and compare notes with Mr and Mrs Cross. The witnesses agreed that the animal was 'very large, quite black, and shaped like a female lion'.

The animal was seen again in the summer, 1974 by a South Molton businessman, his wife and two friends who were picnicking at Hacche Moor: 'All four of us saw it clearly, no doubt about what it was, a very large, black cat and I said at the time it had probably escaped from a zoo or circus.'

The situation became further complicated that year when a fawn-coloured big-cat put in the first of several appearances. It was seen by Mrs Cooper of Merton who described it as 'a stone-coloured puma' with long hind legs, and a very distinctive cat-like gait. It was bigger than a Labrador dog. Mrs Cooper saw the animal twice: once on the road between North Molton and South Molton, once between South Molton and West Buckland.

At 8.00p.m. on a summer evening in 1977 a driver saw a sandy-coloured, puma-like animal run across the road in front of his car as he was travelling between Bovey Tracey and Haytor Vale. He stressed that its appearance and movement were feline. Between 1978 and 1979 there were several more reports of a golden-brown big-cat in the Moretonhampstead area.

The black animal also appeared in 1978. One witness was Mr W. P. Cornish who was driving towards South Molton when, at Seven Ash near Blackmoor Gate, he saw a 'black panther'. He was able to approach to within twenty feet of the animal before it ran away. Another witness was Mr Charles Pitt who also saw the animal near South Molton. He had stopped his car to avoid hitting a stag which had leapt over a hedge and then jumped the hedge on the opposite side of the road, when:

> . . . a huge black cat landed on the road right in the same spot. It turned towards the car, and gave a frightening scream, and then leapt the hedge after the stag.

In February 1980, the tawny cat was seen again. Police Constable Farquharson was out with the Mid-Devon hunt, when the hounds flushed out a golden, Labrador-sized cat resembling a puma. The dogs chased after the animal but were called back by the hunt master. P.C. Farquharson was surprised to learn from the other hunters that the animal was well-known in the area.

Almost a year later, in January 1981, schoolboys Ben Huggins and Peter Tremere were playing in the woods near Tedburn St Mary when their two Jack Russell dogs ran off, to return a few moments later yelping in terror. Chasing them was a huge black cat which, on seeing the boys, stopped dead and then bounded up a wooded bank and out of sight. At the time the boys kept quiet about their encounter, convinced that no one would believe them, but shortly after, huge tracks were found in the woods. Casts were made and experts said that the prints were probably those of a puma. The reader should perhaps be reminded at this point that pumas are not black, though other big-cats sometimes are.

A few weeks later, a tawny-coloured big-cat was seen by Lesley Bryant of Rudge Farm. Driving down the lane towards her home at about 10.00p.m., she saw a large animal standing on its hind legs with front paws resting on a concrete stand on which the farm's rubbish bags were left. Miss Bryant described the beast as follows:

> It was the same colour as a fawn Great Dane, maybe slightly darker. But it was much too long for a Great Dane, and then I drove the car towards it, and it ran off and I got a back view. It went very fast. It had a blunt-ended tail and sort of cat ears but not pointed. It just turned in that old lane and jumped a five-bar gate with no trouble and disappeared. It was like a racy sort of lioness.

Sightings continued through 1981 and 1982 but the Beast of Exmoor did not really make the headlines until 1983. On 21 April the *North Devon Journal-Herald* devoted most of its front pages to a hunt being mounted by local farmers after an unknown animal had killed large numbers of sheep in the area. Mr Eric Ley of Drewstone Farm had lost about thirty of his lambs, and killings had also occurred at the neighbouring farms of Bickner, Pillavins and Limeslake. The hunt continued until nightfall but failed to track down the killer. The depredations continued, the Exeter *Express and Echo* for 30 April stating that losses of sheep and lambs totalled seventy to eighty. At a Press conference, Assistant Chief Constable Rupert Ormorod announced that he was calling in the Royal Marines.

The events of the following few months were confused. There were numerous sightings of strange animals, some cat-like, some dog-like, and of a variety of colours. After the *Daily Express* offered a reward of £1000 for an unpublished photograph of the beast, reporters and sightseers, armed with cameras, descended on the area. The sheep-killings continued and farmers and marines seemed to be blasting away at anything that moved. Several dogs were shot, including a valuable black Labrador. There was no shortage of theories as to the identity of the Exmoor beast. Several big-cats were suggested, including lynx, leopard, puma, lion, lioness and black panther. A man telephoned the police to say that the killer was a monstrous African badger, while a Canadian Indian living at Redruth, said that some features of the killings were reminiscent of wolf attacks. A letter to the *North Devon Journal-Herald* suggested that the creature was a specially bred dog, intended to be used in illegal dog-fights, which had escaped. At one stage the police said that they believed the beast to be a mongrel greyhound lurcher with a bull mastiff's head. Some theories tended towards the macabre and paranormal. One old farmer thought that the beast was a monstrous escapee from an experimental laboratory, the result of an experiment which had gone wrong. Others pointed out that the mystery was centred on an area steeped in legends of the phantom Black Dog of English folklore.

Disentangling and assessing the confused events of the summer of 1983 is difficult, but one thing does emerge: a black animal like the one reported many times since the early 1970s was still being encountered. A detailed account came from thirteen-year-old Alison Healey of South Molton, who saw the creature on Thursday 19 June. As she was walking near Bishop's Nympton she noticed that sheep in a nearby field were agitated and then saw, at a distance of about eighty yards, a big, black, panther-like animal. She had a clear view of it and was able to produce a sketch. (*See* Fig. 1)

At the end of July the police issued a statement to the effect that the Beast of Exmoor was dead. The beast, a dog, had been shot by a marksman, they said. It had been seriously wounded, they thought, and had crawled away to die. The carcass had not been

Fig. 1. Alison Healey's sketch of the animal she encountered on 19 June 1983.

found but the police said that there had been no evidence to support the view that the beast had been a big-cat.

There may have been a lack of hard evidence to support the cat theory, but there were continual reports, like that from Alison Healey, of cat-like animals. Many farmers were angry with the police statement and the subsequent withdrawal of the marines. They were certain that the beast was still out there!

The sightings continued through 1983 and 1984, some witnesses describing a tawny big-cat, others a black one. A detailed description of the latter came from naturalist Trevor Beer who was investigating the mystery. On a summer's day in 1984 he was walking through an area of woodland on Exmoor where the carcasses of several deer, killed by an unidentified predator had been found. Looking up over a slope he saw the head and shoulders of a large animal appear out of the undergrowth:

> In the green, sun-dappled shadows of the wood it looked black and rather otter-like, a first impression I shall always remember, for the head was broad and sleek with small ears. The animal's eyes were a clear greeny-yellow as I just stood still and stared at it.

As it stared back at me I could clearly make out the thickish neck, the powerful-looking forelegs and deep chest and then without a sound it turned and moved swiftly away through the trees.

That it was jet black I was sure, and long in the body and tail. I guessed at four-and-a-half feet in body length and about two feet at the shoulders.

I dropped my camera bag at the bushes where it had appeared and went after it, instinctively thinking, and hoping, that if it was running away it would continue to do so.

Fig. 2. Trevor Beer's sketch of the Beast of Exmoor.

> Reaching the wood edge I could see the animal already two-thirds of the way across the adjoining field and moving at great speed. It ran like a greyhound, its forelegs pushing through the hind legs and they seemed to go forward in front of its round head as it raced away, then forcing back as the forelegs again came forward to hit the ground together, a beautiful, very large black panther was my immediate thought.
>
> I watched it reach the field edge where it leaped high into the hedge and disappeared over.

Sightings of the Exmoor beast continued. Trevor Beer stated in a BBC natural history programme on 6 March 1986, that he had seen the animal six times since his original encounter. Attacks on farm animals also continued: the *Daily Mirror* for 14 February 1986, reported that an animal believed to be the Beast had struck twice in one month at David Rawle's farm at Parracombe. On the second occasion a ewe was killed and Mr Rawle commented: 'The sheep had a shoulder ripped off. Its killer must be very powerful.'

Scottish Mystery Cats

Those who remain sceptical about big-cats at large in England might find it easier to accept the possibility of such creatures living in the wilds of Scotland where vast tracts of wilderness remain. Food, consisting of wild animals and farm livestock, would be plentiful and the human population, compared with that of the rest of Britain is very small. Although covering an area of thirty thousand square miles, over half the size of England and Wales combined, Scotland has only five million inhabitants.

In recent years big-cats have been reported in several Scottish counties. The sightings have occurred in two main regions, one in the south, stretching from Lothian in the east to Kirkcudbrightshire in the west, and the other reaching from south Inverness-shire to the north coast. These two areas are separated by a wide band of country where there seem to have been only a few, scattered reports. We shall look first at sightings in the southern region.

In March 1982 I appealed through several Scottish newspapers and magazines for information about mystery cat sightings. The response was overwhelming. The majority of the letters came from the south-eastern counties of West Lothian, East Lothian, Midlothian and Berwick, where, in the words of one correspondent, 'the mystery puma was becoming as famous as the Loch Ness Monster!'

One of the earliest sightings was that reported by Mrs E. Hall, who saw the animal at the farm in Whitburn, West Lothian, where she and her now retired husband used to live. Mrs Hall writes:

> Some time after seven in the evening of a summer night in 1973, I was at the window when I saw what I believe was a puma go through the farm yard. It was bigger than an Alsatian dog, light brown in colour and had a square-shaped head. I ran out and tracked it for a mile over the country. I thought it may have come off a circus van. I had thought no more about it until I had begun to hear of sightings in the north of Scotland where sheep were being killed.

Black big-cats have often been reported in Scotland. The following account was sent by Mrs Janet Knox of Thornhill, Dumfriesshire:

> I saw a puma in the autumn of 1975 near Kilmarnock. My mother, myself and my little daughter were picking blackberries from a hedgerow beside an old untarred road, when a puma appeared on the road about 100 yards ahead of us. It stood still and watched us for several seconds and we thought at first it was a black Labrador dog, but when it walked away into the wood we could see its long tail and cat-like way of walking.

A sighting of a more conventionally coloured puma was described in a letter from Janette Bell of Cormiston Farm, Biggar, Lanarkshire:

> About one month after New Year 1976, myself and two others saw a puma in close proximity to the farm. I saw it running away across an open field, towards a strip of scrub wood. I was upstairs at the time and saw it clearly. The animal was dark brown in colour, had a long tail, square, flat head and large paws. The creature was not as long as some of the big-cats, like tigers, one normally sees in zoos. It was a bit shorter. The creature was running, but not at a great speed, and the way it ran struck me too: long, pounding definite strides throwing its front legs up.

I naturally told everyone in the house at the time what I had just seen and they all laughed at me saying I had had too much to drink! I was hurt at their remarks, because I had definitely seen a puma. However, about two days later the byre-man's wife saw it too, entering the same wood, and then my sister-in-law saw it crossing the road from this wood at night. There were never any reports from farm workers that livestock had been interfered with, but my brother did mention that this scrub wood was usually full of pheasant and at the time of the sightings there were none to be had.

Mr Tomlinson of Oldham wrote describing a mystery cat he saw while on holiday near the hamlet of Borgue on the Kirkcudbrightshire coast:

While on holiday at the Brighouse Bay caravan site in May 1979, I saw what I am convinced was a puma. The caravans on the site were usually only occupied at weekends. It being mid-week we were the only people for probably a couple of miles, except perhaps for the site warden.

It was about 7.30p.m. when I heard a commotion amongst a flock of sheep on top of the cliffs. I went to investigate, as there were a lot of lambs. What I saw was a large cat about five feet, maybe more, in length, with very sleek, fairly long hair and a rather bushy long tail. It seemed to run very fast and was very agile, dodging around boulders and gorse bushes with a semi-crouching run. I got to within fifty yards of the animal when it spotted me and made off at great speed.

This is the most southerly Scottish sighting and apparently the only one from Kirkcudbrightshire.

Mr J. M. Jenkins of Edinburgh sent possibly the most detailed and interesting of all the Scottish accounts. He was using a metal detector near a derelict gunpowder factory between Roslin and Rosewell, Midlothian during the summer, 1979. From the corner of his eye he saw a big animal cross the path nearby. He shouted at the beast and it turned, giving him a clear view. Mr Jenkins continues:

It was not more than six feet away, a puma beyond any doubt. It was the colour of a golden Labrador with white showing through and it had a black bar crossing its face. It was not in the least aggressive. I made a threatening gesture with my metal detector and it jumped over the ferns uphill, but stopped again after a few yards and turned to look at me, giving me another good look at it. This animal was pregnant and I was not surprised to read recently in the press that a puma had been sighted at Fountainhall, Midlothian, just four months ago [early 1982]. The female pumas in Edinburgh Zoo are identical to the animal I saw, even to the bar over the face. My sighting was reported to the police in Bonnyrigg and to the farm near the spot.

This creature seems to have been interested in, rather than afraid of, its human observer, a characteristic of pumas. The most interesting feature of this report, though, is the animal's apparent pregnancy, which raises several questions. Was a pregnant puma released from captivity, or have pumas bred in the wild? The former is the more likely supposition, but the latter cannot be ruled out. If the animal gave birth, did the cubs survive? Certainly pumas could breed and thrive in Scotland, as they do so in a far harsher environment in parts of America.

Mrs I. Christie of Glenrothes, Fife, wrote describing a black big-cat. One evening she was driving with her husband, daughter and three grandchildren along a road in the Ochil Hills when they saw an unusual animal by the roadside. The animal had apparently just emerged from a hedge on the edge of a wood and was about to cross the road. Mrs Christie stated:

It was huge, like a big, black cat with enormous green eyes and, on seeing our van, turned and silently went back through the hedge towards the woods. Six people saw it so we could not be in any doubt.

Mrs Christie also mentioned that, earlier in the day, she had seen two dead sheep in the area, and that a nearby flock seemed very restless. She thought that the creature she and her family had seen might have been the killer.

Mrs K. S. McKinnon of Penicuik, Midlothian wrote:

On Sunday 16 May 1982, I was out walking with my husband and children along the track of a disused railway which runs close by Penicuik. I was on a part of the track which had a hill running up to my left, when I saw what I at first took to be a lioness – the animal which I saw was roughly that size and colour with a long tail. Naturally enough, I could not believe my eyes, and studied the animal as closely as possible. It was about 4.00–4.30p.m. on a bright, warm afternoon, so there was good light, and vegetation on the hill was still fairly low.

The animal, which I now believe to be a puma, was alone as far as I could tell, was prowling about on the hillside and appeared to be calm. It was, most definitely, of the 'big-cat' family. My husband also saw the animal, although he did not stop as long as I did for fear of alarming the children. I watched the animal for perhaps five to ten minutes, partly to convince myself that what I was seeing was really there, and partly to see what it did. It continued to prowl about in the one small area and appeared not to notice us on the path below.

When we returned on the same path about one hour later there was no sign of the creature.

On a Sunday morning early in June 1982, Mr Thomas Catleugh from Garvald, Midlothian saw what seemed to be a puma stalking the sheep in a field at Garvald Mains Farm. He stated:

The animal was about twenty inches high with a long body and tail measuring about three feet. It was dark grey in colour and I noticed a dark sheen along its back. As I watched, the animal neared the sheep, moving very stealthily, crouching down on its forelegs. The sheep moved away and it lay down where it had been.

Its large rounded ears lay back on its head and its jaw constantly opened and closed. I have never seen an animal with such a deep jaw. The way it studied the sheep I was sure I was going to see a kill. I was less than forty feet away and I had a very good view, but as I am not all that quick on my feet I thought by the time I warned anyone it would be away.

Mr Catleugh hoped that a car would pass so that he could ask the driver to inform the police, but none did. After about an hour the animal walked away. Mr Catleugh told the farmer, Gavin Hamilton, who called the police and the SPCA. The area was searched but without success.

A few days later a monk at the nearby Nunraw Abbey reported that he had seen the animal run across open fields. Mr John Williamson of the SPCA was certain that a puma was at large, saying:

A sheep was killed last weekend and I have not seen a carcass like that before. Previous evidence linked to the latest story makes me believe that a puma is in the district.

Mary F.'s photographs of the Falmouth Bay sea serpent, 1976.

Enlargement of triple-exposed photograph of Morgawr taken by David Clarke on 17 November 1976.

David Clarke loading his camera shortly before Morgawr appeared.

The Falmouth Bay sea serpent, photographed by Anthony 'Doc' Shiels.

Two of Gerald Bennett's three photographs of the Falmouth Bay sea serpent, 1977.

Monster hunting at Lough Nahooin; Lionel Leslie (left) with Professor Roy Mackal.

Lough Auna, Connemara, County Galway; F. W. Holiday (right) with Lionel Leslie and Holly Arnold.

From the gentle rolling hills of southern Scotland we travel now to a region of rugged mountains, thick forests, and desolate moorland: the northernmost third of Scotland.

Sightings of mystery cats in northern Scotland, like those in the southern half of the country, have all occurred since the early 1970s, with one interesting exception. It was described by Mrs Bridget MacKenzie of Langbank, Renfrewshire:

> In response to your letter in the *Ross-shire Journal* about sightings of pumas: I saw one in Sutherland, on the west coast, in 1957. At the time I was the warden of Achinvar Youth Hostel, which was a small crofthouse about two miles south along the coast from the village of Achiltibuie and about ten miles north of Ullapool. It was just before Midsummer's Day, probably about 18 June as far as I remember.
>
> There were five or six other people, all hostellers, cooking their evening meals, when we heard a sudden great agitation among the sheep in the field to the north. We went outside to see what ailed them. They were all baaing and snorting and moving quickly downhill dashing out of the mist as if a strange dog were at them.
>
> Then we saw it was not a dog. It was a bigger animal very like a cougar I had seen in British Columbia. It was a bright sand colour all over with no markings: definitely a cat and not a dog. Its ears were rounded rather than pointed and set close to its head, which was broad and shaped like a lioness's. The tail was longish and sandy, the same colour as the body, with a tuft at the end. It had rather large feet and its legs were thin. In fact I thought that it looked a bit undernourished.
>
> It was stalking the sheep which were panic stricken. It moved in a sort of feline slink, with its head thrust forward. It passed twenty-five to thirty yards from us, totally ignoring or unaware of us. We were standing in a group in front of the house and the six of us watched it follow the galloping sheep across the slope of the field and over a rise in the ground. It had not caught any by the time it went out of our view and we certainly did not follow it. In fact we all bolted back into the house and shut the door very firmly. It was very menacing, and we all admitted to finding it rather alarming. It was broad daylight when we saw it, about 6.00p.m. We were all sober, young and keen-sighted and were all agreed on what we saw.

The witnesses reported their sighting to the police and to a nearby croft, but apparently there had not been any other reports.

This incident seems to be completely isolated, there being no further sightings, it seems, for another fifteen years. It could be that witnesses simply did not report their encounters, though they might be expected to come forward in later years when pumas became headline news. It is also possible that any big-cats loose in this bleak, empty countryside simply managed to avoid human beings altogether.

On 18 November 1977, Mrs A. Sutherland and her husband were driving towards Kirkcaldy from their home in Halkirk, Caithness. At about 5.45a.m., as they were driving past the cemetery on the north side of Berriedale Brae, an enormous animal leaped across the road. At first they took it to be a dog, but then realized that its appearance was feline with a broad, flat head and long, very sharp-looking teeth.

Mrs Helen Fitch had lived in Central Africa where she had seen big-cats on a number of occasions. Because of this experience she was sure that just such a creature was in a field near her house at Cononbridge, Ross-shire on 30 January 1978:

> Out of the corner of my eye I caught a glimpse of a large dog-like animal carrying a black object in its mouth. I looked again and realized it resembled a big-cat similar to a small lioness or puma. It was dark tan but its tail and back were a darker shade. It was very heavy in the shoulders and hindquarters and its tail curved upwards and curled at the tip. Also its stomach sagged. I was convinced it was a big-cat. I reported it to the police and they came and took plaster casts of its prints. An armed officer also went into the fields and tracked the prints as far as he could, but found nothing.

More prints were found by farmer John Henderson on 6 February, about a mile away from the scene of Mrs Fitch's encounter. In a field next to his garden was a trail of very large paw-prints in the snow. They were between three and four inches in length. A vet, Mr MacJohnston, who examined the prints thought that they belonged to a member of the big-cat family.

On Saturday 27 October 1979, farmer Ted Noble saw what he described as a 'lioness or similar member of the big-cat family' stalking ponies at his farm near Cannich, Inverness-shire. He added that, for over a year, there had been a continual unexplained loss of livestock, particularly foals. This is an interesting point, for pumas are known to have a liking for foals' flesh.

The police organized a search with the help of Eric Stephens, a big-game expert, who commented, 'A lion could easily be living in the area. There is plenty of food: sheep, horses and deer, and plenty of cover.'

On the night of 3 November Angus Monro was driving a minibus along the A839 from Lairg to Embo in central Sutherland, about fifty miles north of Cannich. He had seen wildcats several times in the Highlands but had never encountered a cat like the one he saw that night:

> It was about the size of a Labrador dog, dark in colour, but with a distinctive cat's face. I had just come round a bend and the lights picked up what I thought was a dog at first. I could have run it down and killed it but you wouldn't do that deliberately. It ran in front of me and I was travelling at about 40 mph before I braked. It crossed in front of me and made off into the grass towards the river Fleet. It was definitely a cat but the size of a big dog. I am in no doubt about that. I had a clear view of its head as it turned in my lights.

Another account was sent to me by Mrs Elizabeth Lennie, whose encounter took place in Moray:

> At about six o'clock one evening during the first week of August 1980, we watched a puma in a field about two miles west of Dufftown. It was a sunny evening so we had a clear view. I spotted it walking across a field and we stopped the car and watched it for a time. It was about the size of an Alsatian dog, but had thicker legs with rounded feet. Its tail was as long as its body with the tip turning up. Its colour was dark gold. It was in good condition with a nice coat and seemed mature but young. It was walking with a very smooth movement, ambling along quite at peace. When my husband got out of the car it heard his footsteps, stopped in its tracks, turned its head and looked at us. After a minute or two it continued on its way. There were four of us in the car and we all saw it. I informed the local police, but have not heard anything further.

Since his sighting in October 1979, Ted Noble had continued to find the carcasses of farm animals, mainly sheep, mutilated and with their bones crushed. In August 1980, he saw the mystery cat again. He told the police but they were not very interested, having searched the area without results. Mr Noble was determined to catch the animal, however. He built a large steel cage which he set up near the cottage of a neighbour, Miss Chisholm, who had also seen the animal, and baited it with fresh meat each day. Nothing happened until the 28 October when, as he went to check the trap with his son Julian, he heard a loud growling. The effort and patience had paid off: in the cage was a fully grown female puma.

With headlines such as 'Caged: The Lion of the Glen' and 'Grrr-eat Scot! Farmer Ted Catches the Loch Ness Lion!', the captured puma was national news. Several newspapers published a photograph of the animal snarling defiantly behind bars. For Mr Noble the puma's capture was 'a dream come true' but it was not long before doubts were raised as to the creature's origins. She was elderly, perhaps ten years old, with a rheumatic hip which caused her to limp, and was sufficiently tame to allow people to tickle her behind the ears! It seemed unlikely that this was the beast which had frightened country folk and savaged farm animals. People soon began talking about a hoax, some suggesting that someone wishing to dispose of an unwanted pet had driven it into Mr Noble's cage. Others even implied that the farmer himself had been party to such a ruse. Mr Noble responded angrily, denying that there had been a hoax, with or without his knowledge. He was supported by Bob High, the local secretary of the Farmers' Union, who said that many farmers in the eastern Highlands had seen the animal, or had lost live-stock to it, but were afraid to speak out in case they were ridiculed. Additional support came from Dr Hans Kruuk, of the Institute of Terrestrial Ecology at Banchory, Aberdeenshire. He had analysed droppings from the puma within hours of its capture, and concluded:

> It has been living wild for some time, living off what one would expect in the wild. One of the droppings was ninety-five per cent deer hair, with four per cent rabbit remains and one per cent sheep. The second was ninety-nine per cent sheep with one per cent rabbit.

This dispelled the theory that a pet puma had been driven into the trap, nor would one expect a well-cared for animal to be suffering from rheumatism, though one living in the cold, damp Scottish Highlands might well become afflicted by the condition. Furthermore, if the puma had been reared in captivity it might well develop a trust for human beings which would remain even after several years in the wild. It seems likely that this puma had been free for some time, perhaps several years.

Wherever the creature came from, it soon became apparent that the mystery had not ended. Sightings of big-cats continued, as did attacks on farm animals.

On 6 November two sheep were savaged near Garve, about twenty miles north of Cannich. Dr Kruuk said that they had been killed in a manner 'very typical' of a puma. In the early hours of 4 December, nineteen-year-old Wendy Mann saw a strange, cat-like animal as she was driving along the Lewiston Road on the north side of Loch Ness, near Castle Urquhart. The animal bounded out of the woods, ran along the road in the glare of the car's headlights and dashed up a side road into the darkness. Wendy said afterwards:

> I couldn't believe my eyes. It was a lioness or puma. It couldn't have been anything else. I noticed it had large paws and a long, loping run.

Detective Sergeant John Cathcart visited the scene and interviewed Wendy. He concluded:

> It sounds as if it could be an authentic sighting. The girl is new to the area and did not know about the puma being captured recently only twelve miles away at Cannich, so she was not influenced in any way in deciding it was a puma she saw.

In April 1983, there were several detailed reports of a black big-cat in Inverness-shire. One account came from Mrs Mary Cameron who saw the animal in a woodland clearing near Viewhill Farm, Balloch. She described it as 'cat-like and black in colour, with a long feline tail and much bigger than a dog'. Another witness was Miss Jane MacKay who saw the creature cross a road on the outskirts of Balloch. She described it as 'an enormous black cat'. A local man who wished to remain anonymous said that he and his children watched the animal for some time near an old quarry about one mile east of Balloch. He said that he found the creature's paw-marks after it had run away, and that each print was about six inches in diameter. Mr Eddie Orbell, the director of the Highland Wildlife Park at Kincraig was impressed by the reports and said,

> I am afraid that this does sound like a panther or black leopard, which is a highly dangerous animal. While the puma, as a rule, is a very shy animal, the black leopard is perfectly capable of attacking human beings, in fact it could easily kill a cow or even a horse. The only other animal it could be is a jaguar, but this is very unlikely as they are extremely rare.

Mr Richard O'Grady, director of Calder Park Zoo, Glasgow, also thought that the mystery animal was a panther. He said, perhaps rather defensively, 'It most certainly is not one of ours. It is likely that it has been released by a private owner or a small travelling circus.'

On 17 October 1985, the story of Scottish mystery cats took another strange turn when several national newspapers reported that a huge black cat had been shot and killed near Tomas Christie's estate near Kellas, Moray. In fact this was the fourth such cat to have been killed in this part of Scotland, the previous incidents receiving little or no publicity. The first had been shot in late summer or early autumn, 1983, on Tomas Christie's estate, the second in September 1984, near Grantown-on-Spey, about sixteen miles south of Kellas, and the third in May 1985, near Advie, about eight miles to the north-east of Grantown. The cats were jet-black with a long tail and large upper fangs which protrude over the lower lip. The largest was that killed near Grantown which measured forty-three inches from nose to tip of tail. At the time of writing scientists are not sure exactly how to classify the animal. It could be a new strain of the Scottish Wildcat, or a cross between the Wildcat and feral cats.

The discovery of this animal could explain some reports of black mystery cats in Scotland but it is too small to account for sightings such as that described by witnesses at Balloch in 1983. It certainly could not have made six-inch paw-prints. The animal is also too small to explain sightings of English black mystery cats, such as the Beast of Exmoor, even assuming it could have extended its range so far south. (Trevor Beer is certain that the creature is not the same sort of animal that he encountered.) It also seems doubtful that such a cat, which I gather is not very heavy (one specimen only weighing about eighteen pounds), could have killed a 200-pound ram or a fully-grown ewe, as the Exmoor animal apparently has done.

The foregoing chronicle of sightings is a selection from the wealth of recorded eye-witness reports, covering the whole of Great Britain. Should we then conclude that there really are big-cats at large in the British countryside? There is strangely little tangible evidence to support this possibility. Occasionally, droppings which are difficult to identify are found, as are tufts of unusual hair and paw-prints of controversial origin. Such evidence remains inconclusive, as does photographic evidence. Three photographs are said to have been taken of the Surrey Puma: at Worplesdon in August 1966, at Upper Hale two months later and at Reigate in October 1977. The Worplesdon picture could have been a puma. The Upper Hale photograph, surprisingly, was lost, so its value cannot be assessed. The Reigate photograph is also unavailable for inspection, but it is known to have been taken on a misty morning and to be indistinct. A photograph of a black mystery feline was taken in Ayrshire in 1979, but officials at Calder Park Zoo thought it was just a big domestic cat.

Di Francis included five photographs of mystery cats in her book *Cat Country*, published in 1983. The pictures were taken near Tonmawr in South Wales. One of them shows a large, grey animal on a hillside; two others show striped cats near a dustbin (Di Francis believes these are cubs) and two more show a black, cat-like animal on a hillside. Unfortunately, the pictures in themselves are inconclusive. The animal on the hillside could be a dog, while the striped 'cubs' could be feral cats. The pictures of the black cat are the most interesting, but distance precludes positive identification.

Even more puzzling are the attacks on farm animals. It is possible that dogs, which can inflict terrible injuries particularly when in packs, are the culprits, but those who examine the carcasses – vets, police, farmers, zoological experts – often state that the injuries are quite different from anything they have previously seen. On several occasions the experts have stated that they believed big-cats were the killers.

Of course, we have had hard evidence in the shape of the puma captured at Cannich, Inverness-shire, and the black cats killed in Morayshire. These incidents, though, seem to add to the mystery rather than to solve it. The capture of the Cannich puma certainly did not put a stop to reports of both tawny and black big-cats, and the Morayshire cat seems to be too small to account for most sightings of the latter.

The bulk of the evidence consists of eye-witness accounts. The authorities are able to dismiss many sightings as misidentifications, but there remain a very significant number which cannot be explained in this way, the descriptions matching very accurately the characteristics of big-cats. Those most closely involved in the investigations – the police and the zoo officials – have often stated that they find many of the reports very impressive. Former Superintendent Ronald Hagley, MBE, for example, who headed the Surrey Puma hunt in the 1960s, stated, when I contacted him in 1980, that a large number of reports came from reliable witnesses and probably did refer to a puma or, possibly, a lioness.

If big-cats are loose in the British Isles how have they come to be there? It is unlikely that they have escaped from zoos or circuses. Such escapes are usually notified to the authorities quickly, and the animals recaptured within hours. It is more likely that the animals are bought as cubs, by individuals wanting exotic pets, and then released when they grow larger and become too difficult to handle.

This explanation, though, could not apply as far as the black big-cats are concerned. It is doubtful if pumas are ever black. Certainly none has been captured or killed. Jaguars, which come from Central and South America, are sometimes black, but they are so large and fierce that if any were at large there would be no doubt about it. Leopards, which are smaller, and possibly more retiring than jaguars, are also occasionally black, but are probably less adaptable than pumas, their normal habitat and climate being far more restricted. Furthermore, the possibility of both black jaguars/leopards *and* pumas being loose stretches one's credulity.

Di Francis believes that all the big-cats reported are members of a so far unclassified species of indigenous British big-cats. In *Cat Country* she puts forward much interesting evidence to support her theory. However, although it cannot be entirely ruled out, the theory does seem a little unlikely. Pockets of such creatures might have survived in certain areas – the Scottish Highlands for example, or the wilds of Exmoor – but this does not seem very probable in areas such as Wolverhampton, or Surrey where big-cats have also been reported.

Some researchers have begun to ask if British big-cats – some of them at least – could not be some form of paranormal phenomenon. The concept is perhaps not quite so improbable as it might first appear. The British Isles have a long tradition of giant phantom cats. A ruined hunting lodge on the slopes of Mount Pellier in the Dublin Mountains, built by William Connolly as a hunting lodge but later used by Dublin's Hell-fire Club (an organization similar to its more notorious English name-sake), is said to be haunted by such a beast. According to John J. Dunne in *Haunted Ireland*:

> On the slopes beneath Connolly's hunting lodge, stories of a ghostly black cat abound, and the ferocious creature has been encountered on lonely laneways, on the adjoining estate of Lord Massey and in other buildings in the district. Here, in the townland of Killakee, stood the old Massey mansion, which eventually fell into ruin, and it is in this immediate vicinity that the legend of the phantom cat persists.

A phantom cat with eyes 'as big as saucers' is said to sit on the top of a stone gatepost near Morwenstow on the borders of Devon and Cornwall. One witness was Mr Greig who saw the creature in December 1957, according to Judy Chard in her book *Devon Mysteries*.

A curious animal ghost was said to haunt the lanes and fields in the Godley Green area of Cheshire. It was yellowish or light tan in colour and although often referred to as a ghost dog some witnesses described it as cat-like. A woman who saw the creature at the end of the nineteenth century thought that it was a lion that had escaped from a zoo. On some occasions the beast was said to have been seen chasing cattle, a feature reminiscent of some mystery cat sightings.

A huge, phantom, black cat was encountered several times in the ruins of Borley Rectory in Suffolk, described by Harry Price as the most haunted house in England. One night in summer, 1939, the author, James Wentworth Day, was exploring the ruins with a friend. As the two men stood in the bright moonlight looking up at the empty windows of the house something shot between Wentworth Day's legs and into the house. It was a gigantic black cat. Wentworth Day reported that he had compared notes with a London journalist who had had a similar experience in the Rectory grounds, when what he took to be a huge black cat had rushed between his legs and shot into the house. The journalist made inquiries locally and found that no one owned such a cat, but that many other people had seen the huge phantom feline dashing into the house.

The Scottish Highlands were traditionally said to be haunted by a huge fairy cat, the Cait Sith. The folklorist J. G. Campbell described it as being as large as a dog, black with a white spot on its breast, and with an arched back and erect bristles. An even more fearsome Scottish beast was Big Ears, the monstrous demonic god of the cats.

There is a curious continuity about the theme of exotic felines in the British Isles. After a series of attacks in 1927 on farm animals in Inverness-shire (a county from where so many recent reports of big-cats have come) a 'large, fierce, yellow animal' was shot. The killings continued and a second of the beasts was shot. Shortly after, a third was trapped and the body sent to the London Zoo where it was identified as a lynx. There seems to have been no speculation as to how three lynxes came to be in Inverness-shire. According to Charles Fort (a well-known collector of reports of strange phenomena) a report of this appeared in the *Daily Express* on 14 January 1927.

In his book, *Rural Rides*, published in 1830, William Cobbett, the political radical, tells the now quite well-known story of how, as a boy, he saw a cat which was as large as a dog climb into a hollow elm tree in the grounds of the ruined Waverley Abbey near Farnham, Surrey. His parents did not believe him, and he received a scolding and a beating, but he later wrote:

> I have since many times repeated it and I would take my oath of it to this day. When in New Brunswick I saw the great, wild, grey cat, which is there called a 'Lucifee' and it seemed to me to be just such a cat as I had seen at Waverley.

It has been suggested that Cobbett saw a feral cat, but it is interesting that in Canada 'lucifee' is the name given to the Canadian Lynx. Whatever the animal was, it is strange that William Cobbett's encounter occurred so long ago in what was later to become the heart of Surrey Puma country.

According to Colin Clair in *Unnatural History*, the sixteenth-century historian, Raphael Holinshed, wrote:

> Lions we have had very many in the north parts of Scotland, and those with manes of no less force than those of Mauretania; but how and when they were destroyed as yet I do not read.

It has been suggested by some researchers that alien big-cats could have been transported, or teleported, from their normal environment by some unknown force to the British Isles and it is perhaps relevant to note here a curious aspect of the encounters which Farmer Blanks had with the Surrey Puma. Interviewed by Charles Bowen, editor of the *Flying Saucer Review*, Mr Blanks mentioned that twice when making his routine nightly rounds of his farm, he had been aware of puzzling lights moving from roof to roof of the farm buildings. He could not account for the phenomenon but was rather uneasy because on each occasion they preceded the arrival in the vicinity of the puma.

The paranormal view would at least explain the strangely elusive nature of British mystery cats, and the great discrepancy between the numerous sightings (the reports described in this chapter are a mere fraction of the total) and the lack of hard evidence. In my own view, no single theory is adequate to account for all the different aspects of the British big-cat mystery. I think the only certainty is that sightings will continue. At the time of writing, Farmer Ted Noble informs me that sightings of pumas continue around his farm in Inverness-shire, and *Fleet News* on 12 July 1985, reported another sighting of the Surrey Puma. The witness, Farmer John Ballantyne, stated that the creature followed him through a cornfield on his farm near Crondall, Hampshire. It was only forty yards away and clearly visible. When the animal saw Mr Ballantyne was watching it, it crouched down and then ran off. It was the farmer's second sighting of the puma. He stated: 'I first saw it fifteen years ago. As far as I am concerned it has never left the area.' This sighting is perhaps an appropriate one with which to conclude this chapter, coming as it does from the village where the entire puma saga seems to have begun.

CHAPTER TWO

Sea Serpents

> I've been fishing for forty years and it's the first time I've ever seen anything like that. Folk have told me about monsters and I always took it with a pinch of salt, but now I'm prepared to believe anything I see out there.
>
> Mr George Vinnicombe who saw a sea monster off the Cornish coast in 1976.

For as long as the British have stood on cliffs and beaches and stared out over the rolling waves, or braved the sea in boats to fish, trade and explore, their imaginations have populated the seas with a variety of fantastic creatures. Some of these legendary beasts were based on garbled accounts of animals now catalogued by science, but others have remained outside zoologists' classifications. Are they merely legendary, or do they actually exist? One thing is certain: there have been sober eye-witness reports of sea monsters off the coasts of Britain for over 100 years.

A convenient starting point for our survey of British sea serpents is a report of a monster that was seen off the coast of County Clare in the west of Ireland in 1871. The witnesses, who included 'a well-known clergyman in the north of Ireland' stated that the creature had a horse-like head, large glassy eyes and a 'huge mane of seaweed-looking hair, which rose and fell with the motion of the water'. These characteristics were to be found in later reports.

One of the most impressive of all British sea-monster sightings occurred in 1872 in the Sound of Sleat, which divides the Isle of Skye from the mainland. It was witnessed by the Reverend John Macrae, Minister of Glenelg, Inverness-shire, his two daughters, Forbes and Katie, his grandson Gilbert Bogle, their companion the Reverend David Twopenny, Vicar of Stockbury, Kent and a Highland lad whose name is unknown. On the 20 August, a calm, sunny day, the party set out from Glenelg in a cutter, the *Leda*, for a trip to Loch Hourn.

They were rowing the boat along, as there was not a breath of wind, when they saw a dark mass in the water, about 200 yards to the north of them. As they drew closer, they realized that it was a living creature. It was between forty-five and seventy feet in length, with seven humps and a longer portion which seemed to be the head. As they were watching the animal it began to move towards them at great speed, churning up the water. When it had approached to within 100 yards of the boat the animal sank, though its course could still be followed by the commotion it made at the surface of the calm sea. It altered its course, turning towards Skye, and continued to show itself that day, careering about in the water, about a mile away.

The party saw the animal again the next day, as did several other people, including Finlay Macrae and his friends who were in a boat just inside the mouth of Loch Hourn, and the ferryman at Kylerhea. On 22 and 23 August it was seen by Lord MacDonald and his friends, including the Reverend Mr McNeill, Minister of Skye, who were on his Lordship's steam yacht in Loch Hourn. It was also seen on 23 August by Alexander Macmillan, a boat-builder from Dornie, and his brother Farquhar who were fishing from a boat at the entrance to Loch Duich.

So far we have had reports of a creature with a mane and prominent eyes and an animal with several humps. Our next four accounts describe a sea monster of another type – one with a long neck.

On a sunny September day in 1893 Dr Farquhar Matheson and his wife were sailing in the Kyle of Lochalsh. Between 1.00p.m. and 2.00p.m. they saw something rise up out of the water about 200 yards ahead of them. The object was clearly part of some living creature which, thought the doctor, most closely resembled the head and neck of a giraffe. It was brown, and seemed to be as tall as the mast of the boat. No body was visible above the water, but the doctor felt that the rest of the animal must be quite substantial to support so large a structure. The witnesses followed the creature for about a mile before losing sight of it.

We remain in Scottish waters for our next two reports. The first

Fig. 3. The *Leda* sea serpent, 1872, after a sketch in *Land and Water* magazine (7 September 1872).

incident was described by Gavin Maxwell in his book *Harpoon at a Venture*. One autumn night early in the twentieth century two men and a lad were fishing from a skiff off the Isle of Skye. The lad, Sandy Campbell, was resting for a few seconds from hauling in the net when he saw an object rising out of the water about fifty yards away. The object continued rising till it towered to a height of about twenty feet above the water. Sandy called to the others but got only an angry reply to keep pulling on the net. Finally though, the two men looked up and saw the creature. The object moved to and fro in the air, and it seemed to be joined to a bulky body which was just breaking the surface. As the fishermen stared, the animal slowly sank below the waves, causing a commotion in the water like the wake of a ship. The terrified trio dropped their net and rowed as fast as they could for the shore.

On a fine August day in 1910 Mr W. J. Hutchinson was shooting plover and duck with his father and cousin near the Skerries of Work in Meil Bay in the Orkneys. As they were sailing towards the Skerries they saw several whales leaping out of the water, apparently scared by a huge animal whose head and neck were rising out of the water. The men hurriedly steered away from the creature which, after about five minutes, sank slowly and vertically into the water, without a splash. Mr Hutchinson said that the animal was between 100 and 150 yards away, and that its head was at least eighteen feet above the water. It was a brown colour, with a head like that of a horse or camel.

Our fourth 'long-neck' was described by Sir Arthur Rostron, Commodore of the Cunard Line, in his memoirs *Home from the Sea*, published in 1931. In 1907 he was the Chief Officer of the *Campania* and while coming into Queenstown (now Cobh), County Cork in Ireland, on the evening of 26 April, saw a strange object protruding from the water ahead:

> We swung away a point but gradually grew nearer so that we were able to make out what the unusual thing was. It was a sea monster! It was no more than fifty feet away from the ship's side when we passed, so both I and the junior officer had a good sight of it. So strange an animal was it that I remember crying out, 'It's alive!' I was unable to get a clear view of the monster's features but we were close enough to realize its head rose eight or nine feet out of the water while the trunk of the neck was fully twelve inches thick.

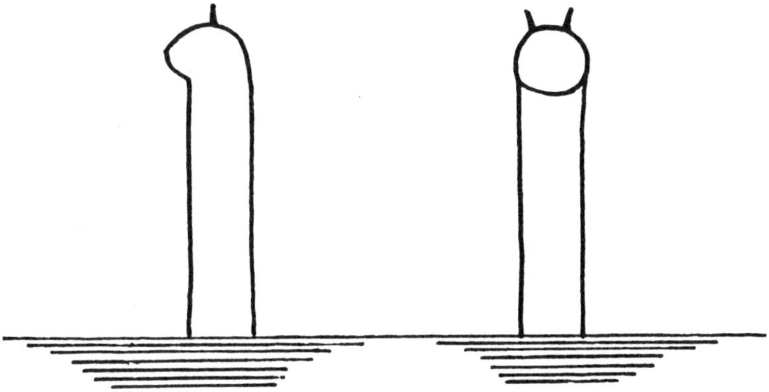

Fig. 4. Sir Arthur Rostron's sketch of the creature he saw off Cobh in 1907.

Sir Arthur Rostron provided Commander Rupert T. Gould, the well-known author and broadcaster, who was fascinated by mysteries of all kinds with a sketch of the animal.

Commander Gould sent a copy of Sir Arthur's sketch to the junior officer, H. C. Birnie, who was now a captain. Captain Birnie confirmed the details of the encounter:

> The sketch you sent me agrees precisely with what I saw in company with Sir Arthur Rostron, the only exception being that when I saw it, it was not perpendicular but at an angle with the surface of the water.

We move to South Devon for our next report, which seems to add another type to our collection of sea monsters – an animal like a giant eel. It was encountered by Captain Ruser and the crew of the German vessel *Kaiserin Augusta Victoria*, off Prawle Point at 6.30a.m. on 5 July 1912, and the details were entered in the ship's log. The creature was about twenty feet long, a foot to eighteen inches thick, and had a distinctive eel-like colour: blue-grey on top and whitish underneath. The animal was whipping the water violently with its tail, perhaps injured or fighting another creature, and at times, said Captain Ruser, nearly the whole of its body was visible.

The following report is unusual in that the creature involved was seen not only on the surface, but was also watched from above through clear water. In August 1919, J. Mackintosh Bell, a Scottish lawyer, was on holiday in the Orkneys. The local fishermen told Mr Bell about a strange creature they had often encountered and on 5 August he saw it for himself. He was out with his friends and several local men, lifting lobster creels between Brims Ness and Tor Ness, when, at about 9.30a.m., one of the fishermen drew everyone's attention to a creature which had quietly surfaced a short distance away. Mr Bell described it as follows:

> I looked, and sure enough, about twenty-five to thirty yards from the boat, a long neck as thick as an elephant's fore-leg, all rough-looking like an elephant's hide, was sticking up. On top of this was the head which was much smaller in proportion but of the same colour. The head was like that of a dog, coming sharp to the nose. The eye was black and small, and the whiskers were black. The neck, I should say, stuck about five to six feet, possibly more, out of the water.

The animal dived, and then swam alongside the boat about ten feet down, being clearly visible through the water. The locals said that they had often seen it swimming in this way after it had appeared at the surface.

Mr Bell said that the animal was about twenty feet long, about ten feet around the body and had an eight-foot-long neck. It was brown, had four flippers and apparently lacked a tail. Mr Bell tried to take a photograph of the animal, but his camera would not function because the shutter was swollen.

A similar creature was encountered in July 1922, in the River Shannon in Ireland. One of the witnesses was Captain Hugh Shaw who was the owner and master of several sailing ships. One afternoon he and his crew were preparing to sail from Limerick when the mate drew everyone's attention to a strange animal which had appeared only a few feet away from the ship.

Captain Shaw said that the animal was black and shiny with a neck about twelve feet long, a small head and bright shining eyes. Behind the neck was a huge, black, cone-shaped hump which protruded a few feet above the surface of the water.

The animal was heading slowly upstream when first seen but, on coming to a bridge, it turned and headed downstream and out to sea. It was seen later by Captain Shaw and his crew about twenty miles below Limerick. Several people on the quayside at

Limerick had seen the animal, including a Mr MacMahon, whose son confirmed the details of the incident many years later to Daniel Doyle, a Limerick librarian.

In 1923, there was a sighting in the Thames Estuary, in an area known as the Black Deep which had been closed to shipping for eight years when the animal was encountered. As one of the witnesses, Captain F. D. B. Haselfoot, commented, 'Its waters were thus entirely secluded for the private activities of any sea monster!' Captain Haselfoot and the crew of H.M.S. *Kellett* were surveying the area on a summer morning when, at about 9a.m., a long neck rose out of the water, about 200 yards away from the ship. It reached a height of about seven feet and then submerged, to reappear shortly after, again rearing out of the water for a few seconds.

In 1928, Michael Peer Groves and his family had a clear view of a sea monster which appeared near their boat off the Isle of Man. They were able to watch the creature for a long time. Seen from the front, the animal's head was diamond-shaped, with huge, forward-looking eyes, a wide mouth and long whiskers, characteristics which suggest that this creature was a mammal. The witnesses were struck by the attractive appearance of the animal and by the incredibly gentle way that it seemed to look at them.

A creature similar to the Isle of Man sea serpent was seen off the Yorkshire coast shortly before World War Two, by Mrs Joan Borgeest. One day Mrs Borgeest was on the beach with several children when, looking out to sea, she saw a huge creature surface about 100 yards away. It was elongated, with a 'flat head, protruding eyes, and a long flat mouth which opened and shut as it breathed; it was a great length and moved along with a humped glide'.

In June 1931, there was another appearance of the many-humped sea serpent, this time off the Suffolk coast. The witnesses were Mrs Sybil M. Armstrong, who had just rented a bungalow at Thorpeness near the cliff's edge, her cook, and her children's governess. On a fine, clear evening with the sea dead calm, the witnesses were eating their supper in the sitting-room which overlooked the sea. At about 8p.m. Mrs Armstrong noticed a dark object moving through the water about 400 yards out from the shore. She went outside and saw that the object was an animal's head with a long back with several humps behind it. She

Fig. 5. The multi-humped sea serpent, 1931, after a sketch by Mrs Sybil Armstrong.

called the others and they dashed along the cliff trying to keep pace with the creature. As they watched, the animal hauled itself up onto a sandbank and then slithered down the far side of the bank into the sea with a great commotion, disappearing from sight.

The following evening Mrs Armstrong looked carefully at the boats of fishermen picking up lobster pots near to where the creature had appeared. She estimated that the animal was five to six times the length of one of these boats, which would have made it between fifty and sixty feet. When it was in the water it seemed almost black, but out on the sandbank it looked lighter, perhaps a tawny brown. It seemed to have a large pair of fins in the shoulder region, and it was the beating of these on the water which had thrown up the great amount of spray.

In 1934, a sea monster was seen ashore, at Filey, Yorkshire, and an account appeared in the *Daily Telegraph* on 1 March:

> Coastguard Meets Monster by Night – Eyes like saucers, two huge humps: When fishermen told us a fortnight ago in Filey that they had seen a Monster of unclassified but awe-inspiring species, about three miles out to sea, we were sceptical. The fishermen, perhaps discouraged, said no more, and we concluded the Monster had gone off to the same retreat as its Loch Ness relative.
>
> Now, however, Mr Wilkinson Herbert, a Filey coastguard, says he saw the thing on shore last night, a dark moonless night. He was walking along Filey Brig, a long spur of rocks running out into the sea, when:
>
> 'Suddenly I heard a growling like a dozen dogs ahead; walking nearer I switched on my torch, and was confronted by a huge neck, six yards ahead of me, rearing up eight feet high!
>
> 'The head was a startling sight – huge tortoise eyes, like saucers, glaring at me, the creature's mouth was a foot wide and its neck would be a yard round.
>
> 'The monster appeared as startled as I was. Shining my torch along the ground, I saw a body about thirty feet long. I thought "this is no place for me" and from a distance I threw stones at the creature. It moved away, growling fiercely, and I saw the huge black body had two

humps on it and four short legs with huge flippers on them. I could not see any tail. It moved quickly, rolling from side to side, and went into the sea. From the cliff top I looked down and saw two eyes like torch-lights shining out to sea 300 yards away. It was the most gruesome and thrilling experience. I have seen big animals abroad, but nothing like this.'

It was, perhaps, an appropriate spot for a sea monster to appear. According to the region's folklore, in the distant past, a dragon had been drowned in the sea here, its mighty bones becoming the rocks of Filey Brig. Mr Herbert's account, and that of J. Mackintosh Bell give us a clear picture of one type of sea serpent that has been seen off British shores. The animal has a bulky body which may show one, two or three humps; a long neck and small head and two pairs of flippers.

On 9 September 1937 a report of a monster appeared in *The Orcadian*. The creature was seen near the Pentland Skerries, a group of islands about halfway between the north-eastern tip of Scotland and the Orkney Islands. The report runs as follows:

Sea Monster near Pentland Skerry – Sea breaking White as on Submerged Rock.

After the relief to the Pentland Skerries on Friday, word was brought ashore that a sea monster had been seen in the vicinity of the Skerries. In a letter, Mr John R. Brown, occasional lightkeeper wrote:

'Mr Scot was speaking last night about a Monster that had been seen about Fair Isle. To tell the truth I never believed much in Monsters myself, but I saw something today resembling nothing I have ever seen before.

'It was about noon when we were working down at the landing at the East End that on chancing to look out to sea I noticed the sea breaking white as on a submerged rock. As I knew there were no rocks at that particular spot, I watched for a little and presently a great object rose up out of the water – anything from twenty to thirty feet and at an angle of about forty-five degrees. It was round-shaped and there appeared to be a head on it, but as it was about half a mile from the shore I could not be sure.

'I called the attention of the other two men but unfortunately before they got their eyes on the spot it had disappeared again, though both of them saw the foam it had made. We watched for a considerable time but it never appeared again.'

In 1966, Mr R. W. Midgley of Boston, Lincolnshire, wrote to the *Skegness Standard* describing a sea monster he had seen as a boy. In 1937 or 1938 he was walking along the sea wall at Trusthorpe when he saw an enormous animal in the water about 400 yards away. It had a long, snake-like body and showed several humps above the surface of the sea.

In 1938, two fishermen from the Suffolk village of Southwold had a frightening encounter with a sea serpent. On 21 October, in the morning Ernest Watson and William Herrington had gone out to lay their nets. It was a clear day with a calm sea. The men were terrified when a huge, grey, long-necked creature rose out of the water about forty yards away. The animal, which had a big humped back, made off at great speed and eventually dived, throwing up a great wash. The men estimated the creature's length at sixty feet.

In his book *Gower Journey*, published in 1950, A. G. Thompson described a sea monster that he had seen off the Gower Peninsula in South Wales. He first thought that the object he saw from a cliff top was a log, but then:

> Suddenly one end moved and it became plain that a head like that of a horse with a mane was standing out of the water and watching something on the rocks at the foot of the cliff. What a thrill! After staring for what seemed minutes the monster appeared satisfied and dived with what looked like two distinct undulations of the hind portion. What an uncanny feeling! The writer waited some half-hour or more but there was no reappearance.

We have already seen one terrestrial sighting of a sea serpent. Twenty-eight years later this remarkable occurrence was repeated. The *Scottish Daily Mail* reported on Saturday 3 February 1962 that, late at night, Jack Hay had seen a thirty- to forty-foot long monster on the beach at Helensburgh on the Clyde. Mr Hay, who was about forty yards from the animal, said that it had a bulky body, long neck and a three foot long head. After remaining motionless for about a minute the creature bounded down the beach and slithered into the water.

In late August 1963, Mr P. Sharman, who was on holiday at New Quay in Wales, saw a strange animal while he was walking along the cliffs. Looking down into a rocky cove, about 100 feet below, he saw a plesiosaur-like animal in the water. It was between thirty and forty feet long, black in colour with a short tail, four flippers and a long neck surmounted by a small head. The creature was surrounded by several seals which were all hurriedly swimming away as if the monster was going to attack them. Mr Sharman commented:

> After I had watched the thing for a few minutes I realized there was a remote possibility that I was looking down upon a floundering basking shark. This seemed more and more probable, so I left the area.

Afterwards Mr Sharman began to doubt his conclusion that the animal had been a basking shark, and indeed his description does not suggest one. The animal would seem to be one of our long-necked sea serpents.

At about 9.00p.m. on 21 June 1965 Mrs Lillian Lowe, from Birmingham, was standing with her husband and her cousin on the end of Mingary Pier, Kilchoan, Ardnamurchan on the west coast of Scotland, looking out to sea. The water was flat calm. Mrs Lowe describes what happened next:

> I saw what I thought to be a seal appear above the water, about a hundred yards offshore. Then, another hump appeared directly behind it and a few feet away. As it moved I came to the conclusion that the two humps belonged to one object. I said 'What's that?' My husband immediately sighted the creature but was silent. He said afterwards he was too amazed to speak. He could see a huge shape about forty feet long beneath the water, and after a few moments said, 'a submarine I think'. He then noticed what seemed to be legs or flippers paddling at the side of the body, creating a turbulence beneath the water. My cousin and I could only see the two humps moving steadily along and waited for a decision as to the identity of the creature, but all my husband could say was that he had never seen anything like it in his life. The two humps were very solid and dark and shiny, and the skin seemed to be like hide.

Mr Lowe had been observing the creature through binoculars and he now handed these to his wife. Just as Mrs Lowe had the creature in view, however, it submerged. They described their encounter when they arrived back at their hotel, but were told that the creature had probably been a basking shark. Mr Lowe had seen basking sharks off Cornwall, though, and they were nothing like the creature he had just seen. The animal seems to have been one of the long-necked type of sea serpent, though on this occasion it kept its neck and head below water, showing two big humps of its body above the surface.

One mid-October day in 1966, Mr George Ashton was strolling along the sea front at Chapel St Leonards, near Skegness, with his wife, May, when they saw an enormous creature moving through the water less than 100 yards offshore. The animal had a snake-like head behind which trailed six or seven pointed humps. It was moving at about eight miles an hour and the couple watched as it travelled from the direction of Chapel Point until it disappeared from view towards Ingoldmells. Several possible explanations flashed through Mr Ashton's mind, including a flight of birds just above the water, or a submarine, but he soon dismissed these as being totally inadequate to account for what he had seen.

For centuries there had been legends about a sea monster in Cornwall's Falmouth Bay, the local people calling it *Morgawr* – an ancient Cornish word which means 'Sea Giant'. In 1876, an intriguing, but infuriatingly brief report appeared in the *West Briton* newspaper:

> The sea serpent was caught alive in Gerrans Bay. Two of our fishermen were afloat overhauling their crab-pots about 400–500 yards from the shore, when they discovered the serpent coiled about their floating cork (buoy). Upon their near approach it lifted its head and showed signs of defiance, upon which they struck it forcibly with an oar, which so far disabled it as to allow them to proceed with their work, after which they observed the serpent floating about near their boat. They pursued it, bringing it ashore yet alive for exhibition, soon after which it was killed on the rocks and most inconsiderately cast again into the sea.

Cornish fishermen seem to have had a rather phlegmatic view of sea monsters, judging from the above account. Obviously such creatures were just one of the hazards that fisher-folk could expect to face. Another puzzling account appeared in the *West Briton* in 1926: two fishermen, Mr Reese and Mr Gilbert, trawling three miles south of Falmouth caught a twenty foot long creature. It had an eight-foot tail, a 'beak' two feet long and six inches wide, four scaled legs attached to the body with armour-like joints, and a wide, flat back covered with matted, brown hair. The creature managed to escape, tearing the net, and leaving a great gobbet of blood. It was reported that the men brought some of the hair ashore, and that Plymouth Marine Biological Observatory was consulted, but was unable to offer any opinion.

Morgawr was reported again twenty years later, on Tuesday 5 July 1949. Harold T. Wilkins and a friend saw:

> . . . two remarkable saurians, fifteen to twenty feet long, with bottle-green colubrine heads, one behind the other, their middle parts under the water of the tidal creek of East Looe, Cornwall, apparently chasing a shoal of fish up the creek. What was amazing were their dorsal parts: ridged, serrated, and like the old Chinese pictures of dragons. Gulls swooped down towards the one in the rear, which had a large piece of orange peel on his dorsal parts. These monsters – and two of us saw them – resembled the plesiosaurus of Mesozoic times.

After these rather vague accounts we move forward to September 1975 when, on a sunny evening, Mrs Scott of Falmouth and her friend Mr Riley saw a long-necked, hump-backed creature off Pendennis Point. It had stumpy horns and bristles down the back of its neck. As the observers stared, the creature dived and, a few moments later, surfaced with a conger eel in its jaws. Mrs Scott said that as long as she lived she would 'never forget the face on that thing'.

Three months later the creature was seen again by Mr Gerald Bennett of Seworgan who described his encounter in a letter to the *Falmouth Packet*, which had printed an article about Morgawr:

> I have myself, during the last Christmas holidays, witnessed the sighting of a similar creature, although until now I have remained reticent about it. It was off the shore at Durgan, Helford, about 4.00p.m. near dusk. When I first spotted it, I thought it was a dead whale, but as I drew nearer it started to move away smoothly and I could see it was not a whale, nor like any creature seen around here. I judged that the part of it I could see above water was about twelve feet in length with an elongated neck.

Another witness was Mr Duncan Viner, a dental technician from Truro who saw the beast in January 1976. Like Mr Bennett, he first took the creature, which had surfaced about 100 yards off Rosemullion Head, to be a whale, as only a smooth dark hump was visible. As he watched, however, it rose in the water and a long neck appeared. The creature looked around and then sank beneath the waves. Mr Viner estimated that the creature's length was between thirty and forty feet.

The creature was seen again in the same area shortly after, the witness being Miss Amelia Johnson from London who was staying with her sister near Falmouth. She described her encounter as follows:

> One afternoon we decided to take a walk, in the direction of Rosemullion. Looking out to sea, I saw a strange form suddenly emerge from the water in Falmouth Bay. It was just like the sort of description one hears of the Loch Ness Monster, a sort of prehistoric monster thing with a neck the length of a lamp-post. I raced back to my sister and told her what I'd seen. She told me she thought I must be 'batty' and when we went back to see if we could see it again it was no longer there.

On 5 March 1976, the *Falmouth Packet* published the first photographs of Morgawr. They had been sent to the newspaper by a lady who called herself Mary F. The photographs had been taken, she said, early in February when she had seen the monster swimming off Trefusis Point. The animal was only visible for a few seconds, and the light was shining into the camera. She described the creature thus:

> I'd say it was fifteen to eighteen feet long (I mean the part showing above the water). It looked like an elephant waving its trunk, but the trunk was a long neck with a small head on the end, like a snake's head. It had humps on the back which moved in a funny way. The colour was black or very dark brown, and the skin seemed to be like a sea-lion's. I'm glad to know that other people have seen the great Cornish sea serpent. As a matter of fact the animal frightened me. I would not like to see it any closer. I did not like the way it moved when swimming.

The photographs do not show any obvious signs of having been faked, and are consistent with other eye-witness accounts. Unfortunately there is no indication of scale, though, and all appeals to Mary F. to forward the negatives for examination have been unsuccessful. Another letter from Mary F. said that the negatives had been sold to an American. Mary F.'s reticence is regrettable but perhaps understandable. Witnesses of water monsters have often been ridiculed, or had unwelcome publicity thrust upon them.

After the publication of Mary F.'s photographs, events at Falmouth took an even stranger turn. At Easter 1976, an attempt was made to 'call up' the monster. Three young witches – Psyche from Inverness, Vivienne from London, and Amanda from Cornwall – swam naked in Falmouth Bay and uttered various incantations. Whatever one's opinions of such practices it cannot be denied that sightings of Morgawr continued. One report came from two London bankers, John Chambers and Tony Rogers. On 4 May, they were fishing near the rocks at Parson's Beach at the mouth of the Helford River when, at about 10.10p.m.:

> Suddenly, something rose out of the water, about 150 or 200 yards away. It was greeny-grey in colour, and appeared to have humps. Another smaller creature also appeared. They were visible for about ten seconds and looked straight at us.

Curiously, John Chambers did not see the second creature. Another sighting was described by a schoolboy called Andrew, to Anthony 'Doc' Shiels, who was investigating the sightings. The boy had photographed a creature he had seen swimming in the Helford River between Toll Point and The Gaw. Like Mary F., Andrew was unwilling to co-operate further, refusing to give his full name or address, so there the matter rests. According to Doc Shiels, the photograph was very murky, but seemed to show two humps and a long neck.

This was indeed a summer of strange happenings in Cornwall. It was at this time that a bizarre flying creature, which soon came to be known as the 'Owlman' first made his appearance. This creature was seen by several witnesses in the vicinity of Mawnan, and is described in greater detail in Chapter Six. As if this was not enough, unidentified flying objects were also reported. The *West Briton*, on 1 July 1976, reported that a group of schoolboys camping near Wadebridge saw a strange light in the sky and heard a 'spine-chilling sound' during the last week of July. At 12.30a.m. on 1 July a woman saw 'three fireballs' over St Mawes.

Doc Shiels was himself destined to witness an appearance of Morgawr. A professional magician and entertainer from the Cornish town of Ponsanooth, he is a colourful and well-known character who has spent many summers busking at seaside resorts and entertaining at fairs and carnivals. His theatrical career, however, represents just one side of his character, for he also has a serious interest in water monsters and other strange phenomena. His showman's reputation has both advantages and disadvantages. On the one hand it has meant that he has not been taken seriously by scientists and the media, who often infer that he fakes the phenomena that he claims to be investigating. On the positive side it has led to his being approached by people with information that they were unwilling to take to newspapers or television. Doc regards water monsters as something more than 'unknown animals' and believes that they can be summoned, or caused to materialize, by telepathy, mental power and witchcraft. He admits that such practices may seem absurd and irrational, but claims that they often work. Speaking of the activities of the three witches he writes:

> They were successful . . . various sightings were reported around that time and a young boy from Helston took a rather murky picture of the sea serpent. . . . The naked witches have been regarded either as a jokey press gimmick or as a complete non-event. The truth of the matter is that the witches played a very important role in a whole series of monster incantations. It should also be remembered that the Owlman showed up for the first time during the Easter weekend of 1976.

One hot morning towards the end of June 1976 Doc Shiels and his family were resting on the sand at Grebe Beach after swimming. Doc periodically scanned the sea with his binoculars, hoping to catch a glimpse of the monster. Three times he saw something in the water but it disappeared before he could obtain a clear view of it. A few moments later he saw two humps which quickly vanished, then a head on a long neck. Doc's wife, Christine, in a letter to the *Falmouth Packet*, described what happened next:

> We missed it that time, but within a few short minutes the kids started pointing and yelling, 'there it is . . . the monster!' Finally I saw

> it (or them) for myself. It was at the edge of my vision and when I tried to focus on the image it simply and suddenly wasn't there. After two or three attempts to get a clear picture of the thing, by staring at it, failing each time, I decided to allow it to be coy, to stay in the 'corner of my eye' so to speak. This worked.
>
> For several seconds I saw a large, dark, long-necked, hump-backed beast moving slowly through the water, then sinking beneath the surface.

Christine Shiels stated that her husband was unwilling to write to the paper himself. He felt that people would disbelieve him, partly because of his showman's image, partly because he was known to be interested in the sea serpent and his sighting would seem to be 'wishful thinking'. Christine also pointed out that Doc was inclined to doubt it himself. He suggested that he and his family might have hallucinated because of the unusual heat and sunlight. He seemed rather disconcerted that he and his family had actually seen the now famous Morgawr.

Meanwhile, other people continued to see the local sea monster. The following sighting was one of the very few of the entire Morgawr saga to be described in the national media. It was reported by two fishermen, John Cock from Redruth, and George Vinnicombe from Falmouth, who saw the creature during the first week of July about twenty-five miles south of Lizard Point. Mr Vinnicombe described the encounter to David Clarke, the editor of *Cornish Life* magazine:

> We were fishing over wartime wrecks in the channel. It was a beautiful calm, clear day. I looked over the starboard side and saw this thing in the water. I thought it was a boat upside down. We went over to investigate and it looked like the back of a dead whale but with three humps and about eighteen or twenty feet long. The body was black but a lighter colour under the water. Then suddenly this head came out of the water about three feet from the body. It just looked at us and my mate and I just looked at one another. He said 'What the hell have we got here?' Then the head vanished and the body sank away. I've been fishing for forty years and it's the first time I've ever seen anything like that. Folk have told me about monsters and I always took it with a pinch of salt, but now I'm prepared to believe anything I see out there.

On 11 August, Morgawr was seen by Patrick Dolan, an art historian from Cardiff, who was sailing from Falmouth to Kinsale, Ireland in his sloop *Daisy*. He was about thirty miles NNW of the Scilly Islands when he saw a disturbance in the water, and a strange creature surfaced. Mr Dolan later described it to the *Falmouth Packet*:

> I could see quite distinctly a kind of worm-like shape in the water and the neck was about eight feet out of the water. It was about forty feet long and propelled itself with an undulating movement. It was moving at ten to twelve knots and overtook me. I must have had it in my vision for about twenty minutes.

Mr Dolan added that he had had a great deal of experience sailing but had never seen anything like this before. The sight of the creature, he said, made him feel 'extremely nervous'.

On the evening of 27 August, Bramwell Holmes, the director of a Penryn furniture company, his wife and son were returning from a trip to St Mawes in their motor-boat when, off Restronguet Point, they saw a disturbance in the water and two humps break the surface. The humps were a mottled greyish colour, and each was about two feet high and five feet across. The witnesses watched the creature for about ten minutes, catching a glimpse of a snake-like head, before it submerged.

Twelve days later the monster was seen by Donald Ferris who, at 7.10a.m. on 8 September, was walking his dog on the beach when he saw what he first thought was an upturned boat drifting towards Gyllyngvase Beach from the direction of Swanpool on the south side of Falmouth. He then realized that it was a living creature, an animal like a gigantic, dark grey eel between fifty and sixty feet long. As Mr Ferris watched, the animal submerged, its back rearing out of the water in a huge hump as it did so.

On 12 September, Morgawr was seen ashore, on Grebe Beach by two holidaymakers from Gloucestershire, Allan White and his sister Sally. They were walking on the beach near Durgan at 8.30a.m. when they encountered the beast:

> We really didn't see it all that clearly but something long and brown definitely slid off the beach into the water. I suppose it was about fifteen to twenty feet long. Neither of us was frightened. It was more surprise than anything else. I've certainly never seen anything like it

> before. . . . I can't really describe it except for the brown colouring. One minute it was on the beach and the next it had gone.

David Clarke, from *Cornish Life*, was writing an article on Morgawr, and had decided to include a description of Doc Shiels and his role in the affair. He arranged to take some photographs of Shiels with the Helford River as a background, and on 17 November 1976 the pair drove to the village of Mawnan and scrambled down the cliffs to Parson's Beach. What happened next was totally unexpected. David Clarke takes up the story:

> I duly took pictures of Doc waving his stick at the waves, and a few more of the river, as fishing boats left the Helford on a rising tide. Doc also took some colour photos of areas where Morgawr had previously been seen. While I was waiting for him, trying to keep warm by throwing stones for my dog to chase, Doc drew my attention to an object half-way across the river – a small, dark head poking out of the water. We both stood on large rocks for a better view and I attached a telephoto lens to my camera. The object slowly moved nearer and I could see that it was definitely a head, probably a seal. It came within seventy or eighty feet and started to move very slowly up and down river in a zig-zag pattern. It was only when I saw it side-on that I observed that the greenish-black head was supported on a long arched neck, more slender than that of a seal. In the wave troughs at least four or five feet of the neck were visible. There was a slow movement of water stretching back behind the head and neck for about ten feet, and at one point a gently-rounded shiny black body broke the surface. . . . The head was rounded with a 'blunt' nose and on the top of the head were two small rounded 'buds'.

At this point Clarke's dog began to bark, and this seemed to scare the creature which slowly sank in a swirl of water.

Doc Shiels described the animal as being about fifteen feet long with an eight-inch head crowned by a pair of stumpy little horns. It was very ugly, he said, with a head like that of a giant snail. He made some sketches of the animal (*see* Fig. 6).

David Clarke had taken several photographs of the creature, and developed his film as soon as he arrived home. He found though, that the wind-on mechanism of his camera had slipped, and that the frames were double and triple exposed. He had previously run a hundred films through the camera with no

Fig. 6. Doc Shiels's sketches of the creature seen off Mawnan between 9.30 and 10.00a.m. on 17 November 1976.

difficulty. Now he was experiencing the ill-luck which seems to haunt those who try to photograph water monsters. However, Clarke sent the negatives to Tim Dinsdale who found that it was possible to develop a print, albeit a far from perfect one, which is reproduced in Plate 8.

David Clarke comments:

> Unfortunately, there are two sets of waves superimposed which gives the impression that it was close by the bank. It also appears so 'seal-like'. In fact at this range it looked nothing like a seal, and this photograph was taken as the head turned away, the outline of its back breaking the surface. What you can see is the back of the head with one of the two small 'buds' or rounded lumps on the left.

Doc Shiels's camera had not malfunctioned, but, as a standard lens had been used, the area of river was very large and the creature very distant. Doc took three pictures; an enlargement of the most interesting is reproduced in Plate 10.

David Clarke was puzzled and worried by the encounter. He said it took a certain amount of courage just to include the sighting in his article: having always been sceptical about the existence of such creatures as sea serpents, he had now been confronted by one at close range. His first reaction was to deny the reality of the experience. He wondered if he had been hallucinating, or if in some way Doc Shiels was playing a trick on him, perhaps with a mechanical monster. However, he had to admit that neither of these theories was likely. What they had seen was solid enough to be recorded on film, and it was obviously beyond even Doc Shiels's capabilities to construct and animate the creature observed.

Doc Shiels had none of David Clarke's doubts and was jubilant at having secured the monster's image on film. He was angered, though, at local reporters' scepticism: 'I know that the thing we saw and photographed was not a seal, a skin-diver, a dolphin, shark or boat . . . or any radio-controlled rubber model.' Doc believes that even if a whole herd of sea monsters appeared before the massed cameras of all the reporters in the south-west it would still not convince them.

More photographs were obtained the following year, by Mr Gerald Bennett who had seen Morgawr at Christmas 1975. Since then he had taken to carrying his camera when he visited Mawnan, the scene of several sightings. On 31 January 1977 he was rewarded by an appearance of the sea monster. He took three photographs, two of which are reproduced in Plates 12–13. Mr Bennett described the back of the creature as resembling that of an enormous crustacean – like a giant lobster. It seemed to be hard and segmented, greenish-black, and bearing what appeared to be a parasitic growth. Judging from the photographs, the creature was heading inland up the estuary, then turned around and made out to sea.

The day after Gerald Bennett's encounter, Ray Hopley, a painter from Ponsanooth, saw Morgawr off Trefusis Point while he was sketching. The sighting was featured in the regional BBC programme 'Spotlight South-West' but when Mr Hopley mentioned that he knew Doc Shiels the episode was treated as a joke. Despite such scepticism, however, people continued to approach Doc with news of Morgawr. He was told by Mr M. L. A. Andrews, executive producer of the BBC programme 'World About Us' that his own mother had seen the monster while sailing between Cornwall and Brittany, and by Mike Truscott of the *West Briton* that he had interviewed a Falmouth policeman who had seen Morgawr, but who insisted on anonymity.

Strange lights were reported again that spring. At the beginning of April 1977, Mrs P. Skentlebury saw a pulsating orange light over St Mawes, and at the end of that month a similar light was seen by a Penryn man. Early in May an unusual light was seen near Truro by Mrs P. R. Packer, while Mr and Mrs Arthur

Wood of Plymouth reported that they had seen a bright green and orange ball of fire over Pendennis Point at 9.00a.m. on Friday 13 May, followed half-an-hour later by the appearance of Morgawr in the sea below Pendennis Point.

In November 1980, Doc Shiels made another attempt to raise Morgawr. On the morning of Sunday 9 November he set out in a boat with several colleagues, an accompanying boat containing a BBC film crew. Doc reported:

> Eventually we decided to head up through the Carrick Roads towards Pill Creek and calmer waters. Barry opened up the throttle and we skimmed along at thirty knots. Just past St Mawes, the three of us in the small boat felt 'something'. I asked Barry to slow down and guide the craft round and round, widdershins, in a gigantic spiral while I bellowed my incantations. Spike was the first to notice it . . . a black hump breaking the surface ahead of us. . . . The hump was visible for no more than a couple of seconds but all three of us saw it.

Unfortunately the other boat was so positioned that the film crew missed the chance to film the brief appearance of the hump. The rest of the morning was spent circling the area, but, although Doc said he felt something beneath them, Morgawr made no further appearance.

On Thursday 13 November Doc was enjoying a lunchtime drink in the Globe Inn on the Falmouth waterfront, when a man aged about sixty came over and said that he recognized Doc from a television broadcast, and that he had seen Morgawr the previous afternoon. It was about 4.00p.m. when he saw the creature off Rosemullion Head, and watched as it moved very quickly towards the mouth of the Helford. Visibility was good, and the animal was under observation for two or three minutes. This witness, who called himself Martin, said that the animal was gigantic, with a body like a whale and a neck like a python. As if this was not enough, he said that his daughter and granddaughter had seen an enormous, bird-like creature fly over the Helford River and into the trees near Grebe Beach.

About half-an-hour later Doc's daughter Kate came into the pub and told her father that she had seen Morgawr that very morning. Like her father, Kate had tried to 'invoke' Morgawr. She had swum naked in the sea at about 7.00a.m. near a cave in the south wall of Pendennis Point. After she had returned to

The culvert between Loughs Crolan and Derrylea where a monster was stranded in the 1890s; Derrylea Lough is in the background.

Lough Mask, County Galway/County Mayo.

Author at Lough Fadda. Incidentally, this is very close to the spot where Alcock and Brown landed after their historic transatlantic flight in 1919.

Lough Auna, County Galway; Air Commodore Kort's cottage is on the right.

Farmer Tommy Joyce, with Shanakeever Lough in the background.

Author (left) with Stephen Coyne at his home in Connemara.

The author at Lough Ree on the river Shannon.

Photograph of the monster in Lough Leane, County Kerry, taken by Pat Kelly in August 1981 (*see* Appendix Two).

shore, just as it was getting light, she saw a large dark hump rise out of the water, some 300 metres off-shore. A small hump then appeared, connected to the first, and then came a long neck. The beast, which was at least twenty-five feet long, raised and lowered its head several times and then sank beneath the waves.

The next sighting of which I have details, did not occur until 1985. One of the witnesses, Sheila Bird, described it in a letter to the *Falmouth Packet* on 31 August:

> For anyone who has actually experienced a sighting of the strange marine creature which has popularly become known as Morgawr, the monster of Falmouth Bay, japes and jokey reports of sightings are particularly frustrating in that they discredit genuine reports and reporters, and thereby discourage serious investigation which could possibly lead to a scientific breakthrough.
>
> This being the case I have decided to place on record my sighting of this creature off Portscatho on 10 July 1985, which I did not report at the time for it coincided with the launching of my book *Bygone Falmouth*, and I was reluctant because it might have been interpreted by some, as a joke to create timely publicity.
>
> Having just met my brother, Dr Eric Bird of Melbourne University, who is a scientist and who had flown in from Australia on that day, we were relaxing on the clifftop to the west of Portscatho at about 8.00p.m., when he leapt to his feet and exclaimed at the sight of an unfamiliar, large marine creature with a long neck, small head and large hump protruding high out of the water, with a long, muscular tail visible just below the surface, propelling itself in a north-northeasterly direction just offshore.
>
> Drawing the attention of two passers-by with binoculars, we were able to scrutinize the grey, slightly mottled creature closely and observe that there was either another hump at the base of its spine, or more likely that the muscular rhythms of the tail created the appearance of a hump. The tail seemed to be about as long as the body and the creature was an estimated seventeen to twenty feet in length.
>
> For several minutes we were able to observe this graceful creature, with its head held proudly as it glided swiftly and smoothly on the glassy surface of the water, illuminated in the clear evening sunlight.
>
> There were a number of birds wheeling around and a couple of boats in the vicinity, but all seemed oblivious of one another.
>
> Suddenly the creature submerged; it did not dive, but dropped vertically like a stone without leaving a ripple, bubble or any trace of

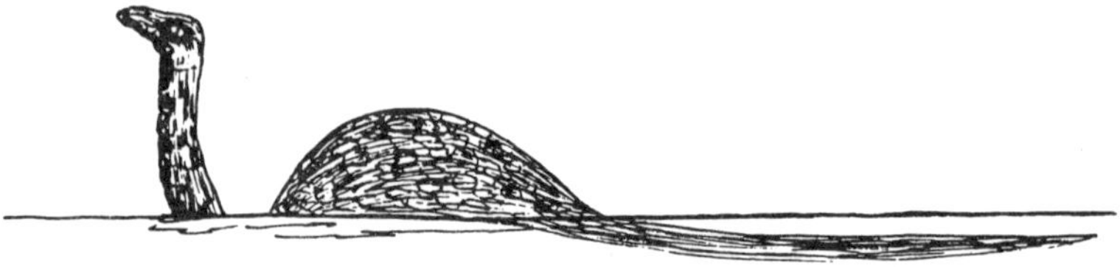

Fig. 7. Sheila Bird's sketch of Morgawr.

where it had been a moment before. We waited hopefully for it to put in another appearance, but it had gone.

I am indebted to Sheila Bird for providing me with a copy of her letter plus a transcription of the conversation that took place between herself, her brother and the passers-by at the time of the sighting, and a copy of her brother's report on the encounter. These are printed in Appendix One at the end of this book. Sheila Bird also sent a sketch of the animal.

About two weeks after Sheila Bird's sighting, which had not yet been made public, two campers, Jenny Halstead and Alice Lee from Hebden Bridge in Yorkshire, saw Morgawr. The *Falmouth Packet* on 26 July reported that they had seen the creature from Rosemullion Head between 6.30 and 7.00p.m. and had watched it for about ten seconds before it sank beneath the waves. The girls had a camera with them, but were too astounded by the animal's sudden appearance to think of using it. They did, however, provide a sketch of the creature which, they said, was like a 'massive overgrown black slug'.

To sum up, there seem to have been four types of sea monster seen off British shores:

Fig. 8. The Falmouth Bay sea serpent, after a sketch by Jenny Halstead.

1. A creature with many small humps along its back; a medium-sized head, and a pair of pectoral fins.

2. An animal having a mane on the neck; very prominent eyes and whiskers on the face and around the mouth.

3. A creature with a long neck; small head; bulky body and four large flippers. It may or may not have a tail. Some witnesses have reported two small horns on the head.

4. An animal resembling a giant eel.

What sort of animals could sea serpents be? Dr Bernard Heuvelmans suggests in his book *In the Wake of the Sea Serpents* that the multi-humped type could be a member of the whale family, perhaps being related to *Zeuglodon*, a genus of the *Archaeoceti* or ancient whales, about which little is known. The zeuglodon, which is thought to have been extinct for some thirty million years, had a long, serpentine body, a pair of pectoral fins and, perhaps, a bilobate tail like modern whales. Some species of zeuglodon were up to seventy feet long. Another possibility, according to Dr Heuvelmans, is that the multi-humped creature is one of the Sirenia, the group which comprises the dugongs, Steller's Sea Cow – now believed to be extinct – and the manatees. The humps on the back of this sea serpent seem, from their relatively small size and large number, to be solid, rather than coils or undulations in a flexible body.

The maned sea serpent could be one of the *Pinnipedia* – the group comprising the seals, walruses and sea-lions. This is suggested by the prominent eyes, whiskers and generally attractive appearance of the animal.

The long-necked sea serpent could also be a pinniped. The webbed feet, appearance of the head, and the fact that it has apparently been seen ashore point to this.

The fourth type of sea serpent could, as its appearance suggests, simply be an enormous eel. The conger eel and moray eel can reach ten feet in length and there is no reason why larger specimens should not exist. Fish keep growing for virtually as long as they live, assuming the environmental conditions are favourable, though the rate of growth slows with age. A twenty-foot eel, such as that reported by Captain Ruser in 1912 is by no means an impossibility.

All this assumes, of course, that sea serpents are what they appear to be – large animals unknown to science – and nothing more. However, some researchers, notably Anthony Doc Shiels and F. W. Holiday, have suggested that sea serpents could be paraphysical beings. They point to the feelings of fear and repulsion experienced by some witnesses such as Mary F. and Mrs Scott; the fact that appearance of sea serpents sometimes coincide with other strange phenomena, as in the Morgawr affair; the apparent impossibility of obtaining conclusive photographs (cameras malfunctioning at the critical moment) and the fact that the monsters' remains are never washed ashore.

CHAPTER THREE

Lake Monsters

> We are in this case convinced that what we saw was not a pike or otter, or any other fish or animal familiar to us, nor was it some inanimate object such as a tree branch carried by the current, for there is no current in this part of the lake. We were convinced that what we saw was a living creature of a very exceptional kind.
>
> Excerpt from a report by three Dublin priests who had seen a monster in Lough Ree on the River Shannon.

Irish Lake Monsters

References to monsters in Irish lakes can be found in very early sources, such as the seventh-century *Life of St Mochua of Balla* and the tenth-century *Book of Lismore*, but they are described in a superstitious and exaggerated way. For less fanciful reports we need to move forward to the latter part of the nineteenth century. Joseph Gallagher, a Donegal man, described a creature seen in Lough Muck in about 1885 to Cyril Dieckhoff, a monk at St Benedict's Abbey on the shore of Loch Ness in Scotland, who in the 1930s was collecting reports of lake monsters. According to Mr Gallagher, the monster was seen by a young woman who had waded out into Lough Muck to pick bog-bean. Hearing a splash she looked up and saw a large animal coming across the lake towards her. She quickly made her way ashore. The creature was seen several times over the next few years, showing two humps above the water.

Mr Gallagher pointed out that as Lough Muck was only three-quarters of a mile long, by half a mile wide there would be very little for a large animal to eat. In fact there have been reports of animals in loughs even smaller than this, as we shall see. It is hard to explain how such small lakes could support large animals, but the reports seem just as reliable as those concerning the larger loughs.

On several occasions, Irish lake monsters have been seen out of the water. Several land sightings are said to have occurred between 1890 and World War One. In the 1890s an animal like an enormous eel was trapped in a culvert between Loughs Crolan and Derrylea in County Galway. The creature was so repulsive that no one would go near it, and it was just left to rot away. When researchers Roy Mackal and F. W. Holiday visited the area in 1968 they found that the stranding was a well-known incident in the local history. They examined the culvert and deduced that the animal would have been about eighteen inches in diameter.

Shortly afterwards a similar stranding occurred at Ballynahinch Lake about four miles to the east. A creature some thirty feet long and 'thick as a horse' became trapped under the bridge which spans the Ballynahinch River near to the castle. In 1969 a local man, Patrick King, who had heard of the incident from his parents, described to F. W. Holiday how a blacksmith from Cashel, Patrick Connelly, forged a large, barbed spear to kill the animal. Luckily for the creature, however, it was washed clear of the bridge by a sudden overnight flood.

Shortly before World War One, a man driving his horse and cart past Lough Abisdealy in County Galway late one night saw an enormous eel-like creature crawling out of the water.

At the turn of the century, a Connemara woman was badly frightened by a monster which crawled out from Lough Auna in County Galway, as Tommy Joyce described to F. W. Holiday:

> This is known by the older people – my mum and dad – that I heard mention it. This would have happened . . . , I would imagine, seventy years ago, because the woman died a couple of years back. She was on the bog over there attending her turf and just as it grew sort of late in the evening – and her bog now, you must remember, ran down to the lake-shore – and she happened to be working the end near the lake. Suddenly there was a commotion in the water and this thing – which she told everyone was a Horse-eel came out of the lake and right up on the turf bank beside her. And she got so scared she ran for her life. . . . It came right out of the lake and up the lake shore to within a couple of yards from where she was working. And her description of it was, at the time – and this has sort of been passed down – that its front appearance was something similar to a horse and it tailed off something like an eel.

Horse-eel is a traditional and widespread Irish term for lake monsters. Thomas Crofton Croker, the nineteenth-century folklorist from Cork, described the Horse-eel as 'a great conger eel, seven yards long and as thick as a bull in the body, with a mane on its back like a horse'.

A monster was seen in Lough Auna on a later occasion. The witnesses were a boy and his mother who were stacking turf at the lough-side. The creature, which was about 200 yards away, seemed to be between thirty and forty feet long, with three or four humps. It had a bristly mane or fin on its back or neck, and resembled a gigantic eel.

The witnesses watched the animal for about fifteen minutes while it rolled and plunged in the water, sending waves right across the lake.

Edith Somerville who, with her cousin Violet Martin ('Martin Ross') wrote the 'Irish R.M.' stories, described in her book *The Smile and the Tear* an encounter with a monster in Lough Abisdealy, the scene of the land sighting described earlier in this chapter. One Sunday morning, shortly before World War One, a young lady, her groom and kitchen maid were driving to church past the lough when:

> . . . suddenly they beheld a long black creature propelling itself rapidly across the lake. Its flat head, on a long neck, was held high, two great loops of its length buckled in and out of the water as it progressed. Obviously a snake and a huge one. The three witnesses stared, doubtful of their own eyes at this amazing sight. The avenue is within a few yards of the water, so they were able to have a clear view of the mysterious monster. For how long they gazed at it I don't know. Unfortunately a virtuous anxiety not to keep her scholars waiting induced the principal witness to proceed on the way to church before the snake submerged.

Lady Augusta Gregory, a friend of W. B. Yeats and one of the founders of the Abbey Theatre in Dublin, discussed lake monsters in her book *Visions and Beliefs in the West of Ireland*, published in 1920. A small lake called Dhulough near Lady Gregory's home was said to harbour a monster and one day she saw the creature herself:

> I was coming home with my two brothers from Tirneevin School, and there as we passed Dhulough we heard a great splashing, and we saw some creature put its head up, with the head and mane like a horse. And we didn't stop but ran.

A County Clare man, referring to Lough Graney, told Lady Gregory:

> The lake down there is an enchanted place, and the old people told me that one time they were swimming there and a man had gone out into the middle and they saw something like a giant eel making for him, and they called out 'if ever you were a great swimmer show us now how you can swim to the shore,' for they wouldn't frighten him by saying what was behind him. So he swam to the shore, and he only got there when the thing behind him was in the place where he was.

One of the most famous of Irish sightings occurred at Lough Fadda in County Galway in 1954. The main witness was Georgina Carberry, a librarian from Clifden who was also a keen and experienced angler. On a June evening Miss Carberry and three friends were fishing from a boat in the lough. After catching several trout they pulled ashore to have some tea. Looking out across the water they saw a dark object coming steadily towards them. Georgina Carberry continues:

> Anyway, next thing, we began to get a bit worried. I was sitting nearest to it and it came in I suppose, oh, to within twenty yards of us. I was the first to move and jumped back and the other three who were sitting behind me did likewise. And as soon as we moved it just came right round . . . swung right around a rock which was near the shore and dived and we could see these awful big rings in the water as it was sinking. Before two minutes it had gone practically up to the island again when it surfaced. We could distinctly see two big humps showing behind its head out of the water. And the tail was noticed, when it swung around the rock. 'Twas a kind of fork – V-shaped – tail. And the mouth, which was open when it came in quite close to us at the shore, and the eyes and that I can't really remember. But I distinctly remember that the whole body had movement in it . . . it seemed like wormy. You know – creepy. The body seemed to have movement all over it all the time.

Miss Carberry was deeply affected by the incident. As she and her friends drove away from the lough she could not help looking back in case the creature had left the water and was coming after them. She had nightmares for weeks afterwards and did not return to the lough for six or seven years. Even then she would not go alone. Her friends were similarly affected.

Perhaps the strangest of Irish sightings occurred at Shanakeever Lough, County Galway, during the mid-1950s. On a rainy, misty day in 1954 or 1955, Patrick Canning went to fetch his donkey which was down by the lough. Walking towards the donkey he saw what he first thought was a foal circling repeatedly around it, but as he drew nearer he realized his mistake. The creature was long and black and had a somewhat horse-like appearance. It had legs and what looked like ears, but from a distance (later measured) of about 200 yards, and with poor visibility, Mr Canning could not be sure of details. The creature, on noticing its human observer, slid down into the lough. Here is how Patrick Canning described the animal's activity:

> It was circling round. . . . It used to go around, from side to side, and come in front. . . . It was going round what you would call gently, you know. It was just like she'd had a foal, d'ye know, and she was going round.

Mr Canning recalled an incident his father had described concerning a strange creature seen on the shore of a lake at Ballynahinch:

> There was a certain house not very far from the lake and the little ones – the children of the house – went out and on the bank there was a grand little foal and they went to tell their parents about it. And the parents came and it went into the lake. It was a Horse-eel. Oh, he told us that several times!

Sceptical people have often asserted that witnesses are deceived by the antics of otters, but this is often the first explanation to be considered by the witnesses themselves – and is soon discarded as being totally inadequate to account for what they were seeing. Typical is the description by Thomas Connelly of his experience on an April day in 1961, when he saw from the window of his cottage some unusual activity in Crolan Lough: 'I thought it was otters,' he said, 'but they were too long in one place to be otters, so I became suspicious like, and went over to see. It wasn't otters.' Mr Connelly went across to a hillock which overlooked the lough and saw about forty yards away a creature which was between twelve and fourteen feet long, an estimate he arrived at by comparing its length with that of his tractor and trailer. It repeatedly dived and re-surfaced, showing about eighteen inches of tail and a portion of its body. Mr Connelly watched the animal for about half an hour. He recalled that as a youngster he was kept away from the lake by his parents, for fear of the horse-eels which, it was popularly believed, could travel overland from lake to lake. He also remembered his parents talking about the stranding of a monster here back in the 1890s, an incident described earlier in this chapter.

On a March afternoon in 1962, Alphonsus Mullaney, a school-master, was fishing with his son at Lough Dubh, about thirteen miles east of Dunmore in County Galway. Feeling a tug on his line he started to pull it in but it snapped and, as he was examining the broken end, his son, a short distance away, screamed. Mr Mullaney looked up and saw a grotesque creature at the side of the lough:

> It was not a seal or anything I had ever seen. It had, for instance, short, thick legs and a hippo face. It was as big as a cow or an ass, square faced, with small ears and a white pointed horn on its snout. It was dark grey in colour, and covered with bristles or short hair, like a pig.

The boy screamed because the beast was trying to climb out of the water, apparently with hostile intent. Father and son hurried away from the lough and reported their encounter to several local men who went down to the lake with guns. There was no sign of the monster, however. The animal, whose head, said Mr Mullaney, most resembled that of a rhinoceros, is quite different from the eel-like animals usually reported, but as there are no grounds for regarding Alphonsus Mullaney as anything but a reliable witness the sighting must be included in the record.

This was not the first monster sighting in Lough Dubh. In 1956, three men had seen an unusual animal swimming there, but were too far away to make out details. In 1960, a local man, Con Mahon, saw three animals in the lough, one large and two smaller, an incident he later described on the radio. Lough Dubh seems to have had a sinister reputation for some time, for, as an old man told an *Irish Press* fishing correspondent, the lake was a strange place: 'queer things had been seen from time to time in the past'.

On 16 June 1963, a calm sunny day, Mr A. R. Lawrence of Tullamore, County Offaly, watched a monster at a distance of about 250 yards in the County Galway end of Lough Mask. Two smooth, black humps were visible, moving slowly and steadily through the water. They protruded about fifteen inches above the water, each being about five or six feet in length, and separated by a distance of between eight and ten feet. Mr Lawrence watched the animal for about a minute and a half during which time it travelled a distance of about 250 yards before finally disappearing behind Inishdura Island. The Scandinavian invaders who overran this area in the seventh and eighth centuries may have seen monsters here and named the lake accordingly. 'Mask' is Swedish for worm or caterpillar.

Farmer Tommy Joyce's house overlooks Shanakeever Lough and it was here in 1963 or 1964 that he saw a large animal, which he first thought to be an otter, break surface among some reeds. As he watched though, the creature heaved a great back, some seven or eight feet long and two feet high out of the water. It then moved away, crushing a path through the reeds, and submerged.

A monster was also seen in Shanakeever by Patrick Walsh. He was out in his boat when he saw a head and neck emerge from the water nearby. He quickly rowed ashore, fearing that the animal would surface under his boat and capsize it. He recalled that two men he knew had seen a creature some sixteen feet long, like a giant eel, in the lough.

> I experienced a sinking feeling as I contemplated this small body of water; not even one substantial animal could have more than a transient relationship with this little pond.

So wrote Professor Roy Mackal of his first glimpse of Lough Nahooin, County Galway, in July 1968. The lough was certainly small – 100 yards long, eighty yards wide and twenty feet deep – yet a few months before Mackal's visit, a local farmer and his family had watched an enormous eel-like animal swimming in its murky peat-stained waters.

At about 7.00p.m. on 22 February 1968 Stephen Coyne went down to the lough-side to bring up some dry peat, accompanied by his eight-year-old son and his dog. It was sunset but still quite light. On reaching the lough Mr Coyne and his son saw a strange creature swimming to and fro. It was about twelve feet long, with a neck nine inches to a foot in diameter, black and smooth. Occasionally it put its head underwater, two big humps showing as it did so, and sometimes a flat tail would appear. The creature seemed to be irritated by the dog's barking and it moved inshore towards the animal with its jaws open, showing a pale interior to the mouth. It moved out again though, when Mr Coyne went over to join his dog. At this point the boy went home to fetch the rest of the family, and when he returned with Mrs Coyne and the other four children the animal was still there. Mrs Coyne said later that the animal had two small horns on its head, and thought that it came as close as four to five yards from the shore, though Mr Coyne thought that the distance was more like nine yards. Eventually as it grew dark, the Coyne family walked home across the bog, leaving the strange creature still swimming energetically around the lake.

The following year, a sheep farmer, Thomas Connelly of Doone, Claddaghduff, saw the Lough Nahooin monster ashore. At about 5.00p.m. on or about 8 September 1969, Mr Connelly saw the animal lying on the turf about fourteen feet away from the lake. As he watched, it slid forward with a rolling motion and slipped into the water, sending up a shower of spray. It stayed visible for a few seconds and then submerged. It was bigger than a donkey's foal, he said, about two to two and a half feet in width, and black in colour. It had four heavy, stumpy legs, and its general appearance was eel-like. Mr Connelly was too far away to make out details of its head, feet or skin texture.

Professor Mackal thought, understandably, that it was impossible for lakes as small as Lough Nahooin to support a population of large aquatic animals, and could only postulate that the monsters must move overland as circumstances dictated, a view supported by sightings like Thomas Connelly's. F. W. Holiday agreed that many Irish lakes were too small to support large animals, but he was to arrive at a much more radical view to explain the presence of monsters in them.

We leave County Galway now and travel to Lough Bran* in

* Lough Bran is named after Bran, the hunting dog of the great Irish hero, Finn Machumhail. The hound was said to have drowned in the lake. Lough Bran has sometimes been referred to as Lough Brin.

County Kerry which has a tradition of monster sightings. A local man described the monster as being about fourteen feet long and resembling a combination of horse and fish. In 1940 the Lough Bran monster was reportedly seen lying on the bank of the lake, apparently basking in the sun. The witness, a fourteen-year-old boy, said that it was black with four short legs.

In 1954, the Lough Bran monster was seen by Timothy O'Sullivan, who farmed near the lake. Early on the evening of Christmas Eve Mr O'Sullivan went to bring in his cattle for milking. Passing the lake, he saw what he first thought were two ducks, but then the 'ducks' rose out of the water and the farmer saw that they were two fins or humps, each about two feet long and two feet high. The distance between them was about twelve feet. Mr O'Sullivan dashed back into the house, loaded his shotgun and, accompanied by his wife, ran back to the lake. The creature, however, was no longer to be seen.

In summer, 1979 two brothers, who farmed near Lough Bran, saw a reptilian creature, black and about ten feet long, swimming in the lake. The animal swam almost the length of the lake, about 600 yards, before submerging. The monster had also been seen several years previously by the men's father. He said that it was as 'black as soot' and was like a cross between 'a giant seal and a dragon out of the pictures'.

Undoubtedly, the most detailed report of a lough monster was that sent by three Dublin priests to the Inland Fisheries Trust after a sighting at Lough Ree, in the very centre of Ireland on the River Shannon. Father Matthew Burke, Father Daniel Murray and Father Richard Quigley were fishing from a rowing boat on the calm, clear evening of 18 May 1960. At about 9.30p.m., while they were about fifty or sixty yards off St Mark's Wood on the eastern side of the lake, they saw a strange object moving slowly along, about eighty yards away.

There were two sections above the water. The leading portion seemed to be the neck. It was between eighteen and twenty-four inches long, about four inches in diameter, and was held at an angle of thirty degrees to the water. The neck terminated in a serpentine head.

Following the neck, about two feet behind, came a hump which was about eighteen inches long at the water-line. The overall length of the two visible portions was about six feet.

The animal was moving slowly and steadily through the water, creating little disturbance, and seemed unaware of, or unconcerned by, its human observers. The priests watched the animal for two or three minutes as it travelled in a north-easterly direction towards the shore. It submerged gradually to reappear a few moments later still following the same course. It was about thirty yards offshore when it submerged for the last time.

The publicity surrounding the priests' sighting prompted other witnesses to come forward. A retired postman, Patrick Hanley described an incident which had occurred some thirty years previously when he was fishing with some of his family in a boat north of Yew Point at the mouth of Bally Bay. Something seized his line and with a strong, steady pull towed the boat out towards the middle of the lake. Mr Hanley was forced to cut the line.

Mr F. J. Waters had two experiences similar to Patrick Hanley's, the first also occurring at Bally Bay, and the second near to Beam Island on the other side of the lake. On the latter occasion, he was fishing for trout with a heavy line when something seized the line and dived straight to the bottom, breaking the line after some seventy feet had unwound from the reel. Most fish are restricted by their enclosed swim bladder to slow movement between different depths, but in the eel the swim bladder is open to the external environment, which allows rapid movement between different depths of water. Indeed, both Patrick Hanley and F. J. Waters thought they had encountered some type of giant eel, a creature far larger than anything previously recorded.

In his book *Thanks for the Memory*, published in 1952, Colonel Harry Rice wrote that a friend of his had seen the Lough Ree monster and had described it as 'like a dozen barrels of porter strung together', while in 1958 two Englishmen were towed by some unseen monster around the lake until forced to cut their line. In February 1960 Patrick Ganley and Joseph Quigley of Inch Turk caught a huge creature in their net while they were fishing for pike, but while trying to haul it aboard their net tore apart and it escaped. 'It must have been as strong as a horse', one of the men later commented. This occurred in some sixty feet of water about half a mile from where, later in the year, the three priests encountered the monster they were to describe so precisely.

A feeling of fear and unease similar to that experienced by Georgina Carberry and her friends was felt by a Dublin man 'L.R.' and his friend who saw a monster in Lough Bray in the Wicklow Mountains in 1963:

> Looking down into the lake, which was perfectly clear in the evening sunlight, we saw a large hump, like the back of a rhinoceros emerge from the water. Ripples spread out to each side of it and then a head, something like a tortoise's, only many times bigger, broke surface. It came up about three feet above the surface of the water, moved slowly around and swam forward a few yards. As it did so the body was clearly revealed, circular and not less than ten or twelve feet in circumference. It was a dark-greyish colour.

The two men watched the creature for about three minutes before it dived, leaving a swirl of water. The men were anxious to know if anyone else had seen the creature, or if there was a natural explanation for the sighting for, as they concluded, 'it was a disturbing experience which still affects us'.

From the Wicklow Mountains we move south and west to Lough Attariff, in County Cork, where the sighting of a monster was reported by Mr W. J. Wood of Bandon:

> In 1966 in the month of June, I was fishing at Lough Attariff, a sixteen-acre lake in the hills between Clonakilty and Dunmanway. The sun was strong with a very light south-westerly breeze into which I was fly-fishing with an expectant eye open for rising trout. Suddenly and quietly a long dark brown object surfaced at about a distance of 100 yards, facing directly towards me. It had the head of a well-grown calf and large glittering eyes almost at water level. The distance appeared to lessen and the creature's approach angle altered until it was parallel to me and about ninety yards distant. It seemed to be about ten to ten and a half feet long and protruded above the surface five or six inches. After about two minutes the animal submerged.

Mr Wood reported seeing another water monster the following year. He was fishing at Lackagh Lake, about fifty miles north-west of Attariff, when a yellowish-brown object about seven feet long broke surface only a few yards in front of him, and after a few seconds submerged.

The Lackagh monster was also seen by a young rugby player who said that it had a long, snake-like body and a small head on which were two stumpy horns. He admitted to being badly frightened.

Sraheens Lough on Achill Island, off the coast of County Mayo, was not unusual in being regarded by the local people as the home of monsters, but in 1968 it was the scene of three dramatic encounters with a creature quite unlike anything previously reported in Ireland.

Sraheens Lough is circular, some 400 feet in diameter, and extremely deep at the centre. A group of Australian students surveying the lough in 1969 described it as 'bottomless' and suggested that it was the crater of an extinct volcano. It is a wild and lonely place; much of the surrounding countryside is covered by dense rhododendron forests which in places run down to the lough's edge.

On the night of 1 May 1968, two local men, Michael McNulty and John Cooney were driving home to Achill Sound from the village of Keel. At about 10.10p.m., as they were driving past Sraheens Lough, an animal 'out of this world' came running up from the lough which was on their right-hand side. It bounded across the road about twelve feet in front of them and disappeared into the undergrowth. Both men were very frightened and quickly drove away from the spot.

Mr Cooney said that the creature was between eight and twelve feet long and about two and a half feet high. It had a long, thick tail, a swan-shaped neck and a head like a sheep or greyhound with glittering eyes. It was dark brown and had a shiny skin and, strangest of all, ran on its hind legs, rocking from side to side as it did so.

A week later the animal was seen again, by fifteen-year-old Gay Dever who, as he was cycling past the lough at about 5.00p.m., heard splashing sounds. He continues:

> When I stopped and looked through an opening in the rhododendrons, I had a shock. Crawling out of the water came the strangest animal I have ever seen. It was much bigger than a horse, black in colour with a long, slender and sheep-looking head, long neck and tail. It moved like a kangaroo and its hind legs were bigger than the front ones. When the nasty-looking thing entered the beach, I left the area as fast as I could.

Two days later, the monster was seen by two girls, twenty-one-year-old Bernie Sweeney and twenty-three-year-old Mary Calaghan, who were returning from a party and trying to hitch a lift back to Achill Sound. Eventually a driver stopped near an opening in the rhododendrons which gave a clear view of the lake. As the car pulled up Bernie looked towards the lough and saw, in the clear moonlight, a big, shiny black creature running towards her. She screamed and ran away from the car down the road. The driver jumped out and asked what was going on, but Mary, who had also seen the creature, was shaking with fright and could only point towards the lough. By this time the animal had entered the water and was on the point of submerging, and all the driver saw was something quickly disappearing below the surface towards the side of the lough where the undergrowth was at its thickest.

This creature was unlike the lake monsters previously reported in Ireland, but the events of May 1968 were not isolated incidents. Dennis McGowan, the storekeeper at Achill Sound, described an earlier encounter with the monster of Sraheens Lough, though on this occasion the animal stayed in the water. The witness was an Englishman who, in July 1966, was fishing for char at the lough, when the calm surface of the water began to boil and ripple and a long neck with a swan-like head emerged. This was followed by a shiny black body and the monster started to swim quickly towards the angler. The terrified fisherman dropped his rod and fled, not stopping until he had reached Dennis McGowan's store where, pale and trembling, he described what he had seen. The storekeeper stated that a monster had also been seen in the 1930s, the locals referring to it as a 'water-horse', but the lough had a sinister reputation before that. A seventy-two-year-old former school teacher, Mary Heaney, recalled that as a child her parents had told her to stay away from Sraheens Lough on account of a monster which lived in an underwater cave. Another resident, Martin Coyne, who was sixty-eight years old, had similar childhood memories, and mentioned another aspect of the mystery – the continued and unexplained disappearance of sheep in the countryside around the lough. Farmer John Madden commented:

> I don't know if it's the monster that gets away with my sheep, but I do know there is something strange on the loose at the lough. The sheep have not fallen over any cliffs, that's for sure. They are very careful climbers and used to the area. And the only other animals present there are badgers, and these are very shy. Who, by the way, has ever heard of badgers attacking sheep?

On occasions, unusual footprints have been found near the lake. Dennis McGowan described a set of paw-prints he saw in the autumn of 1973 as being three-toed, with an impression of webbing between the toes, and twice the size of the paw-prints of a large dog. The tracks came out of the water, continued for about ten feet, and then re-entered the water. The stride was about five feet. Mr McGowan doubted that they were a hoax as people seldom visited the lough.

For our last few reports from Ireland we return to the Connemara area of Galway. On a May evening in 1980, a barbecue party was in progress at the cottage of retired Netherlands Air Force officer, Air Commodore Kort, about 120 yards from the shore of Lough Auna. The Air Commodore and his friends had just gone indoors when, through the window, he saw a dark shape moving through the water about fifteen yards out from the shore. With a guest, Adrian O'Connell, he watched it for several minutes as it moved slowly towards the western end of the lake. Another guest, Farmer Tommy Joyce, mentioned earlier, also glimpsed the creature as it moved into some reeds. The visible part of the animal seemed to be about five feet long and one foot high. Mr Kort commented on the movement of the creature: 'The uncanny thing about it was the gliding movement without any disturbance of the water at the surface.'

When I spoke to Tommy Joyce at his cottage in March 1986, he described an encounter with a monster in Shanakeever Lough which occurred in the summer, 1980. The witness was a soldier in the Welsh Guards who, while fly-fishing in the lough, had noticed a strange creature lying on the surface of the water nearby. His first thought was that his eyes were playing tricks on him, but he soon realized this was not the case. The animal, which had two small horns or protruding eyes, seemed to be watching him. The witness, now feeling uneasy, began to edge away from the creature, but it moved whenever he did. Finally, the man, now very frightened, started to run along the side of the lough, the creature keeping pace with him in the water for a short distance. The witness ran all the way up to Tommy Joyce's cottage where, very breathless, he described his encounter. The soldier, a giant of a man said Tommy Joyce, admitted that he had never been so frightened in his life.

Tommy Joyce himself had a brief sighting of the Shanakeever monster in June 1982. He was in a car travelling past the lough with some German tourists when he saw a big hump in the water. His companions suggested that it might have been debris, but when they returned along the road shortly after, the hump had vanished. Tommy now keeps a loaded camera ready on his dresser in the hope of photographing the elusive monster of Shanakeever Lough.

Scottish Lake Monsters

In Scotland, as in Ireland, lake monsters seem to have been encountered for centuries. There are hundreds of recorded sightings from Loch Ness alone. Here I have simply picked out some of the most interesting accounts from six Scottish lochs.

Loch Arkaig

It was not until the nineteenth century, when wealthy Englishmen began to travel in Scotland and settle there, that sightings received wider publicity. One interesting early description came from the third Earl of Malmesbury, an English politician with estates in Scotland, who in his *Memoirs of an Ex-Minister*, published in 1857, wrote:

> October 3rd: This morning my stalker and his boy gave me an account of a mysterious creature, which they say exists in Loch Arkaig, and which they call the Lake-Horse. It is the same animal of which one has occasionally read accounts in the newspapers as having been seen in the Highland lochs, and on the existence of which in Loch Assynt, the late Lord Ellesmere wrote an interesting article; but hitherto the story has always been looked upon as fabulous. I am now, however, really persuaded of the truth. My stalker, John Stuart, at Achnacarry has seen it twice, and both times at sunrise in summer on a bright sunny day, when there is not a ripple on the water. The creature was basking on the surface; he only saw the head and hind quarters, proving that its back was hollow, which is not the shape of any fish or seal. Its head resembled that of a horse. It was also seen once by his three little children, who were all walking together along the beach. It was then motionless about thirty yards from the shore and apparently asleep. They at first took it for a rock, but when they got near it moved its head, and they were so frightened they ran home, arriving in the state of greatest terror. There was no mistaking their manner . . . and they offered to make affidavit of it before a magistrate.

Loch Eil

In his book *September Road to Caithness*, published in 1962, the writer, 'B.B.', described a monster he saw in Loch Eil on a bright October morning. He was watching some mallard when there suddenly rose out of the calm water a big, black shiny object which resembled the 'blunt, blind head of an enormous worm'. The witness continues:

> It was, I suppose, some fifty yards from where I was standing, and it kept appearing and disappearing, not moving along, but rolling on the surface. The water was greatly disturbed all round the object. It had a shiny, wet-looking skin, but the head (if head it was) was quite unlike a seal's and had no face, or nose, no eyes. It rose quite a long way out of the water, some three feet or more, before sinking back.

In Ireland, Georgina Carberry had likened the monster she saw in Lough Fadda, County Galway, to a gigantic worm. 'B.B.' is one of several Scottish witnesses to make a similar comparison.

Loch Lochy

A report which vividly captures the feelings of people suddenly confronted by a huge unknown animal is that of Mr and Mrs Sargent from Fort William, Inverness-shire. At 2.00p.m. on 30 September 1975 the Sargents and their three children were motoring along the south shore road overlooking Loch Lochy. As they turned the corner by the Corriegour Hotel they saw an unusual wave in the water and, a few seconds later, the gigantic creature that was causing it. The animal was gliding through the water, showing a great black back about twenty feet long. Mr Sargent slowed his van and his wife, fumbling frantically with her camera, jumped out. Unfortunately the creature submerged before she could get a picture. Shortly after, a terrific surge of water broke on the shore below her. Her husband, meanwhile, had stopped the van further up the road. He noticed a second, smaller hump, just behind the first, though his wife, busy with her camera, seems to have missed this. He said that during the sighting, lasting approximately two minutes, he was 'literally stunned and frozen to the spot'. The children were shouting excitedly. Catching up with his wife, he saw that she was visibly shaking. Mrs Sargent commented:

> ... there can be no doubt in our minds about what we saw on Lochy and incredible as it seems (we got no sleep that night talking about it!) it was as real as we are real today, and it will remain one of the most thrilling memories of our lives.

Loch Urabhal

On 27 July 1961, a calm, sunny day, two teachers, Ian McArthur and Roderick Maciver, both local men, were fishing in Loch Urabhal, a fresh-water loch near the village of Achmore on the Isle of Lewis in the Hebrides. The quiet was broken when Maciver jumped to his feet, shouting, 'There's something in the loch!' About forty-five yards away a large creature was undulating vertically in the water. It had a large hump, and a small fin or head about six feet in front of this. The creature appeared three times on the surface while McArthur struggled with his camera. Finally he had it ready, but the creature had submerged for the last time. The witnesses dismissed suggestions that the animal could have been an otter. It did not resemble an otter, was much too large, and did not swim like one. Lake monsters had been reported on Lewis on previous occasions.

Loch Morar

In her book *The Search for Morag*, Elizabeth Montgomery Campbell gives details of thirty-one sightings of a monster, known to the local people as Morag, in Loch Morar between 1887 and 1971. Loch Morar is eleven miles long, and at its deepest about a thousand feet deep. Probably the most dramatic encounter with the Loch Morar monster occurred in August 1969. Between 9.00 and 9.30p.m. on 16 August, two long-distance lorry-drivers, Duncan McDonnell and William Simpson, were returning from a fishing trip on the loch in their motor boat. They were heading towards the islands at the western end of the loch, travelling at a speed of between six and seven knots, when Duncan McDonnell, who was at the wheel, heard a splash and, looking round, saw a large animal following the boat. In a few seconds it had caught up with them and bumped into the vessel. McDonnell grabbed an oar and attempted to lever the beast away, fearing that it might capsize the vessel. At this point, William Simpson dashed into the cabin to shut off the gas-stove, as the collision had spilt a kettle of boiling water and extinguished the flame. He came out just in time to see the oar break and, grabbing his rifle, he put a bullet into the animal. The beast slowly sank, though there was no sign of blood or any injury.

The men estimated the visible length of the creature to be between twenty-five and thirty feet. It had three low humps or undulations which protruded about eighteen inches above the surface of the water, as did the head which was snake-like and about a foot across. The skin was rough and of a dirty-brown colour. Mr McDonnell said that the beast felt very solid as he was trying to push it away with the oar.

Initially the men did not report their encounter to the media, but they did tell a relative who, two days after the incident, gave the story to the newspapers. Several exaggerated and confused accounts were published, some describing a pitched battle between the men and the monster which was said to have bitten the oar in half. In 1970, Elizabeth Montgomery Campbell interviewed Duncan McDonnell who, in her opinion, was a reliable witness. As a footnote it should be pointed out that Professor Roy Mackal, who was investigating reports at Loch Ness at the time of the Morar incident, examined the boat two days after its collision with the monster, and found that the point of impact was marked by scratches and missing paint.

Loch Ness: pre-1933 sightings

The Loch Ness Monster did not become famous until 1933, but encounters with the beast had occurred many years before this. According to E. H. Bright, whose account we will come to shortly, the creature was seen in 1862 by one Jimmy Hossack, though no details of the encounter seem to have been recorded. This seems to be the first sighting at Loch Ness in which the witness's name is known.

In September 1950, *The Scotsman* newspaper printed a letter referring to a sighting of the monster which occurred some time in the nineteenth century:

> The late Dr Galbraith of Dingwall used to tell of how he was visiting on the west coast of this country, and while in a house there a paper came in with an account of the Loch Ness Monster. With them in the house was a man who had returned home after spending most of his life in New Zealand. This New Zealander quietly said: 'I have seen the Loch Ness Monster.'

As a boy the New Zealander was on a boat travelling from Plockton to Inverness. While they were sailing through Loch Ness the monster had suddenly surfaced alongside the boat and swam on a parallel course for a short distance before submerging.

In March 1934 Mr D. Mackenzie of Balnain wrote to Commander R. T. Gould describing an encounter which had occurred some fifty years before. Mr Mackenzie saw the monster in October 1871 or 1872, while he was gathering bracken. He was near Abriachan when he saw what he first thought was a log drifting out into the loch from the direction of Aldourie. The surface of the loch was very calm. As the 'log' reached the middle of the loch, however, it suddenly 'came to life' and, looking just like an upturned boat, went at great speed, churning up the water, in the direction of Urquhart Castle. Mr Mackenzie concluded:

> It was about 12 o'clock on a grand sunny day, so that it was impossible for me to be mistaken. It was an animal of some sort; and I have told this story to my friends long before the present 'monster' became famous.

According to the *Northern Chronicle* for 12 August 1933, an Abriachan stone-mason, Alexander MacDonald, saw the monster several times early in the morning during the late 1880s:

> Mr MacDonald, who was a regular traveller on the Loch Ness mail steamer between Abriachan and Inverness, was often known to arrive at Abriachan Pier in a state of subdued excitement, and after having boarded the steamer he sometimes volunteered the information that he had seen the 'salamander' as he called it.

Another witness was Roderick Matheson whose sighting took place at about the same time. According to the *Glasgow Herald* of 19 July 1933:

> Mr Matheson was part owner of the schooner *Bessie*, which frequently made passages from the west coast to the east via the Caledonian Canal and, of course, Loch Ness. On one of these journeys Mr Matheson, who was mate of the vessel, saw in Loch Ness what he describes as 'the biggest eel I ever saw in my life. It had,' he said, 'a neck like a horse and a mane somewhat similar.'

On 20 October 1933, *The Scotsman* printed a letter from a Mr D. Murray Rose who stated:

> In the summer of 1885, stories were circulated about a strange beast being seen by many people about Loch Ness. It usually only appeared for a few minutes on the surface of the Loch, so that no-one could properly describe it.

In a letter to *The Times* in November 1933, the Duke of Portland wrote:

> I should like to say that when I became, in 1895, thirty-eight years ago, the tenant of the salmon angling in Loch Quoich and the River Garry, the forester, the hotel keeper and the fishing ghillies used often to talk about a 'horrible great Beastie' as they called it which appeared in Loch Ness.

Nicholas Witchell writes, in his book *The Loch Ness Story*, that the monster was seen several times in 1896 by the residents of Fort Augustus, one of whom was James Rose, a local shop-keeper. Apparently the beast showed itself as a large hump moving quickly along the surface of the loch.

Some of the early reports are particularly interesting in that they describe the monster ashore. One such encounter, in 1879, involved a group of children who saw a strange creature on the north shore of the loch. This sighting was described many years later by one of the witnesses, a lady in her seventies, to Edward P. Smith who reported the incident to Tim Dinsdale in 1962. The children had seen the monster on a hot summer day while they were picnicking on one of the northern slopes near to the old graveyard. They had almost finished their meal when they heard a noise on the slope behind them and, turning round, saw an enormous animal coming towards them. It was:

> . . . bigger than an elephant, but about the same sort of colour. It had a head perched on a relatively slender neck, and it turned from side to side and seemed to peer at us, passing us a few yards to one side, and waddling down to the lake where it entered the water and disappeared.

A year later the creature was seen ashore again, by an eight-year-old boy, E. H. Bright, and his cousin. They were walking along the shore near Drumnadrochit when they suddenly saw the monster appear from the nearby woods, about 100 yards away. The animal 'waddled' along to the edge of the loch on four short legs, entered the water and rapidly sank, leaving a tremendous wash. The boys, terrified, ran to their home. E. H. Bright described the encounter many years later, at the age of ninety, to Mr D. J. A. Briggs of Wimbledon, who recounted it to Tim Dinsdale. Mr Bright said that the animal had a long neck, like an elephant's trunk, a small, snake-like head, and was a dark colour.

On a warm Sunday afternoon in September 1909, eleven-year-old Margaret MacGruer, her baby sister in a pram, and her two brothers were on the shore at Inchnacardoch Bay awaiting the arrival of some friends. They were skimming stones across the water when they heard a loud crackling noise in the trees on the other side of the small bay. The crackling grew louder, and suddenly a huge animal came out of the trees and made its way down to the loch. The creature was about twenty feet long, grey in colour and its movement reminded Margaret Cameron of that of a caterpillar. It had two short legs at the front, and its skin seemed to be shiny. The children could not see if the animal had a long neck or a short one as it was facing directly towards them. As the beast entered the water the terrified children fled.

In September 1957, one H.F.W. wrote to *The Scotsman* stating that it was common knowledge at the turn of the century that there was 'something odd' in Loch Ness, but that the local people were afraid of ridicule:

> [you] only heard little bits as you got to know the people. . . . I subsequently had a talk with a priest with whom I had been friends for years, and he frankly said that the story had been going around to his knowledge since before the monastery was built.

Mr F. Frazer of Knockie described to Commander Gould how he had seen the monster on a calm December day in 1903. He was rowing across the loch with two others from Knockie Pier to Invermoriston when, at a point about 400 yards out, they saw an object like an upturned boat moving through the water about 250 yards away in the direction of Fort Augustus. The men rowed after the creature, but it was moving too fast for them to catch up with it and, as they had to catch the Invermoriston steamer, they reluctantly gave up the chase.

During his stay in Invermoriston in 1933 Commander Gould met a Mr John MacLeod who described an encounter which occurred many years previously. Standing on a ledge of rock at the foot of the lowest fall on the Moriston River, overlooking a pool in which the river joins Loch Ness, Mr MacLeod was about to start fishing when he noticed a huge creature, thirty to forty feet long with an eel-like head, lying motionless on the surface of the water. After watching it for a while he threw his line in its direction and the animal made off. Gould writes that Mr MacLeod described his encounter to a Mr J. McC. Robertson in 1908, and to a Mr C. W. W. Broun in 1910.

During World War One, Mr Kenneth Mackay of Inverness was in charge of the Drumnadrochit Hotel. One evening, James Cameron, head keeper at the Balmacan estate, who had been out fishing on the loch, came into the hotel looking pale and shaken and asked for some brandy. He would not say what had upset him. Later on, Mr Mackay accompanied Mr Cameron on his way home, and persuaded him to reveal what had so shocked him. While he was fishing on Loch Ness an enormous animal had suddenly surfaced beside his boat. The shock caused him to collapse in the bottom of the boat. When he came to there was no sign of the creature, and he rowed to the shore as quickly as possible. He would say no more of his experience. Mr Mackay described this incident to Commander Gould.

According to Mr D. Murray Rose, mentioned earlier, the monster was seen again in 1912, but details, unfortunately, are lacking.

At 7.30a.m. on a day early in May 1923, James McGillivray and William Miller saw the Loch Ness Monster about a mile from the Dores-Stratherrick road at a point east of Balnafoich. It was lying on the surface of the water near Abriachan Pier, looking like an upturned boat. It then moved off, describing 'three parts of a circle' and submerged. 'When moving,' said the witnesses, 'it went slowly, but we could see a ripple leaving its fore part.' The creature, which the men watched for between eight and ten minutes, showed ten to twelve feet of its dark body at the surface. Mr Miller's wife had seen a similar creature in Dores Bay in July 1914.

In 1919 there seems to have been another land sighting of the

Loch Ness Monster. The witness was Jock Forbes, then a boy of twelve, and his father, a farmer from Foyers. Many years later Mr Forbes described the encounter to Nicholas Witchell:

> It was a very dark, stormy night. My father and I stopped off at my uncle's house at Scaniport and then continued on our journey. We were about two miles north of Inverfarigaig near the old ferry where the bank isn't very steep when the pony suddenly stopped and started backing away in fright. It very nearly backed us right off the road and down the bank.
>
> Something large was crossing the road about twenty yards ahead of us – it came out of the trees above the road, moved slowly across the road and then down the bank and we heard a splash as, presumably it went into the water.

Mr Forbes could not make out any details, but he stressed to Nicholas Witchell that the animal was very large, extending from one side of the road to the other.

In 1923, the Loch Ness Monster was again seen on land. Early one April morning, Alfred Cruickshank, a chauffeur, was driving alongside the loch's northern shore on his way to meet his employer at Spean Bridge Station. At about 5.00a.m., as he drove up a small hill about two miles north of Invermoriston, his lights illuminated a large moving object next to the road about fifty yards ahead. It had a big humped body about six feet high and twelve feet long, and a long tail ten to twelve feet in length. The creature had four limbs and seemed to be a khaki colour with a lighter underside. The head seemed to be set close to the body. As Mr Cruickshank passed the animal it made a grunting noise. When he arrived at the station his employer asked him what was wrong as he was very pale. Mr Cruickshank recounted his experience, only to be told that he must have been dreaming. The reaction of his friends was equally sceptical. In this sighting the absence of a long neck, and the presence of a long tail, quite the reverse of the usual descriptions, are puzzling, but Mr Cruickshank's view of the animal was fleeting, and it is possible that he mistook the creature's neck for a tail.

The *Inverness Courier* for 6 November 1962, reporting on an outing of Caledonian Canal Authority pensioners, described how during the trip conversation turned to the monster. Mr Simon Cameron of Invergarry recalled how he had seen the animal in

1926 near Cherry Island at the Fort Augustus end of the Loch. He stated:

> It was while I was watching two gulls skimming the loch's surface that my attention was fixed when the gulls suddenly rose screaming into the air. Then before my eyes, something like a huge upturned boat rose from the depths and I can still see the water cascading down its sides. Just as suddenly though, it sank out of sight, but it was an extraordinary experience.

Another witness cited by Commander Gould was Mrs Cumming who, at about 9.30a.m. on an August day in 1929, with her cousin D. McGillivray and her aunt, watched the monster through a telescope from almost the same spot as had William Miller. The creature, which appeared as a dark hump as bulky as a horse's body, was close to the shore at a point some 300 yards north-east of Abriachan Pier, and stayed motionless for about ten minutes. It then sank, throwing up spray.

On the calm, clear evening of 21 July 1930, Ian J. Milne from Inverness was fishing from a boat with two friends, R. C. M. Macdougal and G. D. Gallon, off Tor Point, Dores Bay. At about 7.30 there was a loud splash and the men saw a large animal travelling through the water about 300 yards away at a speed of about fourteen to fifteen knots. The creature showed two or three humps above the water and was about twenty-two feet long. A peculiar undulation, similar to the motion of a caterpillar, ran along the animal's back. The creature threw up a bow wave about two feet high which rocked the boat from side to side. The animal, which reminded Mr Milne of a huge conger eel, was in view for about three and a half minutes, describing a semicircular course before submerging. Commander Gould, who interviewed Mr Milne, also contacted the other witnesses who confirmed his account.

Loch Ness: post-1933 sighting

At 10.10a.m. on 1 October 1933, B. A. Russell MA, a schoolmaster at Fort Augustus, saw the Loch Ness Monster near Inchnacardoch Bay while he was standing on the rocks about 100 feet above the loch. The water was flat calm and Mr Russell estimated that the creature, which was due east of him, was about

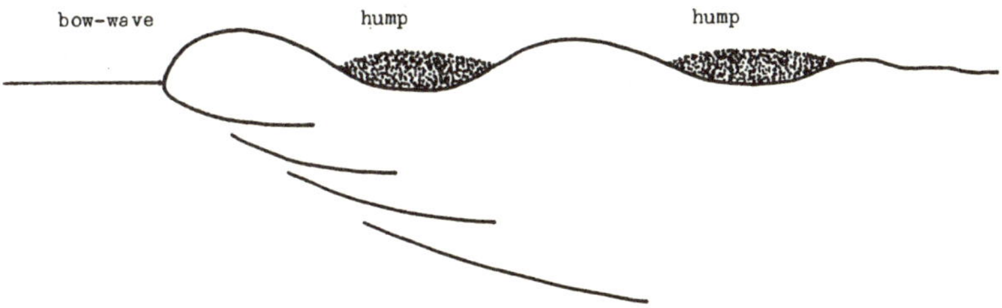

Fig. 9. Mr I. J. Milne's sketch of the creature he saw in Loch Ness on 21 July 1930.

800 yards away. It had a long neck and small head, protruding about five feet out of the water, and swam slowly, keeping a straight course, occasionally turning its head from side to side. The head and neck seemed to twist together, rather than the head pivoting on the neck. A V-shaped ripple spread out from the front of the neck where it met the surface. Mr Russell watched the animal, which was a dark colour, for twelve minutes, timed by his watch, before it submerged. At its closest point it was, he thought, about 700 yards away. Previously Mr Russell had been sceptical about the existence of the Loch Ness Monster, believing that some large marine animal, a seal perhaps, had somehow got into the loch, but his experience dispelled all scepticism.

On the morning of 27 December 1933, Mr G. Jamieson was driving a van towards Invermoriston. He was near Jack's Quarry, about three miles from Fort Augustus, when he saw the monster about 100 yards offshore moving quickly in a southerly direction. The road at this point runs close to the loch and overlooks it. The animal showed two large humps, a long neck and small head and was greyish-black, with a rough, knobbly skin. The larger hump

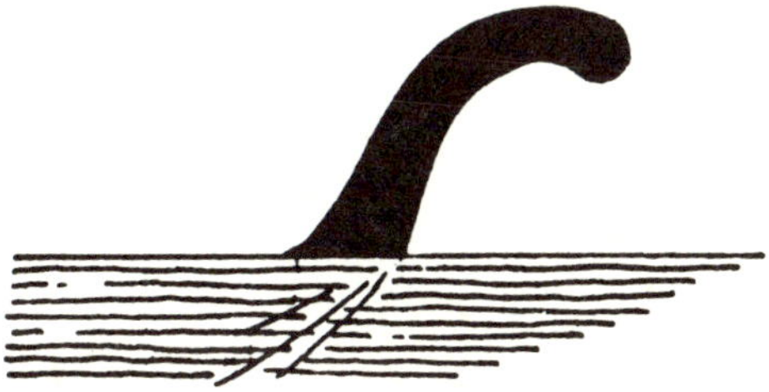

Fig. 10. Mr B. A. Russell's sketch of the creature he saw in Loch Ness on 1 October 1933.

Fig. 11. Mr G. Jamieson's sketch of the creature he saw in Loch Ness on 27 December 1933.

protruded about three feet above the surface of the water and the smaller about two. The animal's length at the surface was between fifteen and twenty feet, but the disturbance of the water at its rear suggested that there was more beneath the surface. Seeing a boat on the other side of the loch, towards which the creature was heading, Mr Jamieson sounded his horn, hoping to attract the crew's attention. At the noise the creature turned its head and dived, leaving a foaming wash. The witness described his encounter to *The Scotsman* and later confirmed the details to Commander Gould. He also provided a sketch.

Several accounts of lake monsters were collected by Dom Cyril Dieckhoff, a monk at St Benedict's Abbey at the southern end of Loch Ness. One witness was a fellow monk, Brother Horan, who saw a monster near the entrance to the Caledonian Canal in May 1934, as Dom Cyril described:

> When he looked up he saw the animal swimming only thirty yards away from him, parallel with the shore and its head turned towards him. Apparently it had no ears, its muzzle was rather blunt, approaching that of a seal – but it was not a seal. It had a graceful neck, three and a half feet in length, held at an angle of forty-five degrees to the water with a broad white stripe down the front.

The animal moved around, occasionally changing direction until, finding a rowing boat in its path, it stopped momentarily and a great commotion appeared in the water to the animal's rear, as if powerful paddles were at work. Then the animal dived, causing a great upheaval in the water.

The following sighting was described by J. Harper-Smith OBE, LLB, Town Clerk of Lincoln. In June 1951, he was staying in Inverness-shire with his son, an army officer. After a fishing trip on Loch Ness in a hired boat they began packing up their equipment at about 9.00p.m. The surface of the loch was flat calm, when suddenly the younger man pointed and said, 'Is that a periscope over there?' His father described what happened next:

> I looked and realized something was coming up out of the water. Within a few seconds a black head was followed by a similar coloured neck several feet long. While we were eagerly looking for the body the head and neck began moving forward at a very fast speed followed by a huge wash. As it came nearer we noticed some oscillations of the head and neck. We began to edge in nearer the shore but when it had come to within about 800 yards 'it' turned and went back up the centre of the loch and shortly afterwards submerged. We put the length of the neck at about five feet and the diameter at about a foot.

In August 1952, Mrs Greta Finlay and her twelve-year-old son Harry, were on holiday in a caravan on the south shore of Loch Ness, about half a mile from Aldourie Castle. At noon on 20 August, she heard splashing in the loch and, walking round the caravan, saw a strange creature about twenty yards out from the shore. She described it to researcher Constance Whyte:

> There were two or three humps and the total length visible was about fifteen feet. The neck was held erect, and where it met the water it enlarged to join a bulky body. The head and neck together were two to two and a half feet in length, the head alone being about six inches long and of about the same width as the neck. What astonished me, apart from the hideous appearance of the head, was that there were two six-inch-long projections from it, each with a blob on the end. The skin looked black and shiny and reminded me of a snail more than anything.

The creature concluded its appearance by submerging rapidly, causing waves to break on the shore. Harry Finlay made a sketch of the animal (*see* Fig. 12).

In later interviews with F. W. Holiday and Tim Dinsdale, Mrs Finlay stressed how repulsive the creature was. 'It was horrible,' she said, 'I never want to see it again. I wouldn't go to look if it was behind six-inch steel bars.' She said she was paralysed with fear and found the mere memory of the creature disturbing. The experience so terrified her son that he gave up fishing altogether.

On a July evening in 1963 two fishermen saw the Loch Ness Monster at a distance of less than thirty yards. They would not

Fig. 12. Harry Finlay's sketch of the monster seen at Loch Ness on 20 August 1952.

give an intverview to the Press, but agreed to describe their experience to F. W. Holiday on condition that he did not reveal their names.

The men were fishing for sea-trout in a boat about 200 yards off Tor Point at the north-eastern end of the loch. At about 10.00p.m. something began rocking the boat. Shortly after, there was a ripple in the water then, suddenly, a monstrous head and neck reared out of the water between twenty and thirty yards away. As the men stared the animal submerged vertically (not by diving) amid a great disturbance of water. It emerged further away, sank and then reappeared at a still greater distance before disappearing finally.

The creature's neck was very thick and powerful-looking, about a foot in diameter and extending about four to five feet above the surface of the water. The head was held at a slight angle to the neck, and reminded the witnesses of the head of a bulldog. No eyes were visible, and the skin was a blackish-brown. The neck was fringed with what looked like coarse hair. The witnesses found the creature extremely ugly.

One August evening in 1963 Hugh Ayton and his son Jim were working in a field on their farm, which overlooked the loch, about two miles south of Dores. Also present were two tourists from Stirling, Fred Gerard and his son Barry, and Alastair Grant, another farmer. At about 7.30 Jim Ayton looked up and saw something moving in a southerly direction across the calm surface of the loch. He shouted to the others and they all watched the object which was big, black and clearly animate. The witnesses ran down to a nearby jetty, scrambled into a boat and set out

The Third Earl of
Malmesbury.

Mr Hugh Ayton.

Mrs Margaret Cameron (formerly
Miss Margaret MacGruer) and
her sister Miss Elizabeth
MacGruer, at the spot from
where they saw the monster in
1909.

'Doc' Shiels's photographs of the Loch Ness Monster.

The late Professor J. L. B. Smith (seated behind the head of 'Old Fourlegs') showing the 'limb' of the coelacanth. (This was the second coelacanth to be caught near the Comoro Islands off the East African coast in 1952.) Will some future scientist be photographed holding the limb of Nessie?

F. W. Holiday (right) with fellow monster hunter Rip Hepple.

Tim Dinsdale on Loch Ness.

Aleister Crowley.

The Reverend Donald Omand
exorcising Loch Ness.

across the loch, hoping to intercept the animal. At first they used oars, but then started the outboard motor. Hugh Ayton takes up the story:

> The thing was still coming down the loch and as we got closer we could see more details of it. There was a long neck coming about six feet out of the water and a head which reminded me rather of a horse though bigger and flatter. The body was made up of three low humps – about thirty to forty feet long in all and about four feet high. The colour was dark and the skin looked rough.

The witnesses approached to within about fifty yards of the animal which suddenly rose up a little in the water and dived, making a great disturbance which swirled the boat round. The head appeared again, momentarily, and then submerged. The creature covered a distance of about a mile, thought Mr Ayton.

On 16 March 1967, John Cameron, a lock-keeper who worked on the Caledonian Canal, was fishing for salmon from his boat opposite Glendoe Pier. At about 3.00p.m., at a distance of about twenty yards, Mr Cameron saw an object ploughing through the three-feet-high waves, against the stiff easterly wind. It was dark brown, about twelve feet long, and had a crinkly skin. Like several other witnesses, Mr Cameron described the monster's back as resembling an upturned boat. He commented to the *Inverness Courier*:

> Believe me, it must be a very large animal as I saw only a part of it, and a powerful animal at that. You should have seen the way it sliced through the waves, quite effortlessly.

In 1971, the monster was again seen by one of the monks from Fort Augustus. On the morning of 14 October Father Gregory Brusey had walked down from the Abbey to the lochside with a friend, Roger Pugh, the organist and choirmaster of St James's Church, Spanish Place, London, to admire the view. It was a bright, sunny day and the water was calm. Looking out towards Borlum Bay the witnesses saw a terrific commotion in the water, and then a long neck which protruded to a height of about ten feet above the surface. The creature swam towards the observers, its neck at a slight angle, and after about twenty seconds slowly submerged. The witnesses estimated that they were about 300 yards away from the animal.

Over the years there have been numerous attempts to photograph the Loch Ness Monster. The results, on the whole, have not been very impressive. The clearest pictures of the monster are probably those taken by Anthony Doc Shiels in 1977. On 21 May in the afternoon, he was observing the loch from below Urquhart Castle when, at about 4.00p.m., a long neck emerged from the water. Doc took two photographs and later described the encounter as follows:

> The camera was a Zenith EM, 35mm SLR, with a 150mm telephoto lens. As I recall, I took the pictures at between f11 and f16 at 1/500 sec. The creature was rather less than 100 yards away, the part of the neck showing above the water-line must have been around four or five feet long. Don't take any notice of what appears to be eyes. I could see no eyes as such in the original. The light patch above the mouth (if mouth it is . . . and I think it is) is merely a reflection off a kind of ridge. The colour of the animal was greenish-brown, with a paler underside. Skin texture, smooth and glossy. The animal was visible for no more than four or five seconds. It held itself very upright, very still, except for a turning of the head and a straightening of the neck before it sank very smoothly below the surface. It had powerful neck muscles. There is evidence, well, possible evidence, of a parasitic growth at the back of the neck, on the dorsal ridge, as a pale yellow-green patch is visible near the water. Also in both pictures, a round pale object floats on the water close to the neck . . . this could be an empty McEwans beer can – so many of them are to be found along the lochside!

Before discussing the photographs it should be pointed out that the original of the second photograph is not available for study. Doc Shiels had a glass copy negative enlargement made by David Benchley, a photo-journalist, and then sent the original negative to a friend, the magician Max Maven, in the United States. The envelope, however, was empty on arrival. Further disaster followed when Doc Shiels dropped and broke the glass negative, though fortunately Benchley had made some trial prints. The difference in contrast between the two prints is due to the fact that Benchley intended to produce copies for newspaper reproduction and this requires photographs with a strong contrast.

The original number one slide was lent to Tim Dinsdale who submitted it, with a sworn affidavit from Doc Shiels, to the Royal Photographic Society. It was examined by Dr Vernon W. G. Harrison, President of the society until 1976. Dr Harrison stated that the transparency showed no evidence of double exposure, retouching or superimposition. He added that the object in the picture had been photographed from a distance through a long focus lens (as Doc had stated), that the object was visible for a few inches below the surface of the water, and that the way the reflection of the object in the water was distorted by wavelets was entirely natural. He concluded that although it was possible that the photograph had been faked, either by photographing an object held up in the water by a submerged diver, or by photographing a painting executed by a skilful artist, this was very unlikely.

Another examination was undertaken by author and researcher Colin Bord, who for twenty years has also been a professional photographer. He spent a considerable amount of time studying the original 35mm transparency through a high-powered magnifier, and also projected it onto a screen with a magnification of ×40. He concluded:

> If these pictures are faked, I cannot detect how it was done. Such fakes certainly could not be called 'crude'. If they were produced by double exposure or superimposition they would need the services of a skilled laboratory staff and have to be the work of a skilled and well-equipped photographer. Having met the man, I do not think that either his photographic equipment (a fairly simple SLR) or his knowledge of photo techniques are up to it. The alternative is that he took a boat out into the loch with a buoyant life-size model aboard, popped it into the water, went ashore, photographed it twice in such a way that it changed shapes between shots, and went out again to retrieve it. All this on an afternoon in May at a famous tourist attraction. I find it simpler to believe in the existence of water monsters.

Possible Explanations

Can sightings of lake monsters be explained in terms of known phenomena? One writer who believes the answer is 'yes' is Ronald Binns. He cogently argues his case in a very interesting book entitled *The Loch Ness Mystery Solved*, published in 1983. Although most of the book is concerned with Loch Ness he extends his conclusions to cover reports from other lakes and from the sea. He bases his case on five main suppositions:

1. That witnesses have repeatedly misinterpreted known animals and phenomena.

2. That witnesses are conditioned by previous publicity into seeing what they expect to see, ie lake monsters.

3. That some of the evidence is the result of hoaxes.

4. That the Loch Ness affair was virtually created by the Press in 1933, and that the mystery did not exist before this time.

5. That the negative evidence against the existence of the Loch Ness Monster is overwhelming.

Ronald Binns argues that people simply misidentify what they see at Loch Ness and other lakes, mistaking various known animals and all manner of inanimate objects for monsters. He ascribes many of the sightings of lake monsters to otters. According to Corbet and Southern's *Hand-book of British Mammals*, the maximum recorded length for an otter is six feet, but such lengths are rare. Most otters are between three and a half and four and a half feet in length. A group of otters playing at the surface might look momentarily like the humps of one large monster, but sightings of more than a few minutes duration could not be explained in this way.

In my view it is unlikely that otters are behind the land sightings of the Loch Ness Monster. The otter is small, sleek, fast-moving and one of the most attractive of mammals. Could any witness, however imaginative, mistake such a creature for a gigantic, ugly, ponderous bald-skinned monster? A further drawback of the otter theory is colour. Otters are brown. Numerous witnesses of the Loch Ness Monster, including some of those who saw it on land, have stated that it is grey or 'elephant coloured'.

Deer occasionally take to the water at Loch Ness, and from a distance might deceive some observers, but close sightings seem to merit some other interpretation. Ronald Binns ascribes the Finlays' sighting to a deer: '. . . there can be little doubt that what she and her son saw in August 1952, was a roe deer . . . Harry Finlay afterwards did a sketch of their monster, which in its shape and proportions greatly resembled a deer'.

In fact Harry Finlay's sketch (see page 104) does not particularly resemble a deer. It could quite reasonably be said to resemble a plesiosaur, though I am not suggesting that this was what the animal was. Furthermore, could the Finlays, even if they were unfamiliar with wildlife, mistake a deer for a monster which left them 'paralysed with fear'? Further, deer are not 'black and shiny' as they described the monster. Finally the Finlay's monster concluded its appearance by submerging, which would certainly seem to rule out a deer.

Undoubtedly some sightings can be explained as birds, such as the Great Northern Diver which frequents several Scottish lochs. Seen singly, at the surface, with their long necks held erect, these birds might be mistaken for monsters. However, birds could not account for close sightings, nor those such as the Sargents' at Loch Lochy where a twenty-foot hump was seen at the surface.

None of the animals cited above could, in my view, account for the sightings described earlier in this chapter, neither could inanimate phenomena such as logs, rocks, wind disturbances, wakes of boats etc.

It cannot be denied that people on occasions see what they expect to see, having been pre-conditioned by media reports. However, in my experience people generally have very little knowledge of lake monsters, and indeed no great interest in them. Furthermore, there have been detailed and reliable reports from lakes far from the tourist areas.

Binns himself believes that most witnesses are honest and that hoaxes account for only a small proportion of lake monster reports. He regards the Shiels 1977 Loch Ness photographs with some scepticism, dismissing one as: 'an unconvincing picture of a motionless head and neck'. In fact the two photographs show that the object has moved between shots, and those professionals who have undertaken a detailed analysis of the photographs, such as Colin Bord, are inclined to regard them as genuine. Ronald Binns is also sceptical about Shiels's photographs of Morgawr, taken in 1976, but it should be pointed out that David Clarke, the editor of *Cornish Life* magazine was present when they were taken and has confirmed the details in that magazine.

Ronald Binns firmly believes that the Loch Ness affair was created by the Press in 1933. Although it was at this time that the monster became a national institution, as I described earlier, monsters have apparently been encountered at Loch Ness and other Scottish and Irish lakes since the mid-nineteenth century. I have notes on thirty sightings of, or references to, lake monsters between 1850 and 1933. Some of these early reports were of the Loch Ness Monster on land, and the Spicers' sighting in 1933, far from being the first land sighting as Binns states, was actually the eighth. The first was in 1879. Early accounts describing a creature with a bulky body, several humps, a snaky neck and small head, agree quite closely with later reports. It is true that many of these early sightings were not reported at the time, but the probable explanation for this seems to be that the witnesses feared ridicule, and came forward in the 1930s when there was a more favourable climate of opinion.

It is certainly true that, considering the intense investigation of Loch Ness, the results have been inconclusive in scientific terms. One would have thought that, by sheer chance if nothing else, an investigator would have been on hand with a cine-camera at the right moment to take the final conclusive film. Again, one would have thought that if large animals had been living in the loch for years their skeletons would be lying on the loch bottom. Attempts to locate and trawl up such remains, though, have been unsuccessful*. The lack of such hard proof is hard to account for, but I feel the negative evidence is insufficient to outweigh the many impressive eye-witness reports.

There are certainly many valid points in *The Loch Ness Mystery Solved*, but I feel that the hypothesis is stretched too far, and that the author is unfair to the efforts of the monster-hunters. At times, it is true, they have been over-enthusiastic, too ready to accept dubious evidence and not rigorous enough in their approach. However some, for example Professor Roy P. Mackal (a qualified biologist) and Commander Gould (an experienced investigator), have been highly scientific in their approach, demonstrated in their books *The Monsters of Loch Ness* and *The Loch Ness Monster and Others*. Both writers reject much of the evidence on the same grounds as Binns, who actually uses several quotes from Gould to support his arguments, but conclude that a proportion of the evidence cannot be explained by known phenomena.

Furthermore, as Ronald Binns himself admits early in his book, the sceptical scientists have not always been the most

* A sonar 'picture' of a somewhat plesiosaur-like shape some thirty feet long lying on the bottom of the loch in about 300 feet of water was obtained in 1976. See *Search at Loch Ness* by Dennis L. Meredith. It is possible, of course, that the monsters are invertebrates in which case there would be no hard remains.

objective of people. They have made some absurd statements about the Loch Ness Monster as he points out on p. 34, 'Commander Gould had an easy task in demolishing the extravagant explanations put forward by zoologists who ought to have known better (sunfish, ray, catfish, salamander, turtle, whale, squid, crocodile and seal)'.

Ronald Binns uses the discovery of the coelacanth to support his argument that scientific recognition swiftly follows new discoveries – saying that the coelacanth 'although decomposed, was instantly recognized as such'. This is belied by Professor Smith's own story of his disheartening and incredibly uphill struggle to obtain recognition of his discovery, recounted in his book *Old Fourlegs*. His amazing fish was dismissed out of hand by many biologists who did not even go to see the remains – one asserting that the fish was obviously a common rock cod with a deformed tail! The only person who 'instantly recognized' the fish was Professor Smith himself. On many occasions scientists have been remarkably unwilling to accept new discoveries.

I am not suggesting that we accept every eye-witness report of a lake monster uncritically, but we should at least keep an open mind on the question. It should be remembered that the okapi, the gorilla and the giant squid were for years known from eye-witness accounts, dismissed as nonsense in exactly the same way as sceptics over the years have dismissed the evidence for lake monsters.

What are Lake Monsters?

There has been much speculation over the years on the possible nature of lake monsters. Commander Gould suggested that the Loch Ness Monster could be a form of giant, long-necked amphibian. Roy Mackal followed this line with a hypothetical species of embolomer, an order of amphibia which lived in the Carboniferous Period which ended 270 million years ago. Peter Costello favours a species of giant, long-necked seal, while F. W. Holiday postulated a form of giant, worm-like invertebrate. A form of giant eel has been suggested and an ever popular theory is that of a surviving species of plesiosaur. Doc Shiels has recently put forward a hypothetical species of cephalopod and this is discussed in Appendix Four.

One could discuss at length the merits of the various theories, but until something more in the way of conclusive evidence is uncovered my own opinion is that the most likely suggestion to account for the majority of reports is the giant eel.

The Psychic View of Lake Monsters

In recent years some researchers have come to believe that lake monsters are not what they seem at first, i.e. flesh and blood creatures that have evaded the scientific net. At first sight there seemed no reason to doubt that they had a physical existence: there were numerous eye-witnesses, many of unimpeachable integrity, and the creatures had been tracked on sonar, filmed, photographed and, on some occasions, apparently rammed by boats. Various experiments were devised to catch one of them, secure a tissue sample, or simply obtain indisputable photographic evidence. Given time and a little luck, the monster hunters thought, the problem could be solved and the sceptics finally confounded. However, as time went by it became clear that the problem was not going to be solved so easily. Not only did it seem impossible to obtain hard evidence, but a whole series of bizarre and uncanny features gradually forced their way into the hunters' awareness, causing them to re-examine their beliefs about the nature of the creatures they were pursuing.

To begin with, there was the fact that lake monsters were often reported to be seen in tiny stretches of water which could not possibly support one large animal, let alone a breeding colony. It would be convenient to dismiss sightings of monsters in lakes such as Lough Nahooin, but the reports seem just as reliable as those from larger lakes, such as Loch Ness. It has been suggested that the creatures are amphibious, and that they move from lake to lake as circumstances dictate, but if this were the case surely they would be seen on land more often, like eels when they are travelling overland.

Another strange feature of a number of lake monster reports is the reaction of some of the witnesses. It is natural that someone encountering a lake monster should be surprised and a little frightened, but several witnesses have testified to entirely disproportionate feelings of extreme fear, loathing and repulsion, not tempered in any way by curiosity or interest at such an unusual sight. One witness at Loch Ness, Mr Spicer, said that the animal he saw crossing the road in front of his car at the side of the loch was: '. . . horrible – an abomination . . . loathsome. It seems futile to describe it, as it was like nothing I had ever read about or seen. It was terrible. It looked like a huge snail with a long neck.'

Other witnesses, Mrs Finlay for example, have likened the Loch Ness Monster to a giant snail or slug. Two other witnesses who found their encounter with Nessie extremely disturbing were Mr and Mrs Jenkyns who watched the creature for about half an hour from their lochside home: 'I felt that the beast was obscene,' said Mr Jenkyns, 'The feeling of obscenity still persists, and the whole thing put me in mind of a gigantic stomach with a length of writhing gut attached.'

Another witness deeply affected was Georgina Carberry who said that the creature she saw in Lough Fadda was '. . . wormy. You know, creepy. The body seemed to have movement all over it all the time'. Miss Carberry said she had nightmares for weeks after the incident. It will be remembered that 'B.B.' who saw a monster in Loch Eil compared it with a giant worm.

The reaction of some witnesses was disbelief in what they were seeing, as if their brains could not accept the existence of such strange creatures. F. W. Holiday, after chasing a large, yellowish object down Loch Ness in 1965 wrote in his report, 'It could have been a boat,' but later said, 'Yet manifestly it was not a boat, as I could see through my 10× binoculars; nor did I believe it to be a boat.' Gavin Maxwell once saw three black humps in Loch Ness which he immediately assumed were boulders. On reflection he realized they could not be boulders and looked again. The 'boulders' were gone. A similar experience befell his brother, Major Eustace Maxwell who, driving past Loch Fyne in his car saw what he first took to be a sandbank. As he drove on he realized it could not possibly be a sandbank and reversed to the spot to find the 'sandbank' gone. In July 1968, Dr Kenneth McLeod, the Commissioner of Public Health for Cortland, New York, was driving past Loch Ness with his father when he saw a grey-black object travelling down the loch in the same direction as the car. Mr McLeod senior could not see the object from where he was sitting, and his son did not draw his attention to it, nor mention it later when they stopped for tea in Fort Augustus. A similar lethargy or indifference overcame the Jenkyns during their sighting. They had a loaded camera nearby, but did not think of using it, nor did they think of telephoning their neighbours. At one point Mrs Jenkyns actually went to sleep on her sofa for a few minutes.

Another curious aspect of the lake monster phenomenon is that it seems strangely impossible to obtain photographic evidence. For years, researchers have been trying to obtain clear photographs and films of lake monsters, but no matter how much effort and ingenuity they put into the task, fate always thwarts them. The 'Loch Ness Hoodoo' as some monster hunters call it, was well known to F. W. Holiday who described a classic case in *The Dragon and the Disc.* On 26 August 1968, Holiday was watching from a cine-camera platform at Abriachan on the south side of Loch Ness. There were two other platforms on the north side, so that, between them, the three cameras had the eastern half of the loch covered. Holiday's previous experience suggested that he would need to watch Loch Ness for about 500 hours to obtain a sighting, and as he had already spent some 700 hours on watch since his last encounter, a sighting seemed long overdue. At about 9.30a.m. Holiday, somewhat bored, broke off to stroll across and chat to the Picketts, a family camping about fifty yards away. He had been talking for a few minutes when, looking towards the loch, he saw an enormous three-humped object ploughing through the water. He wrote, 'I stared at this spectacle for about two seconds without speaking. The experience seemed curiously unreal and I remember registering the idea that I must be suffering from some sort of hallucination.'

He was not hallucinating, though, as the Picketts could see the thing as well. Holiday raced back to the camera, but as he reached it he heard Mrs Pickett shout, 'Oh, it's gone down.' When he looked towards the loch all he could see was a patch of foaming water. Not only had the monster evaded Holiday's camera, but it had managed to avoid those on the opposite shore. It had surfaced, and submerged, in a tiny blind spot where trees and rocks concealed it from the two cameras on the north bank.

This was not the first time that Holiday had come frustratingly close to filming the Loch Ness Monster. In June 1965 he watched, with Mr and Mrs Eaves, a couple on holiday, as a black hump rose out of the water off Whitefield. He managed to locate the hump in the cine-camera's viewfinder but, just as he was about to start filming, the object 'collapsed in a sort of muscular spasm'.

Similar experiences have befallen other researchers. On 4

August 1970, Alan Butterworth of the Loch Morar Survey was watching the loch with binoculars, his cine-camera ready nearby. He saw what he first thought was a familiar islet, then sweeping further along with his glasses he saw the real islet. Turning back to the first object he saw it was an animate hump some fifteen feet long and three to four feet high, but before he could reach his camera the hump had submerged.

The two fishermen mentioned earlier who saw a monster in Loch Urabhal struggled to position and focus their camera as the creature surfaced and submerged repeatedly in front of them. After they had it ready though, the animal did not reappear.

One day in 1965, one of the Loch Ness Investigation Bureau's cameras, which was positioned on a platform near the Clansman Hotel, was taken away for servicing. The next morning the staff of the hotel had a good view of a hump moving about close to the shore.

At about 6.00p.m. on the 28 July 1970 the Anderson family saw a large brown hump moving about in the water close to Urquhart Castle. Literally only minutes earlier an LNIB observer whose camera overlooked the area had packed up for the day and gone home.

In 1971 Tim Dinsdale was manning a camera post when a long neck broke surface only 200 yards away. Dinsdale was so surprised that he was momentarily paralysed and missed the shot.

Sometimes the very apparatus itself seems to prevent the observers from recording the photographic proof that they so desperately desire. In October 1970 the Academy of Applied Science's sonar equipment recorded a four minute contact with a large animate object, but the camera which should have filmed the image on the sonar scope jammed. In the winter of 1976/1977, when sonar again detected a large moving object, the underwater camera which should have filmed it failed to function, and it was later found that the casing of the electronic flash unit was cracked. Hugh Grey who took five shots of the monster in 1933 found that four of them came out blank. In 1952 Lachlan Stuart tried to take five pictures of the monster, but after the first shot the camera jammed, preventing further exposures.

Even when photographs are obtained the tribulations may continue, as Doc Shiels pointed out after photographing the Loch Ness Monster in 1977:

My 1977 photographs of Nessie have had some adventures, all part of the cosmic trickster's game. My original no. 1 colour slide went astray for days on end at the *Daily Record* office in Glasgow. Other photographs, from the same strip of film, vanished entirely after being inspected by the picture editor, Martin Gilfeather. My original no. 2 slide somehow escaped from its carefully sealed envelope somewhere between Cornwall and Boston, Mass, USA. The only direct, negative, monochrome, glass copy-plate made from that slide (by David Benchley of Cornish Photo-news) was accidentally dropped and broken (by me!). It's a disturbing fact that hardly any of the original negatives of the better known Loch Ness Monster photographs taken since 1933 have survived. Nessie Pix are supernaturally accident-prone.

Sometimes the hoodoo seems to affect the health of the hunters themselves. While at Lough Nahooin Ted Holiday was plagued by neuralgic pains in his jaw, and influenza-like symptoms. His colleague Ivor Newby was similarly affected, and they continued to suffer until they left the area. Doc Shiels writes that he has experienced similar ill-effects while monster hunting, and Tim Dinsdale has had some unpleasant experiences at Loch Ness. Dinsdale had a particularly bad time while observing the loch from a tiny beach not far from Foyers. In many ways it was a perfect hide – quiet, secluded and safe enough to leave equipment there unguarded – yet there was something strange about the place. Four out of five of his expeditions based there resulted in illness or injury. On one occasion he seriously injured two fingers, trapping them in his camera apparatus. Finally he left the spot, convinced there was a malevolent influence there. He later found that the area had an unusually violent past, and wondered whether this could have left a permanent 'residue of evil' at the spot. Dinsdale experienced a similar feeling of unease at another location, a stretch of shoreline below the estate of Tychat where he sometimes moored his boat at night. 'This was so powerful,' he wrote, 'that I had to force myself to overcome it, and so real I mentioned it to people at the LNI.' This area too, it seems, had a troubled past. It was said that the Urquhart witches, hundreds of years ago, were forced to bear the stones for Urquhart Castle. The rock from which they got their first sight of the castle became known as The Rock of Curses. The witches used to meet at a rock known as The Harp which is within the boundaries of Tychat Farm.

Mention of witchcraft at Loch Ness brings to mind the notorious Aleister Crowley who lived at Boleskine House near the loch between 1900 and 1918. He chose this place because he believed it to be a potent psychic energy centre, a suitable place for his experiments in black magic. Crowley attempted to repeat the Abramelin Ritual, a ceremony devised by the sixteenth-century occultist Dr John Dee, and which was intended to summon demons. Crowley's biographer, John Symonds, believed him to have been successful and later wrote, 'The lodge and the terrace became peopled with shadowy shapes.' Something seems to have gone wrong, though. Crowley never finished the ceremony and could not control the things he had invoked, and illness, madness and death descended on people living in the house and its environs. Even after Crowley's departure many people said that the area had an evil atmosphere. The story has a curious postscript. In 1969, three American students found an old tapestry rolled around a conch shell in the cemetery below Boleskine House. It seemed to be Turkish in origin, and may well have been one of Crowley's possessions. Among the designs on it were humped worm or serpent-like animals. The cloth had apparently been used fairly recently in some form of black magic ceremony and then hurriedly hidden. The following year F. W. Holiday was invited to a dinner by researcher Robert E. Love where one of the guests was a Dr M. Dee. It turned out that he was a relative of the famous necromancer.

The Reverend Dr D. Omand undertook an exorcism of the locality in 1973 in an attempt to dispel the evil atmosphere which he felt to be still hanging over the area:

> I never exorcised the monster, as is supposed, but Loch Ness and the land immediately around it. My reason was to overcome the spirit of evil which I have located in and around the various waterways in which monsters have been sighted. This spirit of evil was a danger not so much to local inhabitants as to strangers attracted to the locality in the hope of getting a viewing. People who do open themselves through curiosity are immensely receptive and therefore very easy to possess . . . 'Nessie' or whatever one chooses to call the phenomenon, is harmless, but evil often attaches itself to the innocent.

The Reverend Omand believes that the Loch Ness Monster is a ghost, a 'manifestation of something which was a physical reality in those waters centuries ago'.

Could lake monsters really be some form of psychic manifestation? If so, how do they originate? Some possible answers are given in the final chapter.

CHAPTER FOUR

The Black Dog

> The Black Dog has perhaps more vitality, and survives in more locations than all the apparitions that in the olden times were sworn to by persons of the highest veracity.
>
> Richard Jefferies, *Wild Life in a Southern County*. 1879.

During the early hours of a winter morning in 1972, Tom Morgan,* a Dartmoor farmer, and his wife were awakened by a scratching noise outside their bedroom door. Armed with a poker, he opened the door and peered out into the gloomy corridor. At first he could see nothing, but as he walked towards the top of the stairs he saw a big black dog. He was about to seize it and throw it out of the house, when it moved towards him, and the startled farmer saw that it had huge, fiery-red eyes. Mr Morgan, taken aback, struck out at the beast with his poker. There was a blinding flash of light and the dog disappeared. The shaken farmer and his wife searched the house. There was no trace of the mysterious black dog, but it had left a trail of destruction, with every window broken, a complete electrical failure and the yard covered with broken tiles from the house and surrounding buildings.

The unfortunate Morgans had encountered one of the oldest phantoms known to mankind – the Black Dog. This creature huge, jet black, shaggy-coated and fiery-eyed; has been encountered all over Europe and in North and South America, but its real 'home' seems to be the British Isles, where it has been seen in every part of the land, from Cornwall to the north of Scotland, from East Anglia to the west of Ireland. Four areas in particular – north-west England, East Anglia, Lincolnshire and the West Country – bristle with legends and sightings of the beast. In

* This is an alias. The sighting was described in *The Unexplained* magazine. I have been unable to obtain further details of this dramatic manifestation.

Wiltshire alone there are at least forty sites traditionally haunted by the phantom.

A rich folklore surrounds the Black Dog: it has been regarded as a demon, sometimes as the Devil himself. Witches' familiars were often said to take the form of a black dog, and practitioners of the black arts were believed to change themselves into such creatures, or even to create them by the power of thought. Black Dogs were sometimes regarded as portents of bad weather, misfortune or death. In some areas they were regarded as the spirits of specific people, usually those who had led a particularly evil life. Places where violent or tragic events had occurred were often believed to be haunted by Black Dogs, as were the locations of buried treasure. Although usually hostile, the beast was believed in some areas to be benevolent, protecting travellers from footpads, and leading back to safety those who were lost.

It would take a book in itself to deal adequately with Black Dog folklore and this chapter is concerned mainly with eye-witness accounts of the phantom. Before moving on to these, however, we should look briefly at the beast's regional names, which by their very number testify to a deeply-held and widespread belief in the Black Dog.

In the north of England the Black Dog was known as Trash, Skriker or Skryker, and the Barguest. Trash comes from the squelching, splashing noise the beast made as it trotted along, like someone walking in worn-out shoes or 'trashes'. 'Skriker' comes from the unearthly howling the phantom made, scrying being an old word, Norse in origin, for crying or howling.

The origin of the term Barguest, which has a variety of spellings, is obscure. The folklorists John Harland and T. T. Wilkinson suggest that, as in the north of England gates were often called 'bars', the name could mean gate-ghost, guest being a corruption of the Anglo-Saxon *gast* meaning spirit. They point out that the Barguest was often said to perch on gates or fences and spring on to the shoulders of lonely travellers. Some researchers have suggested that the name comes from the Anglo-Saxon *burh* and *gast* which would mean town ghost. Other folklorists disagree, pointing out that the Black Dog more often haunts country areas. David Hunt suggests that the name comes from the German *berg* and *geist* which gives us 'hill ghost', or from *bär* and *geist* which means 'bear ghost', the phantom according to Hunt sometimes appearing bear-like. Jessica Lofthouse favours

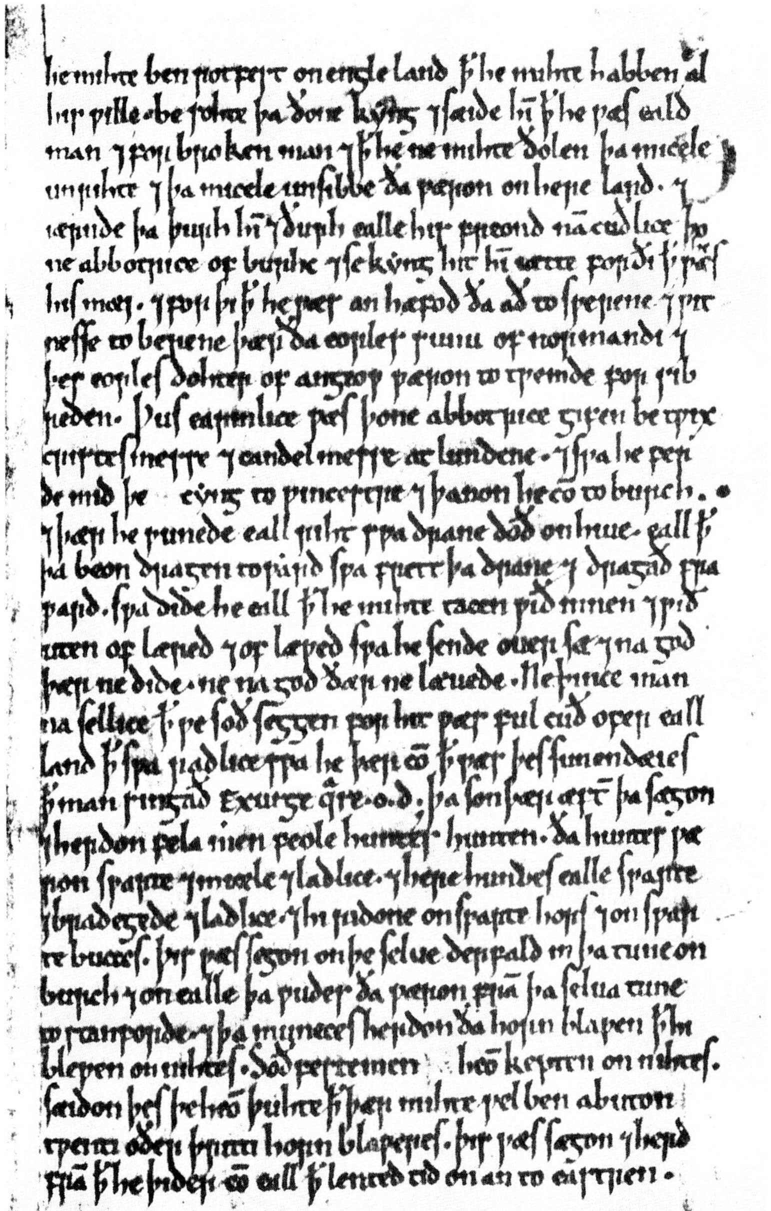
hie mihte ben forþfer on engleland þ he mihte habben al
his wille. Be sohte þa done kyng & sæide him þ he wæs eald
man & forbroken man & þ he ne mihte dolen þa micele
unrihte & þa micele unsibbe ða wæron on here land. &
wernde þa þurh him & þurh ealle his freond namcuðlice þo
ne abbotrice of burhc. & se kyng hit him geatte forði þ he wæs
his mæi. & forþi þ he wæs an hæfod ða að to swerene & wit
nesse to berene þær ða eorles sune of normandi &
þes eorles dohter of angeow wæron to twæmde for sib
reden. Þus earmlice wæs þone abbotrice gifen betwyx
cristesmæsse & candelmæsse æt lundene. & swa he wær
de mid þe kyng to wincestre & þanon he co to burch.
& þær he wunede eall riht swa drane doð on hiue. eall þ
þa beon dragen toward swa fretet þa drane & dragað fra
ward. swa dide he eall þ he mihte taken wið innen & wið
uten of lered & of lewed swa he sende ouer sæ & na god
þær ne dide. ne na god ðær ne læuede. Ne þince man
na sellice þ we soð seggen for hit wæs ful cuð ofer eall
land þ swa radlice swa he þær co þ wæs þes sunendæies
þ man singað Exurge quare o D. þa son þær æft þa sægon
& herdon fela men feole huntes hunten. Ða huntes wæ
ron swarte & micele & ladlice. & here hundes ealle swarte
& bradegede & ladlice. & hi ridone on swarte hors & on swar
te bucces. Þis wæs segon on þe selue deorfald in þa tune on
burch & on ealle þa wudes ða wæron fram þa selua tune
to stanforde. & þa muneces herdon ða horn blawen þ hi
blewen on nihtes. Soðfeste men heom kepten on nihtes.
sæidon þes þe heom þuhte þ þær mihte wel ben abuton
twenti oðer þritti horn blaweres. Þis wæs sægon & herd
fram þ he þider co eall þ lented tid on an to eastren.

Page from the *Anglo Saxon Chronicle* for the year 1127. There were several copies of the Chronicle, which was begun in the Ninth century, compiled in different parts of England. This extract is from the Laud Chronicle, written at Peterborough between 1121 and 1154. The Laud Chronicle is now in the possession of the Bodleian Library, Oxford. To locate the section describing the Black Dogs look for 'Exurge Quare O.D.' on line 20.

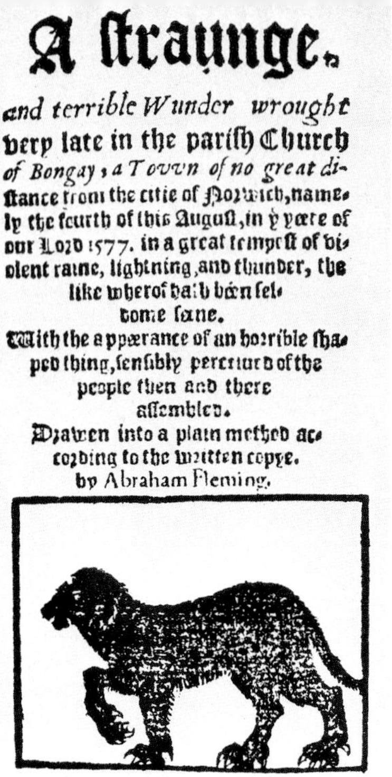
A straunge.
and terrible Wunder wrought
very late in the parish Church
of Bongay, a Tovvn of no great di-
stance from the citie of Norwich, name-
ly the fourth of this August, in ye yeere of
our Lord 1577. in a great tempest of vi-
olent raine, lightning, and thunder, the
like whereof hath been sel-
dome seene.
With the appearance of an horrible sha-
ped thing, sensibly perceiued of the
people then and there
assembled.
Drawen into a plain method ac-
cording to the written copye.
by Abraham Fleming.

Title page of Abraham Fleming's booklet on the Black Dog.

Marks on a door at Blythburgh Church said to have been made by the Black Dog.

The Black Dog Inn in the hamlet of Black Dog, Devon.

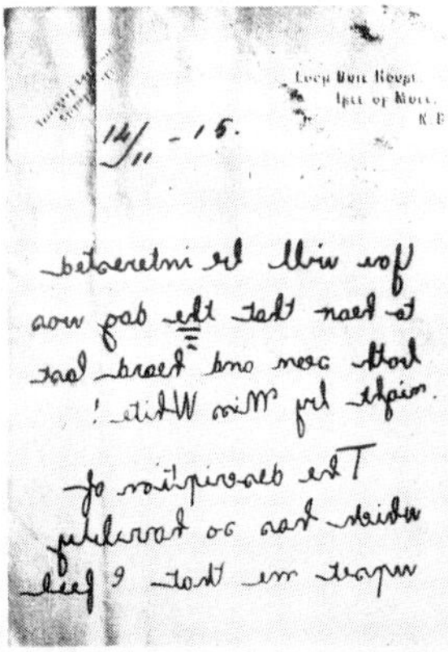

Loch Buie House
Isle of Mull
N.B.

14/11 - 15.

You will be interested
to hear that the dog was
both seen and heard last
night by Miss White!
The description of
which has so terribly
upset me that I feel

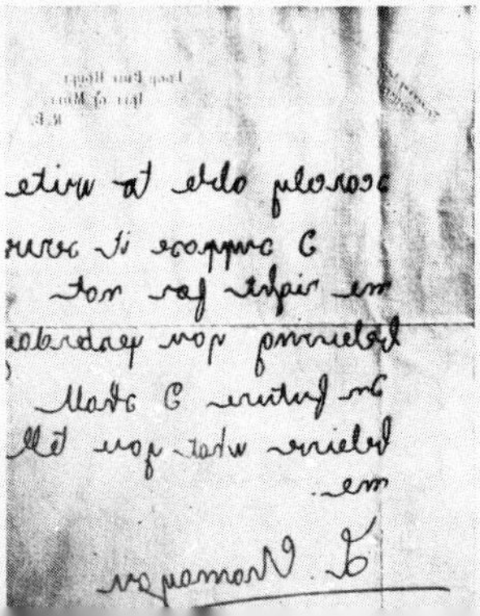

scarcely able to write
I suppose it serves
me right for not
believing you yesterday
In future I shall
believe what you tell
me.

Letter in mirror writing about the Black Dog of Lochbuie.

Two views of the Peddars Way 39: Near Little Massingham, Norfolk; 40: Crossing Harpley Common, Norfolk.

Sir Walter Scott's earlier suggestion, that the name comes from 'bier ghost', after the spirit that followed the bier on which a corpse was carried. C. Hardwick suggests that Barguest may be a version of 'boggart', a name which could apply to many types of supernatural being. Yet another possibility, put forward by Lewis Spence, is that Barguest is a corruption of 'barrow ghost' and refers to the spirit that issued from the fairy mound or prehistoric barrow. He points out that dogs were often buried with corpses in ancient times so that the canine spirits could guard their masters' graves.

A Westmorland name for the phantom was Capelthwaite, which apparently came into use after a Black Dog attached itself to a farm of that name. Padfoot was another north-country name sometimes used when referring to the Black Dog, but it was also applied to other animal phantoms.

East Anglian names included Old Shock, Black Shuck, the Shuckey Dog and the Shug Monster. These may come from *Scucca* or *Sceocca*, Anglo-Saxon names for Satan, or possibly from 'shag' or 'shaggy' after the beast's tousled coat.

Scarfe is a Suffolk name for the phantom, Skeff is used in Garveston, Norfolk, and the Black Dog that haunts South Town Road in Yarmouth is known as Old Scarpe. These names might come from the Old English *sceorfan* meaning to gnaw, bite or scratch, or Old High German *scarpon* meaning to cut to shreds, East Anglian Black Dogs being regarded as highly dangerous. It is possible that Skeff may refer to the animal's coat, which one East Anglian witness described as 'skeffy' but I have not been able to confirm this derivation.

Galley Trot is another East Anglian name. Alasdair Alpin MacGregor suggests that this is a corruption of *gardez le tresor* – the phantom often being looked upon as a treasure guardian. The name could also come from *gally* an old word meaning to frighten and the German *trötsch* meaning elf or spirit. Spence suggests that it combines *trötsch* with the Frisian *glay* or *gley* which means shining, after the glow which is produced by the phantom. J. Wentworth Day writes that in some inland Norfolk villages the Black Dog is known unaccountably as 'Owd Rugusan'.

In the Midlands, Hooter was a commonly used name for the phantom, and in Somerset it was often referred to as the Gurt Dog or 'great dog'. In Lincolnshire the beast was sometimes called Hairy Jack, this name in particular being applied to a black dog which haunted an old barn near Willoughton Cliff. Another Lincolnshire bogey was the Shag Foal, which could appear in a variety of forms including that of a black dog.

The Isle of Man's Black Dog was known as the Mauthe Doog or Moddey Dhoo. The Pooka was an Irish shape-shifting spirit which could appear as an ass, a horse, a bull, a goat and a black dog. The name, which has a variety of spellings, may derive from the Irish *puc* meaning a buck goat. In Scotland the Black Dog was known as the Muckle Black Tyke, and, in Gaelic, as the Choin Dubh. In Wales he was called Gwyllgi – the Dog of Darkness – and on the Island of Jersey he was known as *Le Tchan de Bouôlé* – the Dog of Bouley.

A phantom known in many parts of Britain was the Church Grim, 'grim' being an old north European name for a spirit. The Church Grim usually took the form of a black dog and was said to guard churches from witches, evil spirits and the Devil.

There are undoubtedly other names I have missed, but we will now turn to some eye-witness accounts, according to the regions in which they have occurred.

East Anglia

We begin here with what seems to be the first English account of these apparitions. It comes from the *Anglo-Saxon Chronicle* for the year 1127:

> Let no-one be surprised at the truth of what we are about to relate, for it was common knowledge throughout the whole country that immediately after his arrival [the arrival of Abbot Henry of Poitou at the Abbey of Peterborough] – it was the Sunday when they sing *Exurge Quare o*[*bdormis*], *D*[omine] – many men both saw and heard a great number of huntsmen hunting. The huntsmen were black, huge and hideous, and rode on black horses and on black he-goats and *their hounds were jet black with eyes like saucers and horrible* [my italics]. This was seen in the very deer park of the town of Peterborough and in all the woods that stretch from that same town to Stamford, and in the night the monks heard them sounding and winding their horns. Reliable witnesses who kept watch in the night declared that there might well have been as many as twenty or thirty of them winding their horns as near as they could tell. This was seen and heard from the time of his arrival all through Lent and right up to Easter.

Whatever incident was behind this account, it has obviously been reported in a superstitious and credulous way, but the description of the phantom dogs will be repeated time and again in more recent and sober reports.

Probably the first detailed account of a Black Dog was that provided by Abraham Fleming. Fleming, who was born around 1552, was the Rector of St Pancras, Soper Lane, London from 1593 until his death in 1607. On Sunday 4 August 1577, he was among the congregation at the church of Bungay in Suffolk, when shortly after 9.00a.m. a thunderstorm arose. Fleming published a booklet describing what happened next, from which the following is an extract:

> Immediately hereupon, there appeared in a most horrible similitude and likenesse to the congregation then and there present a dog as they might discerne it, of a black colour; at the site whereof, togither with the fearful flashes of fire which were then seene, moved such admiration in the minds of the assemblie, that they thought doomesday was already come.
>
> This black dog, or the divil in such a likenesse (God hee knoweth all who worketh all) running all along down the body of the church

Fig. 13. The Black Dog weather vane in the market place at Bungay.

with great swiftnesse and incredible haste, among the people, in a visible fourm and shape, passed betweene two persons, as they were kneeling upon their knees, and occupied in prayer as it seemed, wrung the necks of them bothe at one instant clene backward, in so much that even at a moment where they kneeled, they strangely died . . . There was at ye same time another wonder wrought; for the same black dog, still continuing and remaining in one and the self same shape, passing by an other man of the congregation in the church, gave him such a gripe on the back, that therewith all he was presently drawen togither and shrunk up, as it were a peece of lether scorched in a hot fire; or as the mouth of a purse or bag, drawen togither with string. The man albeit hee was in so strange a taking, dyed not, but as it is thought is yet alive: whiche thing is mervelous in the eyes of men, and offereth much matter of amasing the minde . . .

After creating havoc at Bungay, the Black Dog went into the church at Blythburgh, about seven miles away, and

. . . placing himself uppon a maine balke or beam, whereon some ye Rood did stand, sodainly he gave a swinge downe through ye church, and there also, as before, slew two men and a lad, and burned the hand of another person that was there among the rest of the company, of whom divers were blasted.

The marks on a door at Blythburgh Church are said to have been made by the Black Dog, and the creature's visit to this part of Suffolk is also commemorated by the weather vane in the market place at Bungay. Fleming's account is certainly a dramatic one, and unique in ascribing several deaths to the Black Dog, but it contains features which have been repeated in other Black Dog incidents through the years.

Other East Anglian churches have reportedly been visited by Black Dogs, including Leiston in Suffolk, where the phantom was seen by Lady Rendlesham and Lady Walsingham. One night towards the end of the last century they waited in Leiston churchyard in the hope of seeing the Black Dog. They were not disappointed. The dog, huge and black with glowing eyes, came bounding up the road, leaped over the churchyard wall and disappeared among the gravestones. Lady Walsingham described the encounter to J. Wentworth Day when he was staying at Merton Hall in the early 1920s.

Fig. 14. Leiston Church, Suffolk, where Lady Rendlesham and Lady Walsingham saw the Black Dog (picture provided by the Reverend Ivan Mann).

Three Norfolk churches haunted by Black Dogs are Buxton Lamas Church, where the phantom is seen in the road nearby; Geldeston Church, where the beast haunts nearby land, and the church at Overstrand, where it appears in the churchyard.

Visitations by East Anglian Black Dogs seem often to have been accompanied by lightning, fire and explosions (the Bungay incident is an early example). In 1893, two men, driving their cart along a road at Rockland, Norfolk, found their way blocked by a huge, fiery-eyed black dog. The driver, despite the warnings of his companion, drove the cart straight at the thing which disappeared in a ball of fire, the air being heavy with the smell of sulphur. In an incident at Hatfield Peverell, Essex, it was reported that a waggoner, who went to strike a black dog blocking his way, was burnt to ashes, along with his horse and cart, in the ensuing conflagration. A correspondent to *Notes and Queries* for 18 May 1850, writing on East Anglian Black Dogs, stated that one witness 'on bringing his neighbours to see the place where he saw it, found a large spot as if gunpowder had exploded there.'

As in other areas, East Anglian Black Dogs were regarded as portents of death. Christina Hole in her book *English Folklore* points out that the terror caused by an encounter with the Black Dog could be enough to cause the fulfilment of the traditional prophecy, and cites a case which she herself heard described while staying with a friend in Norfolk when a child. Her friend's mother described how, some thirty years before, her brother had been sent on an errand at dusk. He arrived at his destination to find the house shut up and deserted and had just turned to leave when a huge black dog rose up silently from the ground and put its paws on his shoulders. The boy was terrified, but broke free and ran home. He told his parents of the encounter and, seeming to have recovered from his fright, resumed his study for a forthcoming examination. In the middle of the night, however, he died, apparently from the delayed effects of the shock he had received earlier. The people who owned the house to which the boy had been sent had no dog of their own.

Fortunately most encounters with Black Dogs are not so tragic. Many are like the following case which involved Mr Wilson from Hempnall in Norfolk. One night in 1921, he arrived home after cycling from Norwich, looking pale and shaken. His mother, Mrs Sophie Wilson, asked him if he was ill, and he replied:

> No. Coming down Market Hole I had a bad turn. I saw what appeared to be a big dog, about to cross in front of my bike, and I thought I should be thrown off, but it just vanished. When I got off my bike and looked round there was nothing to be seen.

In 1933 the BBC broadcast *The Dark Shore*, a radio programme concerned with ghosts and witchcraft in East Anglia. The producers heard several accounts of Black Dogs, one from a young farmer from Sheringham in Norfolk, who stated that one clear summer evening he had watched Black Shuck cross the road in front of him and walk through a closed five-barred gate. Another account came from a middle-aged couple from Coltishall, who after a stroll on a fine summer evening had stopped on Coltishall Bridge. The man was just striking a match to light his wife's cigarette when Black Shuck 'as big as a calf and as noiseless as death' passed by within a foot of them.

Black Dogs have been seen to walk through solid barriers on several occasions. Just before World War One a black dog seen at Barham, Suffolk, vanished through a brick wall, and similar cases in other areas are described in the following pages.

Black Shuck has often been seen at Coltishall Bridge, sometimes appearing there without its head. East Anglian Black Dogs often materialize with portions of their anatomy missing or with the heads and limbs of other animals. Sometimes Black Shuck appears with its head missing but with its saucer eyes in their correct position. Another variation is the cyclopian Black Dog with one huge eye in the middle of his head. A black dog with a monk's head is said to haunt the area around Clopton Hall, near Great Bealings, Suffolk, and a hybrid known as the Shug Monkey haunts the road between West Wratting and Balsham in Suffolk. It has been described by several witnesses as a big, rough-haired dog with an ape's head and huge, shining eyes.

The following is a classic Black Dog incident. One evening in the autumn of 1938 Mr Ernest Whiteland was walking home from Bungay to Ditchingham, on the border between Norfolk and Suffolk, when he saw a huge black animal about seventy-five yards away coming towards him. Mr Whiteland continues:

> As it came close I could see it was a large black dog, trotting along the same side of the road as I was on. It was a lovely evening – no wind and everything so still and quiet. As it came to about nine or ten yards away, I could see that it had a long, black, shaggy coat, and was about twenty-eight or thirty inches tall. I moved into the middle of the road to let it pass. When it got level with me, it vanished. I looked around to see if I had made a mistake – to see if it was still running along, but could not see it. I then went and looked over the hedge, expecting to see it on the meadow, or hear it, but could do neither. I stopped, it seemed to me for some minutes. Then a sudden fear came over me, and it did not take me long to cover the distance to my house.

A curious case occurred at Hilgey in Norfolk in 1945 when a man heard, but did not see, what he thought was Black Shuck. He became aware of a faint howling which slowly became louder, until it was 'ear-splitting'. It was accompanied by the sound of a chain being dragged along the road. The man, now quite frightened, broke into a run, slowing down as the howling died away. The witness later wrote:

> I later realized that this was the first time I had been afraid of a dog, my hair was standing on end, but why I could not understand. . . . I love dogs and have never been afraid of the fiercest in my life.

East Anglian Black Dogs were often said to be accompanied by the sound of rattling chains, and a man who saw Black Shuck near Gorleston, Norfolk, during the last century said that the phantom was laden with rattling chains.

Author John Harries described how he was followed by a mysterious black dog on a November night in 1945. He was cycling from East Dereham, Norfolk to the RAF station of Swanton Morley where he was based. The dog, which resembled a black Alsatian or Labrador joined him shortly after he set out from East Dereham at about midnight, and loped along behind him. Whenever he stopped and looked round the dog stopped too. Its jaws were open and its tongue hung out but there was no sound of panting. Harries became rather nervous and pedalled as fast as he could, reaching a speed of about twenty miles an hour on the flat road. He finally arrived at the RAF base and, looking back once more, saw the dog still trotting along. Then, in a patch of darkness near some trees it simply vanished. Harries looked all around but there was no sign of it. Subsequently he asked people who lived near that stretch of road if they owned a black dog, but none did. Had he seen Black Shuck?

The town of Hockley in Essex was traditionally haunted by a black dog, and Eric Maple in *The Realm of Ghosts* described an encounter with the beast which occurred in 1958. An old lady was walking home one winter's evening when she was suddenly joined by a gigantic black hound. It accompanied her for a short distance and then simply disappeared. The witness, interestingly, said the encounter took place at the spot where a gibbet had once stood.

Sightings of Black Dogs in East Anglia seem to have diminished as time has gone by, and the few recent reports are less dramatic than earlier accounts. In 1972, Graham Grant, a coastguard on duty at the Gorleston Rescue Headquarters, reported seeing the Black Dog:

> Looking to the north, at about 04.45 at daybreak, on Wednesday last, 19 April I saw a large, black, hound-type dog on the beach, about a quarter of a mile north of the look-out. What made me look was that the dog was running then stopping as if looking for someone. As I watched, it vanished before my eyes. I kept on looking for a time but it did not reappear.

Mr Grant pointed out that there was nowhere the dog could have hidden as that part of the beach had recently been levelled by bulldozers. Further, he was a newcomer to the area, and had not heard of legends of the Black Dog.

East Anglian Black Dogs seem on the whole to be unpleasant manifestations. They are at best indifferent to their human observers, and at worst downright hostile. Indeed the Black Dog was often regarded by East Anglians as the Devil himself.

Lincolnshire

Moving north into Lincolnshire, we find that Black Dogs have been regarded in a very different light. Here they were believed to be benevolent, and there are many stories of them looking after lonely travellers.

One report of such a beast came from Mrs L. of Willoughton, who described to folklorist Ethel Rudkin an incident that had occurred about 1917. She set out at dusk one evening to visit a sick friend who lived at Kennington Farm. As she was walking up the hill which led to the farm she was joined by a big black dog which emerged from a hole in the hedge. Mrs L. liked dogs and was glad of the animal's company. The dog accompanied her almost to the farm, leaving her at a gate which led on to some allotments. Mrs L. left the farm at about 10.00p.m. and was rather nervous at the thought of walking home alone. To her relief she was joined by the dog again at the allotment gate, and the beast accompanied her until she reached the hole in the hedge, into which it disappeared. Mrs L. was very glad of the beast's company, being quite convinced that it was there to protect her. She had spent some two hours at her friend's house, and thought it 'nice of the old dog to wait for her'.

A Mrs C. from Boston wrote:

> My father was a lay preacher for many years (attached to the Methodist Church) and was a man of exceptional physique and iron nerve; fear was almost unknown to him. I have many times known him walk upwards of twenty miles on a Sunday to fulfil his appointments. He was returning home one Sunday evening in the depth of winter after taking one of these appointments on the Alford circuit, and on his way home he had to go down what was then known as Mumby Long Lane. Almost immediately he entered it, apparently from

nowhere, came a large Black Dog, and walked by his side. Though possessed of such wonderful nerve, I have frequently heard him say that he would rather deal with a man at night than a dog, so he tried to get rid of it, but it continued to walk by his side until the end of the lane was reached, and then vanished as mysteriously as it came. He always maintained that the dog was providentially sent that night to protect him from something or someone who had no good intentions towards him.

Another friendly Black Dog was described by a schoolmistress who said that when she cycled home from Kirton to Manton she was often joined by a big black dog which trotted amiably along beside her. She said that she liked to know he was there. Similarly, a woman walking home one night from Crosby to Scunthorpe was joined by a huge black dog which trotted along behind her. Presently she passed a group of labourers and heard them saying what they would have done to her if 'that (something) dog hadn't been with her'. When she arrived home she called her husband to see the animal but it had vanished. This was described to Ethel Rudkin by the witness's daughter.

Despite the foregoing, it was not a friendly black dog that was encountered by Sidney Benton of Horncastle in the early 1920s. During the winter of 1921/22 Mr Benton was working at a small dairy. His deliveries often took him to one of the oldest parts of the town, and his route went past an old iron foundry, over a bridge, past the back of the vicarage and the old churchyard. One evening something was waiting for him on his return:

On this particular evening I had made my deliveries and had just climbed over the small wooden palings on my way back to the dairy, when all at once, right in the centre of the path, appeared two great bright shining eyes.

I called out, thinking the dog from the dairy had followed me, but got no answer. I climbed back over the fence and stood there almost petrified with fear. I don't know how long I stood there but suddenly the eyes were just blotted out. I must have been braver then than I am now, for I took my courage in both hands and got back over the fence and walked back over to the spot where the eyes had been.

Mr Benton later found that a friend had had a similar experience in the same place several years earlier. He was also told by an old lady that the spot had always been said to be haunted, after several people had been drowned when ice gave way on what used to be the moat of an old castle standing on that site.

The areas haunted by Black Dogs in Lincolnshire appear to have two things in common: the presence of water and the presence of thick undergrowth, in the form of hedges and trees. Among the rivers and streams haunted by the Black Dog are the River Till, where the phantom has been seen near the bridge; a stream which runs under the Wrawby road outside Brigg where the phantom has been seen near a culvert, and a stream near Belle Hole Farm near Kirton, where the beast was believed to 'live' in a burrow in the bank. The phantom is also said to haunt a bridge over a stream between Manton and Scotter, a pond near Willoughton, a pond between Leverton and Wrangle, and another at Blyborough.

Wooded areas where Black Dogs have been seen include Bourne Wood, where the beast would always vanish by a hand-gate at a corner of the wood, and South Kelsey where the phantom was seen walking along a road next to a plantation. The pond-haunting dog of Willoughton invariably vanished by a certain ash tree, and Algarkirk's Black Dog always appeared near a clump of trees. The Black Dog of Moortown Hall always appeared at a particular part of a hedgerow, and, describing a hedge-haunting dog, a farm labourer said, 'If 'e passed you, an' you watched 'im after 'e'd passed you, 'e'd go into th'edge which'd crackle just as if a gurt bullock was pushin' 'is way thruff.' He added that the beast would always join him at the same part of the lane, and, in Lincolnshire generally, Black Dogs seem to be creatures of habit, appearing in the same places and patrolling the same routes. A youth who cycled regularly between Leverton and Wrangle at the turn of the century and who often saw the Black Dog, said that it would always dash out of a drove-end behind him and lope along to another lane down which it turned.

The inconsistent nature of Black Dog manifestations is illustrated by several Lincolnshire reports. Sometimes the beast seems solid: The farm labourer's account testified to the creature's ability to force its way through a hedge, and the dog haunting the road to Moortown Hall has been felt by several witnesses brushing against their legs. At Willoughton in 1933 a man was pushed up against his gate-post by what felt like a very large, but unseen, dog with its paws on his shoulders. To others in the same locality it appeared visually but without substance. A lady followed by the phantom near Blyborough fishpond struck at the creature: 'Quick as lightning I upped wi' the umbrella I was a-carryin' an' lammed 'im one as 'ard as I could.' The umbrella, however, went straight through the Black Dog which trotted on beside her.

Worcestershire

We move westwards now from Lincolnshire to the county of Worcester, where two Black Dog encounters occurred at roughly the same time. The witness in the first case was a four-year-old girl evacuated during World War Two with her mother from London to a cottage in Bredon. Thirty years later she wrote to Janet Bord:

> My encounter took place one late afternoon in summer, when I had been sent to bed but was far from sleepy. I was sitting at the end of the big brass bedstead, playing with the ornamental knobs and looking out of the window, when I was aware of a scratching noise, and an enormous black dog had walked from the direction of the fireplace on my left. It passed round the end of the bed, between me and the window, round the other corner of the bed, towards the door. As the dog passed between me and the window, it swung its head round to stare at me – it had very large, very red eyes, which glowed from inside as if lit up, and as it looked at me I was quite terrified, and very much aware of the creature's breath, which was warm and strong as a gust of wind. The animal must have been very tall, as I was sitting on the old-fashioned bedstead, which was quite high, and our eyes were level. Funnily enough, by the time it reached the door it had vanished. I assure you that I was wide awake at the time and sat for quite some long time wondering about what I had seen, and to be truthful, too scared to get into bed, under the covers, and go to sleep. I clearly remember my mother and our host, sitting in the garden in the late sun, talking, and hearing the ringing of the bell on the weekly fried-fish van from Birmingham as it went through the village! I am sure I was not dreaming, and have never forgotten the experience, remembering to the last detail how I felt, what the dog looked like, etc.

Three aspects of this sighting are of particular interest: the scratching noise which preceded the beast's appearance, reminiscent of the Dartmoor farmer's account; the animal's hot strong breath, and the fact that the witness was aware of the normal everyday activities of the world outside. These imply that the experience was 'real' – that the Black Dog was actually there. If not, the witness had an hallucinatory experience of an extraordinarily strong and all-enveloping nature.

Our other Worcestershire account comes from the author Stephen Jenkins who, during Christmas 1943, was staying with an uncle at Bewdley-on-Severn. He writes:

> On Christmas Eve I went to see some people who had a house on the hill near Tickenhill Palace, a Tudor mansion (with a brick facade added in 1738). The place is now called Tickenhill House.
>
> The road was narrow and ran between huge hedges, climbing steeply to the hill behind Bewdley. The day was sombre, and the clouds thickened as the light waned so that no star was visible. By nightfall a river mist was mingling with hill fog, and visibility was limited, which added to the wartime blackout and made for a very dark night. At the foot of the hill an immense black dog slipped out of the vapour and trotted past me. It was almost waist high and I noticed two things about it. The first was that its eyes glowed faintly, although I carried no torch, and there was no natural light of any kind. The second was that there was no click of paws on the metalled road in the profound stillness. My shoes were rubber soled and heeled, so I was making no noise of any kind myself.

Devonshire

The county of Devon, and particularly Dartmoor, are rich in legends of the Black Dog. Indeed, it was the stories of phantom hounds from this vast desolate expanse of moorland which provided Sir Arthur Conan Doyle with the inspiration for *The Hound of the Baskervilles*. An early account of a Black Dog on Dartmoor comes from J. L.W. Page in his book *An Exploration of Dartmoor* published in 1889:

> On an occasion just before the opening of the railway from Okehampton to Lydford a coach was crossing the moor from Lydford, when the driver cried out: 'There, there, do you see that?'. Running alongside the coach, and keeping pace with it without apparent effort, was a large, sinister-looking black hound. 'That's the

thing that haunts Dartmoor,' the driver went on excitedly, and he lashed his horses to a gallop. The hound still kept up with the coach without seeming to move any faster, and it was not until the coach had gone a considerable distance that the great dog was left amidst the gloom in its rear.

Moving eastwards, a lane which runs along the boundary between Devon and Dorset at Uplyme has long been reputed to be haunted by a black dog and was called Dog Lane because of this, the phantom also lending its name to an adjacent public house. One encounter with the beast occurred in 1856. The witnesses were a local couple and the woman described the incident as follows:

As I was returning to Lyme one night with my husband down Dog Lane, as we reached the middle of it, I saw an animal about the size of a dog meeting us. 'What's that?' I said to my husband. 'What?' he said, 'I see nothing.' I was so frightened I could say no more then, for the animal was within two or three yards of us, and had become as large as a young calf, but had the appearance of a black, shaggy dog with fiery eyes, just like the description I had heard of the 'black dog'. He passed close by me, and made the air cold and dank as he passed along. Though I was afraid to speak, I could not help turning round to look after him, and I saw him growing bigger and bigger as he went along, till he was as high as the trees by the roadside, and then seeming to swell into a large cloud, he vanished in the air. As soon as I could speak, I asked my husband to look at his watch, and it was then five minutes past twelve. My husband said he saw nothing but a vapour or fog coming up from the sea.

This account focuses attention on the very nature of the phenomenon. One person could see the phantom while her companion could not. Was it just imagination on the woman's part, or was she a 'seer', able to see into another dimension or reality, invisible to most people.

Black Dogs often seem to make their habitual patrols on routes which follow ancient pathways and boundaries. A good example of this is the Black Dog of Torrington in north Devon, which was investigated by Mrs Barbara Carbonell, who travelled around this region during the 1920s, recording details of local history and folklore. She became interested in stories of the Black Dog and found that many legends and sightings were clustered around a particular stretch of road that ran from Torrington to Copplestone, a distance of some twenty miles.

Beginning at Copplestone, Mrs Carbonell was told by several local people that the Black Dog had often been seen near the Cross, actually a squared granite pillar some fourteen feet high, inscribed with Celtic symbols and known to date from before the sixth century. It is in the centre of a junction where three roads meet.

From Copplestone the road is accompanied by an ancient lane which runs into the cross-roads at the hill-top village of Down St Mary, which has an ancient Saxon church. Several villagers related how the Black Dog ran up the old lane on dark nights, past the smithy and between the church and the school. The dog was said to knock down the corner of the school, which juts out into the road, the noise of falling masonry being heard, but no damage was ever seen. One old man said, 'I've a-heard the stones fall as he goes roarin' by and I've heard the same from my father and grandfather time and again. It's true right enough.'

Another local man described an encounter which occurred when he was a boy. He and several friends had been making their way home after a choir supper at Christmas. As they passed the smithy they heard the Black Dog coming up the lane, and fled into a field. They saw a dog 'the size of a calf' black and with glowing eyes rush past the smithy and towards the school, baying loudly. As it passed the school a noise 'like stones falling in a quarry' was heard. The boys waited until the baying died away and then 'us ran for it to get back home'.

Leaving Down St Mary, the old land joins the main Torrington road which runs through Stopgate, Blackditch and Aller. Much of this stretch has a deep ditch which indicates where a much older road ran. The Black Dog was seen on the Torrington road on numerous occasions by a man who, for forty years, drove a miller's wagon between Copplestone and Torrington. Mrs Carbonell writes:

> He seemed to consider it nothing unusual to see 'they sort of things' while admitting that he was 'scairt' the first time, hastily getting under the shelter of the van hood (his van was, of course, a heavy fourwheel one with a stretched canvas hood) when the dog 'appeared' the first time. Rather than remain seated on the side of the

> shaft, as was his custom, he said that as the years went on and he became familiar with the Dog's appearance he did not trouble to do so, often walking at the head of his team regardless of the 'gurt hound' running beside him, 'so big as a calf' were his words.

At Wembworthy there were only vague tales of 'something' haunting the road, and the same was true at Hollocombe and Week Hill. Mrs Carbonell noticed, however, that the inhabitants of Week Hill, though shaking their heads, when asked about the Black Dog, gave a secretive look called 'looking sideways' in Devon. Clearly they knew more than they were telling.

Mrs Carbonell found a similar reluctance to talk about the phantom at St Giles-in-the-Wood, but she did obtain some information from Mrs Jewel who kept the village store at Bow, a few miles away. Mrs Jewel used to live at St Giles, and when asked about the Black Dog she responded:

> It's always about there. Everyone knows of it, but it's bad luck to speak of it there, and I'm not sure if it's a good thing for me to tell you of it now, but I've seen it myself several times when I was a child living there, again when I was a young maid, and once again, years later. . . . He's all about in St Giles Parish, but mostly he runs on Week Hill. That's where I first saw the old thing.

Mrs Jewel's earliest encounter with the Black Dog occurred in the early 1870s when she was about ten years old. At about 11.00p.m. she was walking home up Week Hill with her father:

> It was a moonlight night and suddenly a sound of something panting came from behind us, and a great black dog as big as a calf with great shining eyes came alongside us. I caught at Father's hand and cried out. Father said 'tis the Black Dog. Hold my hand, don't speak, walk along quiet and don't cry out.'

The dog accompanied the travellers for nearly a quarter of a mile, its tongue hanging out 'like a great piece of red flannel'. Finally, when the girl and her father turned off the road to enter their cottage, the dog left them, trotting along for a while before finally disappearing. The girl's father said that he had seen the phantom many times, and that it didn't do any harm, but his daughter was terrified and could not sleep that night.

Mrs Jewel saw the spectre again when she was fourteen. She was walking home one night with two other girls and, on crossing a field towards Week Hill, they saw the hound running up the hill, baying 'as loud as a pack of hounds'. On another occasion the hound darted past her as she was approaching her cottage.

Her last encounter with the Black Dog occurred many years later. She and her father were driving home from Torrington Market when, between Allen's Week and Great Torrington, the hound suddenly emerged from the ditch, making the pony shy and bolt. Mrs Jewel was certain that the Black Dog was still seen in St Giles, but that people simply wouldn't speak of it.

Mrs Jewel's account concludes those which came from the original line of sightings, but Mrs Carbonell later heard additional reports from locations slightly further afield. One account came from her own daughter who, with her husband, was driving along the Torrington to Bideford road one night in January 1932. At about 11.00p.m., as they were driving alongside the River Torridge, an enormous black hound suddenly appeared in the road ahead, causing the driver to brake suddenly. The startled travellers were convinced that they had hit the dog, but it had completely disappeared. There was nowhere it could have gone, there being the river on one side of the road and a steep cliff on the other. Mrs Carbonell's daughter described the creature as 'bigger that any dog I've ever seen, quite black'. Her husband, who had always been sceptical about the supernatural, confirmed her description, and stressed the suddenness of the beast's appearance and disappearance.

Mrs Carbonell found that the countryside to the south of Tiverton had a strong association with the phantom dog. Indeed there is a hamlet called Black Dog, with the houses clustered around an inn of this name about a mile south of Thelbridge. A Tiverton man told Mrs Carbonell that he and his father had seen the Black Dog in this neighbourhood and that he knew several others who had encountered the phantom.

It was in north Devon that what seems to have been the most recent sighting of a Black Dog occurred. The witness was Mr Lee, who lived near Molland on Exmoor. On the night of Tuesday 31 October 1984, Mr Lee was driving his Ford Capri towards Molland when, at about 8.30, he saw a huge black animal, like a Great Dane with a long neck and huge head, run down the road towards him:

> I put on my anchors and in the headlights it slowed down and walked right up to the car. I could see its eyes as plain as day, green and glassy they were and he looked right over the bonnet at me, he was that tall, then he just went!

When asked if he meant that the creature ran off, Mr Lee replied:

> Oh no, just went like a light going out, I just couldn't see it any more. It isn't real like an ordinary dog. I could feel the hairs on my neck standing up. I just started the car and drove off, wasn't hanging about with that thing out there!

Derbyshire

At about 8.00 one evening in 1930, Greta Shirt was walking along a lonely lane between Upper Booth and the Lea in Edale in the Peak District of Derbyshire. She saw a dog coming towards her, black and the size of a very large collie and, wondering whose dog it was, went to stroke it as it walked past her. To her surprise she could not feel the animal. She was even more shocked when 'the dog merged through the close, criss-cross wires of the fence, which could not possibly have let its body through'. She immediately looked over the fence, but the dog had disappeared. On arriving home she told her father of the apparition, and he said: 'Well, now that you've seen it I'll admit there is a black-dog ghost along there, but I did not want to tell you till you were grown out of your childhood.' He had seen the phantom himself, several years previously.

Ireland

We travel now to Ireland where the Black Dog was usually known as the Pooka. The Pooka was well-known in the countryside around the north Galway town of Ballygar. A young man was cycling home one evening in 1913 when a big, black dog appeared and trotted along beside him. The creature kept looking up at him in a way which made him feel very uneasy, and the man was very relieved when the dog left him, just before he cycled over a small culvert. On arriving home he described his encounter and found that the dog was well-known in the area, the local people avoiding that stretch of road. Several witnesses stated that the dog vanished before their eyes.

During the late 1930s, there was a long correspondence in the letters column of the *Dublin Evening Mail* about the legends and traditions of the district of Templeogue, a suburb of south Dublin. The area had once been a quiet country village, and one reader described a strange incident which had occurred at a spot known as Pussy's Leap, some forty years earlier:

> It was a moonlight winter evening, about 9.00p.m., and I was walking home accompanied by a servant maid from Cherryfield. As my companion and I approached Pussy's Leap, a black dog crossed our path. It got larger as it ran across, and gradually went out of sight, with the sound of chains.
>
> I need not state here my fears, but I managed to get home without losing consciousness. For years after, I was always afraid to pass the 'leap' at night. Strange, the servant maid did not see the dog, but heard the rattling chains.
>
> Another old legend relates that some seventy years ago a man was killed by a runaway horse at Pussy's Leap, where the Knocklyon road intersects, and I remember well, as a boy, seeing a rough cross in the grass border.

The account contains features we have seen in other Black Dog reports: the expansion of the phantom, the fact that one person could see it while another couldn't, the sound of rattling chains, and the fact that the Black Dog appeared at the site of a violent death.

Another locality with a long tradition of Pooka hauntings is the area around the Loughs Conn and Cullen in County Mayo. Early one evening in the 1930s, a lady was walking with her dog along the road to the west of the Pontoon Bridge Hotel, when she saw what she first took to be a donkey lying in the road about twenty yards ahead. As she looked the creature rose to its feet and showed itself to be a dog, huge and black. The beast looked at the woman, slowly walked on to the grass verge at the side of the road and disappeared. The woman was quite certain that it had not slipped into the undergrowth, for there was none capable of concealing the animal. One interesting feature was the behaviour of the witness's dog. Normally it was fearless when meeting a strange dog, but on this occasion when it saw the black hound it ran, whining, behind its mistress's legs.

Another witness was a local man cycling home late one summer night. Just before he reached the bridge between the two loughs he stopped to pump up a flat tyre. While thus engaged he looked up and saw a big black dog jump over the wall around the woods and stand there looking down at him. Not having the slightest doubt as to the supernatural nature of the beast, he prayed to the Virgin Mary, jumped on his cycle and pedalled home as fast as he could!

The following two cases occurred during the 1950s. The first involved a sixteen-year-old girl who lived with her parents on their farm which was about three miles from Ballaghadereen, County Roscommon. At about 6.00p.m. on a hot summer evening, she was standing in a field beside the house, when a gigantic black hound as high as her shoulder walked past about three or four yards away. As it passed, it turned its head and stared at the startled girl with eyes that seemed almost human in their intelligence. Up to this point, the girl thought that the beast was a flesh and blood animal, but then it walked straight through a solid iron gate some twenty yards away. The girl stood transfixed for a few moments and then ran screaming into the house. Her parents did not believe her story, but nothing they said could convince her that she had not seen the Pooka.

On a light summer night in 1952, as Margo Ryan walked towards her parents' house near Redcross, County Wicklow, the quiet was broken by a soft pattering and a huge, jet-black dog came up alongside her. It seemed a friendly animal so Margo reached to pat it. Her hand seemed to miss the animal, however, so she tried again, with the same result. A third attempt to pat the beast also failed and, a little startled, Margo watched the dog as it moved in front of her and walked on just a few yards ahead. After the girl and her strange companion had covered another fifty yards the dog stopped, turned its head to the left and vanished, in front of Margo's gaze. This, and the sudden realization that the dog's back was much higher than the level of her hand which must have passed through the animal hit Margo forcibly, and she ran home as fast as she could. Unlike the parents of the Roscommon witness, Margo's family believed her, listening to her story with interest and sympathy.

Wales

Black Dogs have also been encountered in Wales. The Reverend Edmund Jones described several cases in his book *A Relation of Apparitions or Spirits in the County of Monmouth and the Principality of Wales*, published in 1813. One witness was a young lady who had to travel one evening to Laugharne, Carmarthenshire. Her mother warned her of a phantom black hound which had been seen by several people near a water-filled pit at the side of the road leading to Laugharne. The girl would not be dissuaded though, and set out on her journey. She arrived at her destination without incident but her return journey was less peaceful:

> On coming back before night, though it was rather dark, she passed by the place; but not without thinking of the apparition: but being a little beyond this pit, in a field where there was a little rill of water and just going to pass it having one foot stretched over it and looking before her, she saw something like a great dog, one of the Dogs of Hell, coming towards her; being within four or five yards of her, it stopped, sat down and set up such a scream so horrible, so loud and so strong, that she thought the earth moved under her; with which she fainted.

A black dog was also said to haunt a spot marked by two ancient stones known as the Devil's Nags on Cot Moor, Pembrokeshire. One evening a Mr W. was travelling through this area when he was seized by some invisible assailant or force and thrown over a hedge. He picked himself up, looked around and seeing nothing resumed his journey. The following evening he passed this way again, but this time with a fierce mastiff for protection. As he reached the Devil's Nags he saw an enormous black dog coming towards him:

> He thought to set his own dog at it but his dog seemed to be much frightened and would not go near it. Mr W. then stooped down to take up a stone thinking to throw it but suddenly there came a fire round the dog so that he could perceive it had a white tail and a white snip down his nose and saw his teeth grinning at him: he then knew that it was one of the Infernal Dogs of Hell.

Another Pembrokeshire Black Dog was described by the witness's grandson to Ethel Rudkin in the 1930s; the encounter had probably occurred about 100 years previously:

> At the time of the described incident, my grandfather was the acting steward of the considerable estate of Camrose and his journeys to the neighbouring town of Haverfordwest were fairly frequent and always on foot. So far as I recollect the story, it was on his way home from Haverfordwest in the darkening evening that he became somewhat alarmed by a considerable commotion in the wood. In his pastoral mind, this could only be caused by a battle royal between some domestic animals and he wondered whose bull had invaded the territory of his neighbour and what dogs were joining in the mêlée. However, he was secure enough in the protection of the hedges and it seemed unlikely that the strife would culminate in the vanquished being forced through the thick trees to drop over the crest of a little cliff into the brook beneath.
>
> A few yards walking brought him to the bridge and here he was terrified to see a huge black dog rise over the trees with a frightful roar and swoop downwards within a few feet of him, to the stream beyond the bridge.

In 1920 J. W. Phillips wrote:

> A Black Dog haunts part of the road from Haverfordwest to Pembroke Ferry about two miles outside the former town. The country people say there is 'fear' at that particular part of the road and do not care to pass there at night. I know of at least five persons who have seen the creature and all describe it as a large black creature between a dog and a calf in appearance. One man met it at 2.00 in the morning when he was on his way to fetch a doctor. I have myself seen it on two occasions.

The description of the creature as being somewhat calf-like is rather interesting, for E. G. Smith, a local historian who lived at Neath Abbey, West Glamorgan, recorded a description of a similar beast in the Vale of Neath. Late one night, a girl was walking home to the farm where she lived and worked when a big 'ambling creature' came up and travelled by her side. She described it as 'somewhat resembling a calf' and on arriving home told her employer that she had seen the Devil. The farmer got his gun and searched the area, but found nothing. In the morning, however, strange paw-marks were found leading to and from the house. After this incident the track became know as the Devil's Pathway. So far as I know this is the only case where a Black Dog is said to have left paw-marks.

The Black Dog has reportedly been seen in the Vale of Neath on numerous occasions, usually at night but sometimes in the morning. People have sometimes seen the phantom roaming the country lanes and taken it for a real animal but, when approached, it vanishes.

Scotland

In the early hours of a morning in 1909, Dr Duncan MacDonald was letting himself out of Lochbuie House, home of the MacLaine family on Mull in the Hebrides, after visiting the elderly and bedridden Murdoch MacLaine. As he opened the front door a black dog rushed past him. Dr MacDonald thought that it must be a family pet and opened the inner door to let it into the house. He climbed into the trap which was to take him to the ferry at Craignure, and mentioned to the driver that someone must have left a dog out all night. The driver very nervously asked the doctor if he had let the animal into the house. When Dr MacDonald replied in the affirmative the driver stated that there was now no hope of the old man recovering, the black dog being a phantom whose appearance invariably foretold a death. Indeed, shortly after, Murdoch MacLaine died.

A few years later, Dr MacDonald's cousin, Reginald MacDonald, also a doctor, had an uncanny experience. One night in 1914, he was returning to his home in Salen after visiting an old man, a retainer of the MacLaine family, at his home in the village of Lochbuie. He was driving up the steep Ardura Hill when he heard the eerie howling of a dog in the woods by the roadside. A few moments later a dog emerged from the trees and ran along the road in front of the doctor's car, illuminated by its headlights, for some distance before vanishing. That night the old man died.

Just before Christmas 1954, Dr Reginald MacDonald's wife, Dr Flora MacDonald, was going through some of her late husband's old papers. Among the documents was a letter in mirror writing. Dr MacDonald held it up to a mirror and found that it concerned the Black Dog. The letter runs:

Telegrams, Lochbuie
Station, Oban

Lochbuie House,
Isle of Mull,
NB

14/11/15

You will be interested to hear that the dog was both seen and heard last night by Miss White!

The description of which has so horribly upset me that I feel scarcely able to write.

I suppose it serves me right for not beleiving [sic] you yesterday. In future I shall beleive what you tell me.

L. Chamanyon

Dr Flora MacDonald thought that the people concerned were guests of the late Sir Stephen Gatty who had a lease of the house in 1915.

Yorkshire

We travel to Yorkshire now, for what must be the strangest Black Dog case of them all. It involved the Reverend Donald Omand, well-known for his activities as an exorcist. The Reverend Omand was ordained as a Free Church Minister in 1937 and entered the Church of England in 1954. He has been the Rector of Winterbourne Abbas and Vicar of Chideock, both in Dorset, and since 1971 has followed his vocation as exorcist full-time. Much of his work consists of trying to rid places, rather than people, of what he considers to be some form of evil influence. One such place is Kettleness on the Yorkshire coast and it was here, during the 1950s, that the Reverend Omand encountered a malevolent Black Dog.

The full story began many years before, when, just before World War One, the young Donald Omand spent a holiday with his parents at Whitby. One day the family visited a desolate promontory, Kettleness, which lies between Sandsend and Hinderwell. Donald was repelled by the place which, in later life, he wrote, seemed 'laden with corruption'. Several years later, at the age of fourteen, he read Bram Stoker's *Dracula* and was astonished and disturbed to come across the passage in which the vampire comes ashore in the form of a huge hound at, of all places, Kettleness!

In the late 1920s, Donald Omand, prior to entering the

Church, was working as a reporter for the *Northern Echo* at Darlington. He was instructed one day to interview a man who claimed to have seen a phantom hound at Kettleness. Donald found the witness to be a down-to-earth fisherman who stated that, on several occasions, he had seen a gigantic black dog appear on Kettleness Point and then vanish a few seconds later. He had never heard of Dracula, the young reporter found.

In the 1950s Donald Omand, now ordained and with a reputation as a successful exorcist, was contacted by a schoolmaster from the Midlands. The latter had been on holiday at Whitby with two friends, and all three, looking out over the shore at Kettleness, had seen a huge black hound moving towards them. After a few moments it disappeared, leaving them with an overwhelming sense of evil. The schoolmaster asked the minister if he could exorcize the area and, after making the necessary preparations, the Reverend Omand travelled to Kettleness with him. Late one evening the pair walked along the shore, which the Reverend Omand felt still had the 'same aroma of corruption'. All was quiet, but then the apparition appeared. Omand wrote:

> What we saw looked like a huge black hound, but bigger than any member of the canine species known to man. It was moving straight in our direction and the schoolmaster's nerve gave way completely. He rushed back to the car.
>
> But I had a job to do, and the sooner it was accomplished the better. I knew that the terrifying spectacle moving towards me had no substance whatever. It was a mere projection, a manifestation of an evil with which I had already contended on hundreds of occasions.
>
> Uncorking the bottle which I was carrying, I commanded the spectre as follows: 'Be gone in the name of the Lord Jesus Christ. Be gone to the place appointed for you, there to remain for ever. Be gone in the name of Christ.'
>
> As I spoke the last words, I splashed holy water in the direction of the apparition, and the latter disappeared as suddenly as it materialized. Then I exorcised all the ground which the spectre had covered and a great heaviness went out of the atmosphere. The menace of Kettleness was ended. The corruption had departed.

Bram Stoker knew this part of the coast well, and the Reverend Omand speculated that the author himself had seen the Black

Dog at Kettleness, and that the experience had inspired him to write *Dracula*.

The foregoing are just some of the numerous sightings of Black Dogs which have been reported down the ages. I have notes on 160 eye-witness accounts, and innumerable local legends and traditions. I hope the reader will agree that the number of accounts and their consistency – the same details are reported over many years and from widely separated areas – argue that at least some witnesses are encountering a genuinely unexplained phenomenon.

Assuming that many of the witnesses have described their encounters truthfully and accurately is it possible to account for the appearance of Black Dogs in our own dimension? There are several recurring features in the reports which may at least provide clues.

An examination of the locations of Black Dog sightings reveals common characteristics. Churches figure prominently, the phantom appearing inside the buildings, in the churchyards or on nearby roads. Several dog-haunted East Anglian churches have already been mentioned, and the phantom has also been seen at the churches of Algarkirk and Northorpe in Lincolnshire, at a church at Chippenham, Wiltshire, and at Burnley Parish Church.

The presence of water is another common feature. This seems particularly true of Lincolnshire Black Dogs, but it has been noted in other areas. Black Dogs have been seen on the banks of the River Torridge and the River Tamar in Devon, and the Londonderry Black Dog, witnessed often, was seen actually in a river. Another aquatic Black Dog haunts Armbroath House, Thirlmere in Cumbria where it is seen swimming across the lake. The Black Dog of Creag an Ordain, Sutherland, has been seen splashing out of a loch, and the Black Dog of Hergest Court in Herefordshire materializes beside a pond. The Pontoon Pooka appears near two loughs, and a stream runs under the road at the Black Dog haunted Pussy's Leap. There is a Poulaphuca or 'Pool of the Pooka' in the Wicklow Mountains, and a Pool of the Black Hound near Dean Combe in South Devon. Many coastal areas are haunted by the Black Dog.

Prehistoric sites seem to be favourite haunts of Black Dogs. One such is the appropriately named Doghill Barrow near

Stonehenge, Wiltshire. A Black Dog also haunts the West Kennet burial mound, Wiltshire, traditionally visiting the site at sunrise on the longest day of the year. In Hertfordshire the phantom has been seen near the ancient site of Six Hills near Stevenage. In the West Country, Black Dogs have been seen at the Long Stone, Minchinhampton, Gloucester; Wambarrows near Winsford, Somerset; Whiteborough, a tumulus near Launceston, Cornwall, and Braunton Burrows in north Devon The Devil's Nags in Pembrokeshire are haunted by a Black Dog, as is a stone circle between Amlwch and St Elian's Church in Anglesey. In Scotland the Black Dog haunts the ancient sites of Dun Borbe in the Outer Hebrides; Castle of the Black Dog (*Casteal a Choin Dubh*) Craignish, Argyll; and Fort of the Black Dog (*Dun a Choin Dubh*) Knapdale, also in Argyllshire. Dermot MacManus writes that there are numerous Rath Phucas in the Irish countryside, a rath being an ancient hill fort.

Black Dogs also haunt ancient trackways, such as Peddars Way in Norfolk, a Roman road which probably followed a prehistoric route across the Breckland, and the road from Torrington to Copplestone in Devon, much of which follows an ancient track. In Lincolnshire the Black Dog patrols an old green lane between Manton and Scotter, and an ancient trackway near Willoughton.

Other topographical features mentioned in Black Dog reports are: gates; gaps in hedges; crossroads; smithies; clumps of trees, and bridges. Black Dogs also haunt, like other phantoms, localities where violent or tragic events, such as murders, suicides and executions, have occurred.

Sometimes Black Dogs seem to have their origins in the very ground itself. The Shag Dog of Birstall, Leicestershire was said to emerge from a hole in the ground, known locally as Shag Dog Pit, and at Thackergate, Lancashire a Black Dog comes out of a pit. The Black Dog of Belle Hole Farm near Kirton, Lincolnshire was said to live in a hole in a river bank. The unfortunate boy who was so terrified by the Black Dog in Christina Hole's account said that the beast rose straight up from the ground. A Black Dog encountered near Tring, Hertfordshire by two travellers in the nineteenth century concluded its appearance by sinking into the ground, and Trash, the Black Dog of Lancashire, was also said to depart in this manner.

Having looked at where Black Dogs appear we should also examine the manner of their appearance. On numerous occasions

Black Dogs have been associated with lightning, fire and explosions. Could some form of electrical phenomenon be involved in the creation of these phantoms? Several Black Dog accounts contain features which are reminiscent of ball lightning, a phenomenon which itself has only comparatively recently been accepted by scientists. Fireballs can appear in the open or inside houses, in calm weather or during storms. They seem able to pass through solid objects, and often conclude their appearances by exploding violently. During thunderstorms over London on 17 July 1964, a fireball struck a school in Shoreditch, breaking windows and throwing glass, bricks and coping stones into the street. These effects are identical to those experienced by the Dartmoor farmer who encountered the Black Dog in his house.

Another common feature of Black Dog and ball lightning cases is the smell that is produced. People who have encountered ball lightning often describe a sulphurous smell (possibly ozone) as have Black Dog witnesses.

In his book *The Elements Rage* Frank Lane points out:

> It is very dangerous to touch a fireball. An inquisitive child once kicked one and thereby caused an explosion which killed eleven cattle and threw the child and a companion to the ground.

Similarly one old treatise warns that encounters with the Black Dog would result in the witnesses being 'thrown down and severely bruised and it is well if they do not get their ankles sprained or broken'.

Several witnesses of the Black Dog (for example a Westmorland man who encountered the phantom one night during the last century) stated that it threw them into or over hedges. This is paralleled by the experience of Professor M. Dandois, a surgeon at the University of Louvais, France, who on 6 March 1894, was walking home after a visit to a patient when the sky darkened and a fireball appeared next to him, exploding violently and throwing him over a hedge and into a field. He lay unconscious for about fifteen minutes, and was numb in an arm and a leg for a short while afterwards.

The injuries that some Black Dog witnesses have received could have been caused by violent electric shocks and the injuries that the witnesses in the Bungay case received are interesting in this respect. The famous pathologist, Francis Camps, once described a case in which the skin of an electric shock victim resembled that of a crocodile, being hard, blackened and wrinkled. One of the Bungay witnesses was said to have been 'wrinkled and scorched like a leather purse in a hot fire'. I am not suggesting that Black Dogs can be explained away as ball lightning – the eye-witness accounts are too detailed and specific for this – but the same sort of energy could play a part in both phenomena.

Further thoughts on the creation of phantom Black Dogs are expressed in the final chapter of this book.

CHAPTER FIVE

Many Kinds of Life

> Thus these beings appear to us, not in order to stay among us or become allied to us, but in order for us to become able to understand them. These apparitions are scarce to tell the truth. But why should it be otherwise? Is it not enough for one of us to see an Angel, in order for all of us to believe in the other Angels?
>
> Paracelsus (1493–1541) in a treatise entitled *Why These Beings Appear to Us.*

The strange creatures so far described have fitted neatly into separate categories, but there are accounts of beings which cannot be so easily categorized. This chapter is a collection of such reports, and describes some of the most bizarre creatures ever encountered.

The Owlman of Mawnan

This creature was seen during the Morgawr appearances at Falmouth Bay in 1976. June and Vicky Melling, aged twelve and nine years respectively, were on holiday with their parents. On 17 April, Easter Saturday, the girls saw an enormous feathered bird-man hovering over Mawnan Church. They were so scared that the Melling family went back home to Preston three days early. June provided a sketch of the creature (*see* Fig. 15).

The creature was seen again on 3 July in the same location. Two fourteen-year-old girls were camping among the trees near Mawnan Church. At about 10.00p.m. they heard a strange hissing noise and, looking round saw a figure in the trees about twenty yards away. Sally Chapman described it to Anthony Doc Shiels:

> It was like a big owl with pointed ears, as big as a man. The eyes were red and glowing. At first I thought it was someone dressed up,

Fig. 15. June Melling's sketch of the creature she saw near Mawnan Church on 17 April 1976. (By courtesy of the Fortean Picture Library).

playing a joke, trying to scare us. I laughed at it, we both did, then it went up in the air and we both screamed. When it went up you could see its feet were like pincers.

Barbara Perry added:

It's true. It was horrible, a nasty owl-face with big ears and big red eyes. It was covered in grey feathers. The claws on its feet were black. It just flew straight up and disappeared in the trees.

Doc Shiels separated the two girls and asked them both to draw the creature (*see* Fig. 16).

The following morning the Owlman was seen by two more girls, Jane Greenwood and her sister, who were on holiday in Cornwall. They saw the creature near Mawnan Church, and Jane later described it in a letter to the *Falmouth Packet*:

It was in the trees standing like a full-grown man, but the legs bent backwards like a bird's. It saw us and quickly jumped up and rose straight up through the trees. My sister and I saw it very closely before it rose up. It has red slanting eyes and a very large mouth. The feathers are silvery grey and so are his body and legs, the feet are like big black crab's claws. We were frightened at the time. It was so strange, like something out of a horror film. After the thing went up there were crackling sounds in the treetops for ages. Our mother thinks we made it all up just because we read about these things, but that is not true. We really saw the bird-man, though it could have been somebody playing a trick in very good costume and make-up. But how could it rise up like that? If we imagined it, then we both imagined it at the same time.

The creature was reported again in June 1978, when a sixteen-year-old girl saw 'a monster like a devil flying up through the trees near old Mawnan Church'. On 2 August, three young French girls also saw the Owlman near the church. They said it was like 'a great big furry bird with a gaping mouth and big round eyes'.

When I discussed the Owlman with Doc Shiels in 1985 he confessed to being baffled. It seemed almost too strange to accept and he wondered if it were all a hoax, but when interviewing Sally Chapman and Barbara Perry he felt that they had been badly frightened and were telling the truth.

Fig. 16. The Owlman of Mawnan, after sketches by Barbara Perry and Sally Chapman. (By courtesy of the Fortean Picture Library).

Mawnan Church, scene of the Owlman encounters.

Orford Castle, once the home of a wild man.

Carving of a wild man in the porch of Peasenhall Church, Suffolk.

The Hexham Heads.

Creature encountered in the grounds of Borley Rectory by Mrs Margaret E. Wilson on 22 August 1938.

John Aubrey.

One of the apparitions materialized by Franek Kluski.

A bird-like apparition materialized by Franek Kluski.

A creature similar to the Owlman had been encountered in southern England thirteen years previously. On 16 November 1963, four young men walking along a country road near Sandling Park, Hythe, Kent, saw a bright light moving above the woods at Slaybrook Corner. As they watched, the light descended in their direction, disappearing behind some trees. The witnesses, now rather frightened, broke into a run, becoming aware that an oval-shaped golden light was moving along about ten feet above the ground in an adjoining field, keeping pace with them. The light again vanished among trees, and then a dark figure appeared, shambling across the field towards them. It was man-sized, black all over, appeared to be headless and had two huge bat-like wings. The men fled. Over the next few weeks strange lights were seen over the area but the winged creature was not seen again.

The Brentford Griffin

It is hard to imagine a more unlikely setting for a griffin than the West London district of Brentford but such a beast has reportedly been seen flying over the area by several witnesses. About the middle of 1984, Kevin Chippendale was walking down Braemar Road, a street of terraced houses, at about 5.00p.m. Glancing upwards, he saw a strange creature flying level with the top of the appropriately named Green Dragon tower blocks. He described it as resembling a dog with wings, having a long muzzle and four legs with what looked like paws. It was a dark colour, at least the size of a large dog, and Mr Chippendale thought he could discern eyes and a tail. The wings were flapping very slowly, as if in slow-motion. It was in view for several seconds before moving out of sight behind the terrace of houses. He was very perplexed but told no one of his sighting at the time. Some six months later, in February 1985, he saw the creature again, at the same time of day and in the same location. Again it flew in front of the tower blocks before disappearing behind the terraced houses. On this occasion he realized that it was very similar to the creature on the sign of The Griffin public house on the corner of Braemar Road. Mr Chippendale then described his sightings to his colleagues, one of whom, Angela Keyhoe, said that she had seen, from a bus, a big, black, bird-like creature, perched on the top of the gasometer next to the Watermans Arts Centre. Other passengers also saw the creature. Another sighting was reported by John Olssen, a psychologist, who had seen the 'griffin' while jogging along the river bank in the early morning.

In March 1985, there was much publicity in the local Press about the griffin sightings. It was also featured in London Weekend Television's *The Six O'Clock Show.* This programme has tended to treat the paranormal somewhat facetiously and unfortunately some 'spoof' reports were included in the item, supplied by author Robert Rankin, who had also been involved in the preparation of the newspaper articles. He admitted to investigator Andrew Collins that he wanted to publicize his novels which were on sale at the Watermans Art Centre in Brentford. However, Mr Rankin also said that he was certain some of the sightings were genuine and that, when living in the area some years earlier, he had heard vague rumours and third-hand stories.

Andrew Collins was sceptical about much of the Brentford Griffin affair, but having interviewed Kevin Chippendale was convinced of his integrity. He also pointed out the curious role which coincidence had played in the story. In addition to The Griffin public house, the Griffin Brewery, using a griffin as its trademark, is at nearby Chiswick. Brentford Football Club's ground is called Griffin Park and the coat of arms for Brentford and Chiswick, designed in 1932, features two griffins holding a shield.

Wild Men

Many accounts of strange beings are found in the writings of the medieval chroniclers, such as William of Newbridge, Gervase of Tilbury and Ralph of Coggeshall. Ralph, who was Abbot of the monastery at Coggeshall in Essex in the early thirteenth century, in his *Chronicon Anglicanum* gives a puzzling account of some sort of wild man caught near Orford in Suffolk:

> In the time of King Henry II, when Bartholemew de Glanville kept Orford Castle, it happened that the sailors there, fishing in the sea, caught a wild man in their nets, whom they brought to the Castellan as a curiosity. He was completely naked, and had the appearance of a man in all his parts. He had hair too; and though the hair of his head seemed torn and rubbed, his beard was profuse and pointed, and he was exceedingly shaggy and hairy about the breasts. They had him

guarded for a long time, by day and night, lest he should escape into the sea. What food was put before him he ate eagerly. He preferred raw fish to cooked; but when they were raw he squeezed them tightly in his hands until all the moisture was pressed out, and so he ate them. He would not utter any speech, or rather he could not, even when hung up by his feet and cruelly tortured. When he was taken into the church he showed no sign of reverence or even of belief, either by kneeling or bowing his head at the sight of anything sacred. He always hastened to bed as soon as the sun sank, and stayed there until it rose again. Once they took him to the sea-gate and let him go into the water, after placing a triple row of very strong nets in front of him. He soon made for the deep sea, and, breaking through all their nets, raised himself again and again from the depths, and showed himself to those watching on the shore, often plunging into the sea, and a little after coming up, as if he were jeering at the spectators because he had escaped their nets. When he had played there in the sea for a long time, and they had lost all hope of his return, he came back to them of his own accord, swimming to them through the waves, and remained with them for another two months. But when after a time he was more negligently kept, and held in some distaste, he escaped secretly to the sea, and never afterwards returned.

Creatures similar to the Orford Wild Man figure prominently in British folklore. Medieval paintings, drawings and architectural sculpture, particularly that of East Anglian churches, frequently depict hair-covered, man-like figures. Sometimes they are shown walking upright, perhaps carrying clubs and shields, and sometimes going on all fours. They were known as the Wild Men of the Woods, or the Wudewasa and were said to dwell deep in forests, or among hills and mountains, sometimes emerging to carry off people, particularly women. A legend from the Nanhrynan area of North Wales concerns a huge man covered in reddish hair who stole farm animals and produce, often entering houses to do so. The villagers made several attempts to catch or kill him, but he was too strong and quick. Eventually his downfall was brought about by a farmer's wife who, instead of retiring to sleep one night, waited for the marauder, armed with a hatchet. Eventually the beast appeared, climbing in through a window, and the woman struck at him, cutting off his right hand. The injured wild man fled, leaving a trail of blood which next day was tracked to a cave under a waterfall. The wild man was not to be found, but he troubled the local people no more. The cave is known to this day as the Cave of Owen Langoch, or Cave of the Hairy Man.

A curious folk tale of the nineteenth century, from the Flintshire area, may be relevant here. It concerns one Richard Roberts who abandoned his once regular Sunday worship to wander instead in the fields and woods. After some months he unexpectedly reappeared at church. Pressed for an explanation for his sudden return, he told the rector that one morning, while he was gathering nuts, he reached for a particularly well-laden branch and was horrified when a huge hairy hand emerged from the undergrowth and reached for the same bush. Roberts fled, not waiting to see the owner of the hand who, he was convinced, was Satan himself.

It is possible that legends and accounts of wild men arose from encounters with degenerate or mentally deficient people rejected by society and reduced to living off wild plants and animals and occasionally pilfering from farms. However, one would have thought that such outcasts would have been quite common in earlier times, and would have aroused no great fear in normal people. Ivan T. Sanderson, the well-known zoologist and investigator of strange phenomena, made the interesting suggestion that accounts and legends of wild men arose from encounters with surviving Neanderthal men, the last remnants of a race which was once widespread over Europe.

Wolfmen

British folklore, like the folklore of many other countries, has traditions of creatures that combine human and wolf characteristics. There was, for example, the Wulver of the Shetlands, as described by Jesse Saxby in *Shetland Traditional Lore*:

> The Wulver was a creature like a man with a wolf's head. He had short, brown hair all over him. His home was a cave dug out of the side of a steep knowe [knoll, mound or hillock] half-way up a hill. He didn't molest folk if folk didn't molest him. He was fond of fishing, and had a small rock in the deep water which is known to this day as the 'Wulver's Stane'. There he would sit fishing sillacks and piltaks for hour after hour. He was reported to have frequently left a few fish on the window-sill of some poor body.

The famous writer on the supernatural, the Reverend Montague Summers, described what was claimed to have been an actual encounter with a werewolf phantom in Wales in 1888.

An Oxford professor, his wife and a friend had rented a cottage for a summer holiday in a mountainous area of Merionethshire. While fishing in a nearby lake one day, the professor found a huge, dog-like skull. He took it home for further examination and placed it on a shelf in the kitchen. That evening, while the two men were out, the professor's wife heard snuffling and scratching noises at the kitchen door. Fearing that a savage dog was outside she went into the kitchen to check that the door was securely fastened and saw a hideous face, part wolf, part man, at the window. The creature grasped the window ledge with paws that were like hands, and glared at the woman with horribly intelligent red eyes. The terrified woman ran through to the front door and bolted it. A few moments later she heard a loud panting outside and the latch rattled as the creature tried the door. The animal prowled around the cottage, snarling and growling and trying to find an entrance. Finally, however, the noises died away and the woman heard the voices of her husband and his friend approaching the cottage. She described her ordeal to the men who, having made sure the cottage was secure, put out the lamps and sat quietly, armed with sticks and a gun. The Reverend Summers continues:

> The hours passed slowly, until when all was darkest and most lonely the soft thud of cushioned paws was heard on the gravel outside, and nails scratched at the kitchen window. To their horror, in a stale phosphorescent light they saw the hideous mask of a wolf with the eyes of a man glaring through the glass, eyes that were red with hellish rage. Snatching the gun they rushed to the door, but it had seen their movement and was away in a moment. As they issued from the house a shadowy undefined shape slipped through the open gate, and in the stars they could just see a huge animal making towards the lake into which it disappeared silently, nor did a ruffle cross the surface of the water. Early the next morning the professor took the skull, and rowing a little way out from the shore flung it as far as possible into the deeper part of the tarn. The werewolf was never seen again.

The Reverend Summers adds a brief note on two other cases of phantom werewolves in Wales:

> There is a story of a werewolf which was seen by certain shepherds on lonelier hill-sides at night about the middle of the Eighteenth century, and there is a tale of a woman who was terribly scared one evening owing to the appearance of a great furry dog with the eyes of a man which, so far as I can learn, must have been about 100 years ago, but both of these grow faint with the passing of time.

Another encounter with a werewolf in Merionethshire was described to Elliott O'Donnell by a Miss Jean St Denis. Miss St Denis was in the habit of sketching the landscape from the platform of the small railway station near the farm where she was staying. One evening at dusk, as she was packing up her equipment, she noticed a figure sitting on a truck a short distance away. The figure was indistinct in the growing darkness, but seemed to be staring at her. Miss St Denis then realized that the station was deserted, apart from the figure on the truck. In an attempt to elicit a response she asked it the time. There was no reply, and the woman, now very nervous, hurriedly departed.

Miss St Denis soon realized that she was being followed. She walked for some distance, occasionally glancing over her shoulder, with the figure still in pursuit then, realizing that the darkest, loneliest part of the road was just ahead, decided she must act. She turned round and cried: 'What do you want? How dare you . . .'. She stopped in mid-sentence, horrified at her pursuer's appearance. The creature had a grey, naked, man-like body, and a hideous wolf's head with blazing eyes. The woman shone her small torch full in the face of the thing which shrank back, put two paw-like hands in front of its eyes, then faded away.

Elliott O'Donnell relates this incident in *A Casebook of Ghosts*, in which he writes of other werewolf encounters described to him at first hand. One of these involved a young couple, Mr and Mrs Anderson, who had inherited a considerable sum of money and had built a large villa in the countryside of Cumberland. They had not been in their new house long when their three children and the servants began to complain of strange noises at night – growling and what seemed to be the padding of animal feet. The Andersons decided to sit up late in their children's bedroom to listen for the noises themselves.

Between 2.00a.m. and 3.00a.m. they heard growling immediately below the bedroom window, but when Mr Anderson opened the window and peered out there was no animal to be seen. Shortly after, the Andersons heard the opening of the front door, which they had carefully locked, and the sound of some big, soft-footed animal coming up the stairs. Mr Anderson waited until it reached the bedroom and flung open the door. The corridor was empty.

The following morning the grounds were searched but there was no trace of any intruder. Shortly after this, the strange noises ceased, but the most frightening incident was still to come. On Christmas Eve the children were sent to bed at 10.00p.m. and two hours later Mr Anderson went upstairs with a sackful of presents to leave in their stockings. As he walked along the passage to their room he heard faint yelping, like that of a wolf, coming from outside the house. He stopped and listened and the yelping was repeated, much nearer this time, followed by a moaning, snarling noise ending in a whine. Mr Anderson, now very frightened, struggled on with his bulky sack and entered the children's bedroom. He was not alone. Close on his heels was a huge, grey, upright figure with a wolf-like face, glowing eyes and white, pointed teeth. Mr Anderson and his children could only stare in horror at the creature. At this point Mrs Anderson appeared with a candle and the apparition vanished.

The Andersons put the house up for sale, but before leaving they made a thorough search of the grounds and surrounding countryside. In a cave behind the house they found several bones, among them the skull of a wolf and a headless human skeleton. Mr Anderson burnt the bones, after which there were apparently no further manifestations at the house.

O'Donnell described another werewolf case:

> A woman I met in Tavistock told me she had seen a ghost which she believed to be that of a werewolf, in the Valley of the Doones, Exmoor. She was walking home alone, late one evening, when she saw on the path directly in front of her the tall grey figure of a man with a wolf's head. Advancing stealthily forward, this creature was preparing to spring on a large rabbit that was crouching on the ground, apparently too terror stricken to move, when the abrupt appearance of a stag bursting through the bushes caused it to vanish.

Another account came from Mr Andrew Warren who encountered a werewolf apparition in the Hebrides. He was fifteen years old at the time, and for several years had been living with his grandfather, an elder in the Kirk of Scotland. His grandfather was keenly interested in natural history and geology and the house was filled with rocks and fossils that he had found in the surrounding countryside. One morning he came home very excited and told the boy to come and look at some curious remains he had found in a dried up tarn. They consisted of what appeared to be a human skeleton with a wolf-like head.

The boy helped his grandfather to carry the bones back home. That evening he was alone in the house, his grandfather and other members of the family having gone to church. Sitting reading, he heard a noise at the back of the house and got up to investigate, but found all secure and no signs of an intruder. He sat on the kitchen table, where the strange bones had been laid, listening to see if the noises would recommence. He was staring down at the floor, his mind blank, when he heard a loud rapping of knuckles on the window pane. He continues:

> I immediately turned in the direction of the noise and saw a dark face looking in at me. At first dim and indistinct, it became more and more complete, until it developed into a perfectly defined head of a wolf terminating in the neck of a human being. Though greatly shocked, my first act was to look in every direction for a possible reflection – but in vain. There was no light either without or within, other than that from the setting sun – nothing that could in any way have produced an illusion.
>
> I looked at the face and marked each feature intently. It was unmistakably a wolf's face, the jaws slightly distended, the lips wreathed in a savage snarl, the teeth sharp and white, the eyes light green, the ears pointed.

The boy could only stare, horrified, at the creature, which raised a slender human-like hand with long, curved finger-nails. Fearing that it was going to smash the window, he ran out of the kitchen, locking the door behind him, and stayed in the hall until the family returned, by which time the creature had departed. The following day the boy and his grandfather returned the bones to the place where they had been found. The creature was seen no more.

In some respects the Summers and O'Donnell reports are unsatisfactory. There is a lack of basic information such as dates, precise locations and names of witnesses. Furthermore, they seem to have been written up in a rather dramatic way, and the recurring motif of the finding of collections of mixed human and animal bones is rather suspicious. However, it seems to have been the fashion at one time for writers to describe true events in a rather story-like manner, and Summers and O'Donnell may merely have added a few dramatic details to what were basically true incidents.

This section concludes with a bizarre and dramatic case of a phantom werewolf in which basic details are not lacking. It all began on a February afternoon in 1972 when eleven-year-old Colin Robson, weeding the garden of his parents' home in Rede Avenue, Hexham, Northumberland, unearthed a carved stone head. He called his younger brother to look at it and, digging further, the boys found another head. The artifacts were slightly smaller than tennis balls and extremely heavy. One of the heads was skull-like and seemed to be masculine, while the other resembled the head of a witch. They were taken into the house and, shortly after, a series of strange events occurred. The heads would apparently turn round by themselves, several household objects were found inexplicably broken, and one of the Robsons' daughter's bed was showered with pieces of glass. Then, a few nights after the discovery of the stone heads, Mrs Robson was awakened by screams coming from the house of her next-door neighbour, Mrs Ellen Dodd. The next morning she learned the reason for the commotion. Interviewed later by BBC reporter Luke Casey she said:

> Next morning I asked her what had happened, and she said this horrible thing had come into her bedroom. One of the children was ill with toothache and she'd been in the bedroom with her, and this thing came in the bedroom. It was half man, half beast. Of course we laughed, but it sounded so horrible y'know, something like a werewolf, and her husband came running in to see what it was, but this thing had gone padding down the stairs, and she could hear it y'know, padding down the stairs as if on its hind legs, and when he went downstairs the front door was open so evidently it had gone out of the front door.

It was shortly after this that Dr Anne Ross took charge of the stone heads. Dr Ross is an authority on Celtic culture, and the author of several books on the subject. She was convinced that the heads were about 1800 years old and used by the Celts in their religious rituals. Such heads were a common feature of Celtic life, and Dr Ross already had several. A few days after Dr Ross added the heads to her collection she had a very disturbing experience. Recounting her story to Luke Casey, she said that she awoke from her sleep feeling very cold and extremely frightened. She looked towards the door and saw a strange figure:

> It was about six feet high, slightly stooping, and it was black, against the white door, and it was half animal and half man. The upper part, I would have said, was a wolf, and the lower part was human and, I would have again said, that it was covered with a kind of black, very dark fur. It went out and I just saw it clearly, and then it disappeared, and something made me run after it, a thing I wouldn't normally have done, but I felt compelled to run after it. I got out of bed and I ran, and I could hear it going down the stairs, then it disappeared toward the back of the house.

A few days after this experience Dr Ross had to go to London for the day, leaving her teenage daughter to let herself in when she came from school at 4.00p.m. When Dr Ross returned home at 6.00p.m. she found her daughter pale and very upset. She told her mother that when she opened the front door she saw a huge black creature, like a werewolf, on the stairs. The creature jumped over the banister, landed with a soft thud in the hall and then ran, on padded animal feet towards the back of the house. The girl, like her mother, felt compelled to follow the creature which disappeared in the doorway of the music room at the end of the corridor. The girl was then overwhelmed with fear.

The phantom was seen several times by the family after this, usually on the stairs. It always halted half-way down and vaulted over the banisters, landing on its padded feet in the corridor. Sometimes the beast's footsteps were heard without any visual presence, and doors would fly open for no reason. There was a definite evil presence in the house, said Dr Ross, which visitors often remarked upon. The phenomena seemed to have become linked with the other stone heads in Dr Ross's collection, and only ceased when they were all removed from the house. It should be pointed out that Dr Ross lives in Southampton, and did not hear about the manifestation in Hexham until some time after her own experiences began.

The case took a further strange twist when it was claimed by Mr Desmond Craigie, who had lived with his family in the house now occupied by the Robsons, that the two heads, far from being Celtic, had been made by him in 1956 as toys for his two daughters. They had been lost somewhere in the garden where they had been later dug up by the Robson children. It is reported that the heads were examined at Southampton and Newcastle Universities to determine their age and composition. However there had been a lapse of several years before my inquiries to the relevant university departments in 1985, and by then I was unable to obtain any positive information as to the outcome of the tests.

The heads were passed from Professor Hodson, who had no strange experiences during his two year custody of them, to Dr Don Robins, an inorganic chemist who was investigating the affair. Dr Robins did not see the phantom werewolf either, but felt strongly that there was some sort of unpleasant influence emanating from the 'witch' head. He commented:

> There was no doubt that any influence that the heads possessed came from the girl. I felt most uncomfortable sitting there with them looking at me and eventually we turned them round. As we did so, I had the distinct impression that the girl's eyes 'slid round' watching me.

One day Dr Robins left the heads in his study, returning shortly after to pick up a book. Outside it was a fresh, blustery day, but the atmosphere in the house was very close and still. The air in the study seemed 'almost electric with a stifling breathless quality'. Again, Dr Robins felt that any influence was coming from the female head, rather than the skull head. Shortly after this he took the heads to Frank Hyde, an astrologer and dowser. Dr Robins himself had some experience of dowsing, and both men obtained a very strong reaction from the 'witch' head when using angle rods and a pendulum.

The heads were left with Frank Hyde, but it is not known if he had any strange experiences with them. Don Robins writes that Mr Hyde was involved in a serious road accident in 1978 and that all subsequent attempts to contact him have failed. The present location of the heads remains unknown.

Is there any explanation for the strange phenomena associated with the Hexham heads? Don Robins followed the 'stone tape' theory in trying to find a solution, the theory being that events, especially if violent or tragic, can leave a recording on their immediate surroundings. The energy is stored, and may be reactivated, maybe many years later, when the conditions are right. The presence of living people may be a requisite, for example. I believe the stone tape hypothesis received its name after the BBC broadcast a television play on this theme by Nigel Kneale, called *The Stone Tape*. The theory, however, is perhaps most notably associated with author and researcher T. C. Lethbridge. How does the concept apply to the stone heads and the werewolf? The answer may lie in certain aspects of the Celtic religion.

The Celts practised human sacrifice, the victims probably being prisoners caught during battle. The methods of killing are believed to have included burning, beheading, hanging and drowning. An important part of Celtic religion was a veneration for the human head, and such sacrifices were undoubtedly performed before carved stone heads such as those found at Hexham. If there is any truth in the stone tape theory the heads would have absorbed the fear and suffering caused by those savage acts. However, even if the stone tape theory is tenable why should the resultant manifestation take the form of a werewolf? Once again we need to examine the Celts' religious practices and beliefs.

The Celts worshipped a variety of gods, many of whom combined human and animal parts. It is quite possible that a creature with both human and wolf characteristics figured among these deities. The Celts' firm belief in, and visualization of, such a creature could somehow have been recorded by the two stone heads, the process perhaps being facilitated by the blood-letting and the violent emotions of both the victims and their killers. When the heads were unearthed centuries later they 'played back' their recordings. Dr Don Robins believes that some minerals, such as quartz, of which the Hexham heads contain a large proportion, may have the capacity to store information in the form of electrical energy in their crystal structure.

Interestingly, not everyone who had custody of the heads saw the phantom werewolf. Perhaps a very particular set of conditions is necessary to trigger the phenomenon. Some sort of 'psychic awareness' on the part of the witness may be a necessary factor. Even if the heads were not Celtic in origin, is it not, perhaps, possible that they somehow absorbed malevolent influences from the past during their burial in this part of the country, with its ancient Celtic associations?

The Horse-Man of County Louth

On a spring night in 1966, John Farrell and Margaret Johnson were driving along a lonely country road not far from Drogheda, County Louth, in the Republic of Ireland. They were driving past Lord Dillon's estate when a huge animal loomed up in the road ahead. John Farrell braked hard, and he and Miss Johnson were thrown back in their seats. When the girl looked out of the window she saw:

> . . . a huge horse with a man's face and horrible bulging eyes. I could see by John's face that he saw it too. I think I screamed, but both of us were so frightened that we were paralysed. The thing had a horse's body. But it was the face, leering and hairy and huge which shocked.
>
> The animal stretched right across the road and completely blocked the car. It stayed there for nearly two minutes. We were petrified. Then it vanished. John quickly swung the car around and drove it to my home, about a mile away.
>
> We were so frightened that we drove through the gate and knocked it off the hinges. I woke up my father and both of us told him the same story. We don't drink and two of us couldn't have imagined the same thing.

Margaret's father later commented to the Press:

> They must have seen something awful. Both were still terrified when they came in here and each of their descriptions of the ghost tallied, Margaret was very sick for days after the incident.

Shortly after the encounter Lord Dillon was interviewed by the Press. He described an interesting legend concerning his home, Rath House, near which the strange beast had been seen. During the eighteenth century an altercation had occurred on the steps of the house between its then owner, a protestant, and the parish priest. The landlord used violent language to the priest and ordered him off the estate, whereupon the priest's horse reared up and crashed its hoof down on the step, leaving an imprint in the stone. What looks like a hoof-print is still visible on the step today.

The Abbey House Animal

Various strange phenomena have been recorded over the years at Abbey House, a predominantly sixteenth-century building in Cambridgeshire. Several apparitions have been seen, the most curious of which is an animal resembling a large hare with close-cropped ears. It was first seen, apparently, during spring or summer 1904, about six months after Mr J. C. Lawson, a distinguished classical scholar, and his family had moved into the house. One day Mrs Lawson went to fetch her three-year-old son John, from the nursery when he ran out in front of her crying 'Where's it gone, mummy?' When questioned he said that he had seen a 'little brown thing' which ran from the doorway of the nursery to the curtains and then disappeared. Later, Mrs Lawson saw the animal, which she described as

> . . . a nondescript kind of animal resembling a large-sized hare, but with close-cropped ears. It was always seen and heard running about on its hind legs, the patter of its footsteps being very distinct and characteristic. It was never seen standing still or moving slowly. Its haunts were the downstairs parts of the house. . . . It was generally seen in twilight but it was also seen quite clearly by artificial light in the drawing room.

The children named the animal 'Wolfie'. On one occasion Mr Lawson heard it coming down a passage, and then watched as it came into view and dashed past him. He was convinced of the solidity of the thing. The creature was seen about thirty times by the Lawson family.

The animal has been seen by later residents of Abbey House. In 1920 Mr G. Granville Sharp, his wife and daughter, moved into the house. Shortly after, the little girl was frightened by the phantom animal as Mrs Granville Sharp described in a letter to Professor F. J. M. Stratton of the Society for Psychical Research:

> We had been in the old Abbey just a week when I heard, one morning, my little girl Charmian, crying in the hall. I went to see what was the matter and found her in the doorway of the dining room,

> crying hard with the tears rolling down her cheeks. When I asked her what was the matter, she pointed to the far corner of the dining room, by the cupboard, and said, 'Will it hurt me?' I answered her that there was nothing to hurt her, but she would not go into the room at any time.
>
> About a week later the same thing happened again – and this time I asked her what it was she saw, and she said it was an 'animal' as she called it.
>
> From this time she often spoke of the 'animal' and said it came in at the window.
>
> She was only two years and nine months old at this time, and had heard nothing whatever about the subject, nor would she have understood if it had been mentioned.
>
> I, myself, had heard nothing more than that the house was haunted, until afterwards. And she was always with me, and couldn't have been told of it by anyone else.

The animal's last appearance seems to have been in 1947. Mrs Celia Schofield, a friend of the tenant of the house, described in a letter to a friend how her son Christopher, then two years old, had run into the kitchen shouting 'Oh look! tiny doggie,' but no animal could be found.

The Things Under the Bed

In December 1883, Mrs Charlotte E. Field wrote an article for the magazine *Merry England* in which she described the strange things that had happened at her house in Montpellier Terrace, Cheltenham, since her arrival there in 1874. These included crashing noises, as if heavy objects had fallen, running footsteps, talking and whispering sounds, and the appearance of two apparitions, one of a girl, and one of a woman. More frightening than all this, however, was the following incident, which was later described by Mrs Field's two daughters. The younger girl stated:

> My sister always teased me for being afraid of ghosts; but, one night, she herself got really frightened. She was standing by my bed, and mother and the maid were talking outside in the passage, when I heard something under my bed, and asked my sister to look. She laughed, and said it was nothing; but while she looked, about a dozen black creatures, like toads, only with horns and a tail, came out from

under the bed, and ran over my sister's foot and across the room, disappearing down the wainscot to return no more.

The incident was confirmed by the elder girl:

> My sister was in bed or standing, I forget which, and I was sitting by her, and our mother was outside with a servant. Suddenly my sister said to me 'There is something under the bed, do look.' I did so and these creatures ran out and one of them ran over my foot.

The elder girl tried to convince herself that the creatures were some sort of mechanical contrivance rigged up by someone who, for some reason, was trying to frighten her family out of the house. 'That is the most pleasant supposition,' she wrote. 'Black things with horns and tails could not have come from a good place, if they were supernatural.'

It is hardly likely that the things were mechanical, particularly as they simply disappeared. What strikes one about this case, as with many others, is that although the creatures could not be 'real' animals they were not only seen quite clearly, but could also be heard and felt.

The Borley Bug

Borley Rectory in Suffolk was probably the most famous haunted house in England. A wide variety of strange phenomena were reported there over a period of some sixty years. One incident which occurred in the grounds of the Rectory in August 1938 (about six months before the Rectory was destroyed by a fire), is particularly interesting. It involved Mrs Margaret E. Wilson, who had travelled to the Rectory on 22 August to make an oil painting of the building. Mrs Wilson arrived at the Rectory shortly after midday and, setting up her easel facing the back of the building, began work. At about 3.00p.m. the peace of the summer day was broken by what sounded like wings beating, or rushing wind. Mrs Wilson says:

> Looking up, I saw the queerest object with impelling eyes advancing towards me at about eye level. It seemed to be coming out of a mist. It was accompanied by a wasp on its left, and this must have been the wings I heard. I had just time to jump up and as they were quite near my face, which seemed to be the objective, I struck at it with my

> mahlstick, and seemed to hit the big object into the grass. The wasp seemed to go off on its own. With alarm I searched for the nameless object I had struck, as if I had not killed it, I thought it was possible it might attack me. I searched but was unable to trace it and eventually gave up looking. Gradually, the unusualness of the creature dawned upon me and the more I thought of it, the less I could understand what it was.
>
> Certainly, I had never seen anything like it before, and should describe it as being quite three inches in length, the body entirely black and composed of sections enabling it to bend and expand with ease. Its eyes were large and the colour of bloomy black grapes. The object was flattish.

When Mrs Wilson arrived home she painted the creature, and then asked her friend, Miss Joyce Mercer, to make a black and white sketch which would be more suitable for reproduction.

The Man-Monkey

On the night of 21 January 1879, a man was driving his cart home from Woodcote in Shropshire to Ranton in Staffordshire. At 10.00p.m., as he was crossing a bridge on the Birmingham and Liverpool Junction Canal (now part of the Shropshire Union Canal), about a mile from the village of Woodseaves, a horrible black creature with enormous shining eyes jumped out of the trees by the roadside and landed on the horse's back. The man tried to push it off, but his whip just went through the creature and in his fright he dropped it. The horse broke into a gallop, the creature clinging to its back. Eventually though, the phantom vanished and the exhausted horse and its terrified owner made their way home, stopping to rest at an inn in Woodseaves where the man described his ordeal. He was so shocked that he spent the next few days in bed. His whip was found next day at the spot where he had dropped it.

The story has an interesting postscript. A few days later, after a garbled version of the story had been circulating, the witness's employer, Mr B., was visited by a policeman who was investigating a report that he, Mr B., had been attacked and robbed on the Big Bridge on the night of the 21 January. Mr B. described the true incident to the constable who responded, in a disappointed manner:

> Oh, is that all, sir? Oh, I know what that was. That was the Man-Monkey, sir, as does come again at that bridge ever since the man was drowned in the cut [canal].

Mr B. described his employee's frightening encounter to the folklorist Georgina F. Jackson just a week after it happened.

The Mocking Beast

Over the years, there have been several encounters with an unpleasant creature at the village school of Goodhurst in Kent. One witness was the writer, Joan Forman, who worked there during the mid-1950s. She was spending the first few days of the summer holiday at the school, most of the staff already having left, and was sleeping alone in the oldest part of the building. At about 3.30a.m., on her second night there, she awoke suddenly out of a deep sleep. Something was crouching on the floor to the left of her bed:

> It was about two feet in length, I suppose, the size of a large cat or a small corgi. It resembled neither of these. It had a pair of huge nocturnal eyes like those of a lemur, and these were the clearest features of the apparition. I noticed them particularly because they were unwaveringly fixed on me. I think it was the most revolting gaze I have ever had to endure, for what emanated from the thing was an atmosphere of extreme malevolence and obscenity. With all its exudation of evil it was at the same time mocking. It stared at me for what seemed half an hour (although I suspect it was only a few minutes in chronological time) and I stared back, playing rabbit to its snake. I could not move to switch on the light, and in any case the creature itself seemed to emit some kind of glow in which I could see the shape of its face and head and the huge eyes, and a dim suggestion of the rest of its body.

Eventually, the room, which had been bitterly cold, grew warmer with the early dawn, and the thing began to fade away, and in a few minutes had disappeared altogether. Joan Forman's successor at the school had a similar experience, though in a different bedroom.

The Big Grey Man of Ben MacDhui

For many years experienced climbers have reported a variety of uncanny experiences on the mountain of Ben MacDhui in Scotland's Cairngorms. These include strange auditory phenomena such as unearthly music, footsteps and voices; overwhelming feelings of depression, anxiety and fear; an urge to commit suicide by jumping from high peaks and, of most interest here, sightings of a giant man-like creature, known in Gaelic as *Am Fear Liath Mor* – the Big Grey Man.

According to writer Affleck Grey, who has made a study of the Ben MacDhui mystery, references to the Big Grey Man go back to the late eighteenth century. Eye-witness accounts, however, seem to be confined to the present century. Two witnesses were Dr A. M. Kellas, a very experienced mountaineer who died tragically on the 1921–2 Everest Reconnaissance Expedition, and his brother Henry Kellas. The latter described the encounter, which took place in 1900, to his lifelong friend W. G. Robertson, who in turn related the story in a letter to the Aberdeen *Press and Journal* in 1925:

> He and his brother, Dr Kellas, had been chipping for crystals in the late afternoon well below the cairn, and were together on the slope of a fold of the hill. Suddenly they became aware of a giant figure coming towards them from the cairn. They saw it pass out of sight in the dip on the side of the fold remote from themselves, and awaited its reappearance. But fear possessed them ere it did reach the top, and they fled. They were aware it was following them and tore down by Corrie Etchachan to escape it.
>
> Mr Kellas said there was a mist on part of the hill but refused to believe that the figure could be the shadow of either his brother or himself, causing an optical illusion. He asked why not *two* figures if that had been the case. . . . No one who knew Mr Kellas or heard him relate his story could doubt this complete faith in his experience.

According to some sources Dr Kellas said that the figure was almost as tall as the ten-foot-high cairn.

Another witness was climber Tom Crowley whom Affleck Grey describes as 'one of the toughest characters I have ever known on a mountain'. On a day in the early 1920s Crowley was descending from Braeraich to Glen Eanaich when he heard footsteps behind him. He saw something which caused him to flee in terror to the glen below – a huge grey figure with pointed ears, long legs and feet with talons which more resembled fingers than toes.

Mountaineer Richard Frere described to Affleck Grey how one of his friends had encountered the Ben MacDhui giant. The witness had been spending a night alone in a tent near the cairn and was lying in his sleeping bag when suddenly something obscured the moonlight which was shining through a crack in the fly-sheet. Overwhelmed with terror he lay rigid, unable to move. Shortly the shadow moved away, and the climber, regaining courage, sprang forward and lifted the fly-sheet. Frere continues:

> The night was brilliant. About twenty yards away (he is curiously certain of the distance) a great brown creature was swaggering down the hill. He uses the word 'swaggering' because the creature had an air of insolent strength about it and because it rolled slightly from side to side, taking huge measured steps. It looked as though it was covered with shortish brown hair (yes, he asserts, most definitely brown), its head was disproportionately large, its neck very thick and powerful. By the extreme width of the shoulders compared to the relative slimness of its hips he concluded its sex to be male. No, it did not resemble an ape: its hairy arms, though long, were not unduly so, its carriage was extremely erect. . . . He tells us that the creature was at least twenty feet in height.

The witness had arrived at his estimate of the creature's height by carefully noting various features of the landscape near to which it had appeared, such as a large boulder, and then applying basic trigonometry. He said that the giant must have been between twenty-four and thirty feet tall.

These three incidents are only a part of the strange story of Ben MacDhui. The subject is dealt with at length in Affleck Grey's fascinating book *The Big Grey Man of Ben MacDhui.*

The Demon in the Stable

In his book *The Middle Kingdom*, published in 1959, Dermot MacManus described how his father had had a frightening encounter with a malevolent supernatural being. As a boy of about fourteen, MacManus senior was playing hide-and-seek with his elder brother among the stable buildings at the family home during the Christmas holidays. He was in one of the granaries above the stables when, lifting a trap door to jump through, he was surprised to see the horses below beside themselves with fear, snorting, trembling and stamping. Looking down into the stable MacManus saw the reason for their terror. Crouched on the edge of the manger, just twelve feet away, and hunched up like a boy squatting on his haunches, was a nightmarish creature. With one of its hands, which was a dirty greyish-brown, all bone and sinew with long curved claws in place of finger nails, it gripped the side of the manger. It glared at the terrified boy with eyes like 'glowing coals of fire' and MacManus stared back in horror for a few seconds before slamming down the trap door. Hurriedly making his way out through the adjacent buildings, and calling out to his brother to follow, he raced back to the house. In the sanctuary of their bedroom the terrified boy described to his brother what he had seen.

A case which bears some similarity to the above was described by Eric Maple in *The Realm of Ghosts*, though he does not give a date or the name of the person involved. The incident occurred at a very old farm known as Devil's House on Wallasea Island, among the marshes bordering the River Crouch in Essex. The house had long been reputed to be haunted. On one occasion a labourer working in one of the barns heard his name called several times and felt a sensation of coldness creep over him, followed by an overwhelming urge to kill himself. In a trance he picked up a length of rope and, fastening one end round his neck, he walked towards a ladder, intending to fasten the other end to a beam. He heard the voice say, 'Do it, do it, do it,' and looking up saw a hideous ape-like creature crouching on one of the beams. It was thin and black and had bright yellow eyes. The sight of it so shocked the man that he awoke from his trance and he fled from the barn.

The Beast in the Orchard

Dermot MacManus also described a frightening experience which befell his grandfather in the late 1860s. At about 12.00 on a warm summer night he was walking through an orchard on the family estate towards the summer-house, where a group of young people were enjoying a party. 'As he reached the glade,' MacManus writes:

> he heard the rustle of dry leaves among the laurels and a large animal ran out, crossing from his left to his right towards the apple trees. It was not three paces from him and he saw it clearly. It was the shape of a fox with a large bushy tail, but of enormous size, more like a wolf than a fox. As it reached the glade he clapped his hands and called, 'Shoo!' whereat it stopped at once, stood up on its hind legs, and turned to face him. It was his own height or more, but to his horror he saw it had no head. In spite of that, he knew it was looking at him and pouring out hate, bestiality and evil.

Mr MacManus made the sign of the cross and called the powers of good to his aid. As he did this the creature dropped on all fours and ran quickly away into the darkness under the apple trees. When he returned to the house he told his wife of his terrifying encounter. In 1901 Mr MacManus, then ninety-one years old, made a signed statement describing the experience which, although it had occurred over thirty years earlier, was still fresh in his memory.

The Vulpine Visitor

A creature somewhat similar to the above was described by Richard Curle in his book *Caravansary and Conversation* published in 1937. He encountered the beast when a boy in Scotland. He was lying wide awake in his bed at about 2.00 one winter's morning, when he heard footsteps approaching the house. They paused momentarily by the back door, then the boy heard them inside the house, first on the flagstones of the lower passage, then coming up the stairs and approaching his room. Curle continues:

> By this time I was sitting up in bed with my eyes glued to the door and with horror in my heart. The handle turned and in the opening stood a creature with the face of a fox, which walked on its hind legs. It was dressed in some sort of way and, would you credit it, wore a top hat, which added an indescribably macabre touch. But its face, I repeat, was fox-like and it had a bushy tail. It was, perhaps, bigger than a real fox, but it was vulpine through and through, although I admit that it had no rank odour.

It gazed at me with a fixed rather than a malign expression, but it did not speak. I shouted out, 'Go away!' – how well I remember the exact words! – and it turned round and went away. I heard its steps follow, in retreat, the precise route they had followed before, unhurried and steady as ever, until at last they died out on the road leading to the woods.

Several explanations have been offered. One is that it was a dream within a dream and that I was asleep the whole time; well, all I can do is to reiterate, emphatically, that I was wide awake. This may not sound convincing, but if one does not know when one is wide awake, what does one know? Of course, I may, for the first and last time, have been subject to an hallucination but, if so, then it was a remarkably thorough one. Still another explanation is that it was a hoax; but who on earth, even if in his dwarfish dimensions he were able to disguise himself as a fox, could make his legs *shrink*?

The thing seems inexplicable to me, who have pondered it for over forty years.

The Monster from over the Hill

In *The Powers of Evil* Richard Cavendish described a bizarre case which involved a person whom he calls Mrs Smith. One evening, about the year 1940, she was chatting to her husband and her neighbours when she said, quite out of the blue, 'It will come over the hill when it comes.' She later had no recollection of saying this, and doubted it even when the others assured her that she had spoken these words. Shortly after though, she became increasingly nervous of being out of the house after dark. About three months later, she woke up in the middle of the night, trembling and shivering. Waking her husband she told him that the thing from over the hill was nearly upon them. Almost at once they heard one of the outside doors opening and the heavy tread of something which sounded wet coming up the stairs. The Smiths clung together, terrified, as a hideous creature came into their bedroom. It was naked, bloated and had a blotched skin of yellow, green and purple with a head that came nearly to a point on top and ear lobes reaching almost to its shoulders. It had a massive bull neck and what appeared to be webbed feet. It crossed to the window, giving the impression of wading rather than walking, and disappeared. Mrs Smith, who said that she and her husband had both seen the thing clearly, later commented:

It was horrible and the absolute essence of evil. . . . I have never experienced anything so dreadful before or since and I hope I never shall, God willing. I still experience the same horror when I talk about it or write as I am doing now. I have never been able to discover why I saw it and I have never been able to find out what it was.

Riders on the Storm

It was pointed out in Chapter Four that Black Dogs often seem to have been associated with electrical storms. On occasions, other weird creatures are said to have appeared during storms, several instances being given in medieval sources. It is hard to assess such reports after so long a time, but they are worth including in the record. The *Chronicon de Melrose*, compiled by the monks at the Cistercian Abbey of Melrose near Galashiels, describes a curious manifestation at Scarborough, Yorkshire:

August, 1065: – Great tempest and thunders at York, when the old enemy was also seen by many in that horrid tempest, mounted on a black horse. The monster was of very large size and preceded the storm. He was always flying towards the sea to tread it underfoot, and was followed by the blast of thunder and the flash of lightning, with horrid cracklings. Indeed, the tracks of this horse, aforesaid, were seen, of enormous size, imprinted on a mountain at the city of Scandeburch [Scarborough], whence he leapt into the sea. Here, on the top of several ditches, men found, stamped in the earth, prints made by the monster, where he had violently stamped with his feet.

Abbot Ralph of Coggeshall, who has already been mentioned, wrote of a strange creature's carcass, which was found after a thunderstorm over Kent in June 1205:

In the holy night of John the Baptist, all night thunder roared and lightning, terrific, incessantly flashed all over England. A certain strange monster was struck by lightning at Maidstone, in Kent, where, in the highest degree, the most horrible thunder reverberated. This monster had the head of an ass, the belly of a human being, and other monstrous members and limbs of animals very unlike each other. Its black corpse was scorched and so intolerable a stench came from it that hardly anyone was able to go near it.

In 1171 a strange animal resembling a pig appeared during a thunderstorm over Hampshire, according to the *Eulogium Historiarum* which was written at Malmesbury Abbey:

> On the night of the birthday of the Lord, there were thunderings and lightnings, of which the like had not been heard before. And at Andover, a certain priest, at midnight, in the presence of the whole congregation, was cast down by lightning, with no other injuries . . . but what looked like a pig was seen to run to and fro between his feet.

The Tudor historian, John Stowe, who was born *c.*1525 and died in 1605, recorded a strange story told to him by his father:

> My father told me that, at St Michael's church, in the Cornhill ward, London, on the night of St James, certain men were ringing the bells of St Michael's, in the loft, when there arose a tempest of thunder and lightning, and a thing of an ugly shape and sight was seen to come in at the south window, and it lighted on the north. For fear whereof, all the ringers fell down and lay as dead for a time, leaving the bells to ring and cease of their own accord. When the ringers came to themselves, they found certain stones of the north window to be razed and scrat as if they had been so much butter, printed with a lion's claw; the same stones were fastened there again, when it was repaired, and remain so to this day. I have seen them oft, and have put a feather or small stick into the hole where the claw had entered, three or four inches deep. At the same time, certain maine Timber posts at Queen Hith were scrat and cleft from top to bottom, and the Pulpit Cross in Paul's churchyard was likewise scrat, cleft and overturned. One of the ringers lived in my youth, whom I have oft heard to verifye the same to be true, and I have oft heard my Father to report it.

Fairies

Belief in a race of beings, usually small in stature, who occupied a shadowy realm half-way between the physical and the spiritual, was once common to all parts of the British Isles. There were many names for the creatures, it often being thought unlucky to refer to them directly. In the Scottish Highlands, for example, they were known as The Good Neighbours or The People of Peace; in the Isle of Man as The Little People, The Little Fellas or Themselves, and in Ireland The Good People and The

Gentry. The Fairy Faith has largely died out, lingering longer in the Celtic parts of the British Isles, but encounters with fairies have continued to be described. Such accounts may tax credulity, but a few samples are given here and readers may form their own conclusions.

One of the earliest accounts comes from the seventeenth-century antiquarian John Aubrey:

> In the year 1633–4, soone after I had entered into my grammar at the Latin Schoole at Yatton Keynel [near Chippenham, Wiltshire], our curate, Mr Hart, was annoy'd one night by these elves or fayries. Comming over the downes, it being neere darke, and approaching one of the faiery dances, as the common people call them in these parts, viz. the greene circles made by those sprites on the grasse, he all at once sawe an innumerable quantitie of pigmies or very small people, dancing rounde and rounde, and singing, and making all maner of small odd noyses. He, being very greatly amaz'd, and yet not being able, as he sayes, to run away from them, being, as he supposes, kept there in a kind of enchantment, they no sooner perceave him but they surround him on all sides, and what betwixt feare and amazement, he fell down scarcely knowing what he did; and thereupon these little creatures pinch'd him all over, and made a sorte of quick humming noyse all the time; but at length they left him, and when the sun rose, he found himself exactly in the midst of one of these faiery dances. This relation I had from him myselfe, a few days after he was so tormented; but when I and my bedfellow Stump wente soon afterwards, at night time to the dances on the downes, we saw none of the elves or fairies.

During the early years of the twentieth century the folklorist and anthropologist W. Y. Evans Wentz travelled around Wales, Scotland, Ireland and the Isle of Man investigating the fast disappearing Fairy Faith. Many people he met claimed to have actually encountered fairies. One account came from Mr T. C. Kermode, a member of the Manx Parliament:

> About forty years ago, one October night, I and another young man were going to a kind of Manx harvest-home at Cronk-a-Voddy. On the Glen Helen road, just at the Beary Farm, as we walked along talking, my friend happened to look across the river (a small brook), and said, 'Oh look, there are the fairies. Did you ever see them?' I

looked across the river and saw a circle of supernatural light, which I have now come to regard as the 'astral light' or the light of Nature, as it is called by mystics, and in which spirits become visible. The spot where the light appeared was a flat space surrounded on the sides away from the river by banks formed by low hills; and into this space and the circle of light, from the surrounding sides apparently, I saw come in twos and threes a great crowd of little beings smaller than Tom Thumb and his wife. All of them, who appeared like soldiers, were dressed in red.

Mr Kermode wanted to get closer, but his friend was impatient to get to the party and struck the wall with his stick and shouted, causing the 'Little People' to vanish.

T. T. Wilkinson, in *Lancashire Folk-Lore* which he wrote with John Harland, described an experience which befell one of his relatives:

He had been amusing himself one summer evening on the top of Mellor Moor, near Blackburn, close to the remains of the Roman encampment, when his attention was arrested by the appearance of a dwarf-like man, attired in full hunting costume, with top-boots and spurs, a green jacket, red hairy cap, and a thick hunting whip in his hand. He ran briskly along the moor for a considerable distance, when, leaping over a low stone wall, he darted down a steep declivity, and was lost to sight.

The following account was sent in the 1920s to E. L. Gardner, a well-known investigator of psychic phenomena. The witness, Mr J. F. White, wrote:

Some years ago I was one of a party invited to spend the afternoon on the lovely slopes of Oxeford Hill, in the county of Dorset. The absence of both trees and hedges in this locality enables one to see without obstruction for long distances. I was walking with my companion who lives in the locality, some little distance from the main party, when to my astonishment I saw a number of what I thought to be very small children, about a score in number, and all dressed in little gaily coloured short skirts, their legs being bare. Their hands were joined, and all held up, as they merrily danced around in a perfect circle. We stood watching them, when in an instant they all vanished from our sight. My companion told me they were fairies, and that they often come to that particular part to hold their revels. It may be our presence disturbed them.

Another account came from a Miss Hall from Bristol who wrote:

> I, too, have seen fairies, but never until now have I dared to mention it for fear of ridicule. It was many years ago; I was a child of six or seven years and then, as now, passionately fond of all flowers, which always seem to me living creatures. I was seated in the middle of a road in some cornfields, playing with a group of poppies, and never shall I forget my utter astonishment at seeing a funny little man playing hide-and-seek amongst these flowers to amuse me, as I thought. He was quick as a dart. I watched him for quite a long time, then he disappeared. He seemed a merry little fellow, but I cannot ever remember his face. In colour he was a sage-green, his limbs were round and had the appearance of geranium stalks. He did not seem to be clothed, and was about three inches high and slender.

Allan Jobson in *Portrait of Suffolk* quotes from the description of a man who saw fairies in Stowmarket, Suffolk, though he does not give a date:

> There might be a dozen of them, the biggest about three feet high, the small ones like dolls. Their dresses sparkled as if with spangles like the girls at shows at Stow Fair; they came moving round hand in hand in a ring; no noise came from them. They seemed light and shadowy, not like solid bodies. I passed on, saying 'The Lord have mercy on me' but them must be the fairies, and being alone there on the path over the field could see them as plain as I do you. I looked after them when I got over the stile, and they were there just the same, moving round and round . . . I might be forty yards from them, and I did not like to stop and stare at them. I was quite sober at the time.

In his book *The Folklore of Orkney and Shetland* Ernest W. Marwick prints a letter from a Mr W. E. Thorner of Luton, Bedfordshire, who described a strange experience which occurred on the Island of Hoy on a winter's day during World War Two. He was walking along the cliff top at Torness, making his way with difficulty against the fierce wind, when he saw a group of small, wild-looking men dancing to and fro. They had round, sallow faces, long, bedraggled hair and unkindly expressions on their faces. They danced with great abandon, at times seeming to throw themselves over the cliff edge. Mr Thorner watched them for about three minutes before leaving the cliff edge.

In *The Middle Kingdom*, Dermot MacManus describes several encounters with fairies. The following incident, which took place around the turn of the century was described to him by a friend, a doctor, who came from County Mayo. MacManus's friend, when a boy, used to bathe in a stream not far from the town of Foxford. One summer afternoon the witness, then about nine years old, was walking home from the pool with a friend, when he saw a small figure dodge behind a large boulder. His companion said that what he had seen was probably just a scarecrow flapping in the wind, but to satisfy their curiosity the two lads went over to the boulder to have a look around. They looked behind the rock and, to their enormous surprise, were confronted by a little man about four feet high. He grinned at the boys, but they were terrified and, after staring for a few moments, took to their heels, not stopping until they reached the town. The little man wore a cap that covered his hair, and a close-fitting collarless black coat buttoned up to his chin. He had a broad, flat face with curly brown whiskers shot with grey. MacManus comments:

> The doctor has assured me that the incident is just as clear to him as ever and that he could lead me to the exact boulder. He is a graduate of Trinity College, Dublin; he served as a British officer in the First World War, campaigning in Salonica and France, and he is a man of intelligence and integrity.

Another account came from a woman of forty-four from the Mount Leinster area of County Carlow. The incident occurred about 1924 when she was a girl of nine. She came from a farming family who lived near the hamlet of Cranagh. One November afternoon she had brought the cows home from the fields and was standing at the farmyard gate waiting for the cattle to pass through when she saw a little man appear from behind one of the cows. He walked quickly, and as he passed by the head of one of the cows it tossed its head and made a pass at him with its horns. As it did so the little man looked at the cow in what seemed to be a friendly manner, and tapped it lightly on the nose with a stick he was carrying in his right hand. Glancing at the girl, and nearly touching her as he went by, he walked straight into a bank of solid earth. He was about four feet tall, looked young and wore a black cap turned up in front, a red coat, and tight buff trousers. The girl told her family about the incident but they merely laughed at her. The witness, though, has never doubted the reality of what she saw.

One clear June evening in 1951, two teenage girls were walking along a quiet country lane in County Wicklow when a little man suddenly appeared from nowhere on the road in front of them. He was between two and three feet high and was dressed all in black with a black cap. He seemed to be young, and looked quietly and intently at the girls, who stared at him in amazement for a few seconds then ran off across a field through a nearby farm gate which they stopped to close behind them. They looked back to see if the little man was still there, but there was no sign of him. Curiously though, balanced on the top bar of the gate was what looked like a 'common tin kitchen clock'. The girls had no idea what this could have been, and neither had MacManus to whom one of the girls gave a signed and witnessed account of the incident.

The following case was described to MacManus by an English lady, Mrs C. Woods. In June 1952, she and her son were staying at Newton Abbot in Devon. One hot day they climbed to the top of Haytor on Dartmoor, and for some reason Mrs Woods decided to walk back down and up again by herself. On her return journey to the top she saw a little man standing against one of the many large boulders which lay on the hill. He moved out about five to six yards from the boulder and stood watching her, shading his eyes with his hand. Mrs Woods continued up the path, feeling rather nervous, until she got to within forty yards of him at which point he dived out of sight behind the boulder. On reaching the summit she told her son of the encounter. He laughed at her but agreed to come down to the boulder to look for the little man. There was no trace of him, however. Mrs Woods stated:

> It was no momentary sight, as I watched him for some time standing there, and I wondered what he was. I had no idea at first that he was a little man; I thought rather of some animal until I got much nearer, and then I just stared and said to myself. 'This is no animal, it is a tiny man in brown.' I felt, and still feel, so convinced.

The little man, she said, was between three and four feet tall, seemed elderly, and was clothed in a brown, knee-length smock, tied at the waist with a cord, brown stockings and what seemed to be a brown cap.

What possible explanation can there be for encounters such as these? All one can say is that, whatever the nature of the incidents, the witnesses were strongly affected by them, and obviously believe that they encountered fairies.

The Shapeless One

After looking at creatures of all manner of shapes we conclude this chapter with a note on a being which has no shape at all. In English folklore the phantom was often referred to as Boneless. One encounter with Boneless, which seems to have taken place early this century, involved a policeman whose beat included the Minehead to Bridgwater road in Somerset. The experience was described by the witness's sister-in-law to the folklorist Ruth Tongue, who writes:

> He told her it was darksome over above Putsham Rise and the tide was in far below – he could hear it plain down two hill fields, and then his lamp lit up a white Summat across the road. It weren't fog. It were alive – kind of woolly, like a cloud or a wet sheep – and it slid up and all over him on his bike, and was gone rolling and bowling and stretching out and in up the Perry Farm Road. It was so sudden he didn't fall off – but he says it was like a wet heavy blanket and so terrible cold and smelled stale.

The experience so terrified the policeman that he requested, and was granted, a transfer to another beat.

Jesse Saxby, in *Shetland Traditional Lore*, published in 1932, described an encounter between a group of Shetland islanders and 'It', though the account reads more like folklore than actual experience. What is of particular interest is the comment of one of the Shetlanders who described the event. It makes a poetic and appropriate ending to this chapter:

> We all ken there's many kinds of life that lives in the air, in the earth and water – forby the clouds above. And we, poor mortals, have no vision to hear or see, or understand the like. We must just leave that to the Powers above.

CHAPTER SIX

Thoughts

> The Western scientists never realize how powerful the human mind is and what miracles it can work.
>
> Statement made by Asian guru in 1912 to a group of Russian occultists.

The eye-witness accounts of the previous five chapters fit into two categories. The first comprises reports which apparently refer to flesh and blood animals. Mystery cats, lake monsters and sea serpents fall into this group. The second category comprises accounts of such creatures as Black Dogs, the Owlman of Mawnan and fairies which, if they are what they seem to be, can only be paranormal in origin. However, it is not always possible to make a sharp division between the two groups. Despite numerous sightings of the Surrey Puma, the Loch Ness Monster and Morgawr, indisputable evidence seems impossible to obtain. Furthermore, there are some decidedly uncanny aspects to sightings of these creatures, as we have seen. Also, although this book has been concerned with mystery animals of the British Isles, sightings of such creatures occur worldwide, our British animals are merely part of a greater pattern.

Increasingly some researchers have come to think that creatures in the first category may have the same paraphysical origins as those in the second. If this is so, how can the continual sightings of these paranormal beings be explained?

There will inevitably be hoaxes and mistakes but, as we have seen, most witnesses appear to be reliable, honest and seeking an explanation for the unusual creatures they have seen.

We seem then to be left with three main possibilities:

That Sightings of Paranormal Animals Are a Form of Hallucination

Hallucinatory experiences seem absolutely real to the person involved, who may not only see animals or people that are not there, but can hear and even touch them. Some accounts of paranormal animals could indeed be hallucinations, but there are drawbacks in applying the theory to all sightings.

We notice that the same types of animals are reported, with very similar details, by many independent witnesses, often over hundreds of years. The Black Dog is an example and if indeed this is an hallucination, why should it be an experience common to so many people?

An answer may lie with the famous psychologist C. G. Jung's concept of the 'collective unconscious'. Jung suggested that an individual's brain, or the subconscious part of it, had access to an immense store of information which it had not acquired from any external source and which it shared with the rest of mankind. The information in this mass memory, thought Jung, could have been inherited genetically, over generations, as unconscious memory. He refers to such items stored in the collective unconscious as 'archetypes'. Is it then possible that Black Dogs, lake monsters and other animal manifestations are such archetypes, and are forced up into the conscious mind as hallucinations under the influence of appropriate external stimulus?

There are arguments against the hallucination theory. In general, hallucinations seem to occur when the human brain is not functioning properly – perhaps when under great stress or fatigue; in the curious half-way state between sleep and wakefulness; in a state of mystical ecstasy, or even under the influence of drugs – whereas many of the paranormal animal sightings have occurred in normal, everyday conditions with the witnesses wide-awake and concentrating on their everyday tasks. Also, on some occasions paranormal animals have been seen at the same timc by several witnesses.

That Paranormal Animals Exist as Independent Beings

It is possible that our phantom animals actually exist – and have always existed – perhaps inhabiting another dimension or plane of existence from which they occasionally emerge into our world. A concept often discussed in the literature of the supernatural is that of the 'astral plane', a realm which is not wholly physical nor wholly spiritual, but somewhere between the two. Richard Cavendish in his book, *The Powers of Evil*, writes that inhabitants of the astral plane include 'innumerable nature spirits, fairies, and other beings of folklore, nymphs and satyrs, trolls and gnomes, elves and goblins'. To this list we might add the Surrey Puma, the Loch Ness Monster, Black Dogs and the Owlman of Mawnan.

Writers such as John Keel have postulated the idea of 'window areas' where our dimension overlaps with another and through which the inhabitants of the parallel universe may make their way into our world. Alternatively, when a sighting of a paranormal animal occurs, the witness may actually be looking through the 'window' and seeing the creature in its normal world.

The creatures of the astral realm might not have form or appearance, being bundles of energy onto which the witnesses' minds impose an identity. This concept was discussed many years ago by W. Y. Evans Wentz, who travelled around Scotland, Ireland, Wales, the Isle of Man and Brittany at the turn of the century, recording accounts of supernatural beings and fairylore, and by the theosophist Edward L. Gardner who wrote:

> The normal working body of the gnome or fairy is not of human nor of any definite form. They have no clear-cut shape normally, and one can only describe them as small, hazy and somewhat luminous clouds of colour with a brighter sparklike nucleus . . . what determines the shape assumed and how the transformation is effected is not clear. One may speculate as to the influence of human thought, individual or in the mass, and quite probably the explanation when found will include this influence as a factor.

This theory would at least explain why the fairies described by so many witnesses are so absurdly like the storybook conception. The witnesses have a preconceived notion and see what they expect to see.

One unpleasant possibility is that the other dimension is inhabited by evil entities which deliberately assume grotesque forms to terrify human beings. John Keel suggests that, throughout history, humans have been plagued by malicious 'ultraterrestrials' who have delighted in frightening and confusing them. Keel, and several other researchers, most notably Jacques Vallee, believe the ultraterrestrials to be behind the UFO phenomenon, and point out the similarity between the alien beings, or UFO-nauts, so often described and the fairies, demons and monsters of folklore. It is possible that the paranormal animals are elaborate holograms – three-dimensional images constructed and controlled by the UFOnauts or ultraterrestrials who keep themselves hidden.

Some clergymen who are practising exorcists believe in the existence of evil spirits which may assume hideous forms as part of their efforts at possession. Leslie Watkins, in *The Real Exorcists*, describes a case involving Father Arnold Clare who succeeded in ridding a seventeen-year-old youth of what seemed to be a possessing demon, the efforts of doctors and psychiatrists to cure the youth's mental disturbance having failed. Two nights after the exorcism Father Clare was confronted in his own home by what he believed to be the demon which had possessed the youth. The spirit had wrecked his study, awakening Father Clare, who hurriedly gathered together his tools of exorcism. He flung open the study door and commanded the demon to show itself and was immediately aware of an evil energy swirling round him. He saw in a corner of the room a hideous creature resembling a 'gigantic man with talons on its webbed paws and with the head of a long-haired ape'. Father Clare flung his censer at the apparition which disappeared in a flash of light, never to return. He was convinced that the demon knew that its most potent weapon was fear and for this reason had assumed this terrifying form. Sensational as this case sounds, Watkins writes that he has spoken to other priests who have had similar experiences and reached similar conclusions. Of course, magicians throughout our entire history have claimed the power to summon and control demons, but the evidence for this rests on their own testimony or that of their committed followers.

That Paranormal Animals are Created by Mental Power

Our third theory combines features from the first and second. It postulates that witnesses' minds actually create the beings they see. The ability to create beings by mental power has long been attributed to psychics, mystics and magicians, the world over. The witches of East Anglia were reputed to be able to create Black Dogs by the power of thought. The lamas of Tibet are also credited with the ability to produce thought forms and, in her book, *Magic and Mystery in Tibet*, published in 1965, Alexandra David-Neel describes how, following traditional Tibetan mental exercises and ritual she succeeded in creating a *tulpa*, a human apparition. The figure, that of a small, plump, jovial monk, was seen not only by herself but by several others, one of whom thought it to be an actual lama. It took several months of mental concentration to bring the apparition into existence, and several more to destroy it.

Another case where a thought form was allegedly created occurred in Russia in 1912, when a group of noblemen, known as the Brotherhood of the Rising Sun, was led in an experiment by a guru of Chinese or Tibetan origin. The guru prudently suggested that they should concentrate on a humorous and harmless creature, such as Puss in Boots, in the uniform of a musketeer. After about half an hour of intense concentration the form began to appear. At first it was just a light cloud but gradually the form of a red-haired cat began to appear. Its dress remained unclear, though, and the guru intervened: 'Obviously you cannot imagine the musketeer's uniform,' he said, 'your thoughts are various. Now, think only of a red-haired cat in common Russian boots.'

> Within a few moments the features of the cat stabilized and on its hind feet was a pair of Russian boots. The *egrigor* was motionless and looked like a poorly developed photograph.

The guru ordered the assembly to cease thinking about the *egrigor*, and slowly the form disappeared. This incident was described by Nicholas Mamontoff, a son of one of the witnesses, in *Fate* magazine in 1960.

Franek Kluski, a Polish medium, also apparently succeeded in creating beings by mental power. He participated in many carefully controlled experiments, producing a variety of thought forms whilst in a state of trance. One creature he regularly materialized was:

> . . . a rapacious beast, the size of a very big dog, of a tawny colour, with slender neck, mouth full of large teeth, eyes which glowed in the darkness like a cat's, and which reminded the company of a maneless lion. . . . The lion, as we may call him, liked to lick the sitters with a moist and prickly tongue, and gave forth the odour of a great feline. . . .

The realistic nature of the apparition is remarkable. Not only could it be seen, but felt and even smelt! Franek Kluski was also able to materialize a huge shambling ape-like creature. One witness, Dr Gustave Geley, present at a seance in November 1920, stated that he felt its shaggy head press hard upon his shoulder and cheek, and when one of the sitters held out his hand it was seized and licked by the animal. Another witness, Colonel Norbert Ochorowitz, described the creature's great strength, stating that it was able to lift a heavy bookcase with ease.

One disturbing possibility is that mind creatures could live on after their creator's death. Tibetan magicians told Alexandra David-Neel that this was possible, and indeed that some *tulpas* were deliberately created with this purpose in mind.

The *tulpa*, the *egrigor* and the Kluski animals were the result of a deliberate process, but perhaps such mind creatures could be brought into existence unintentionally or unconsciously.

Dion Fortune, psychic and witch, described in her book *Psychic Self-Defence* how she unintentionally created a werewolf. She was lying in bed, half asleep and brooding resentfully against someone who had injured her. The thought of vengeance entered her mind and she suddenly thought of Fenris, the huge, malevolent wolf of Norse mythology. 'Immediately,' she later wrote, 'I felt a curious drawing out sensation from my solar plexus, and there materialized beside me on the bed a large wolf.' As she moved, the beast growled at her, but she summoned all her courage and pushed it off the bed. The animal vanished through the wall of the room, but next morning another occupant of the house told of dreaming about wolves, and of waking in the night to see the glowing eyes of an animal in the darkness.

Another occasion when the power of thought might have inadvertently resulted in the appearance of a cat-like animal was reported by Anthony 'Doc' Shiels. After two previous occasions when he had apparently been able to raise a sea serpent and lake monster, in Cornwall in 1976 and Loch Ness in 1977, he tried unsuccessfully to raise a lake monster by the power of thought in Lough Leane, County Cork, in 1980. After several days of failure he met two friends, who related a curious incident; he writes:

> Seamus and Pauline had a strange tale to tell. Around twelve the previous night, they had been driving into Ballyvourney when a large animal stepped into the road, in the full glare of the car's headlights. 'Grey in colour. Shaggy coat. Tufted ears. Big . . . it looked just like a lynx . . . but you don't get lynxes in County Cork.' Now at that time, neither Seamus nor Pauline had any idea that I was a monster hunter;

but the fact that they encountered their Hibernian Lynx at the very same time that we were trying to raise a beastie in Lough Leane is, I'm sure, significant.

Is it possible that mystery animals are brought into existence by the mass exercise of subconscious will-power? Such a process could perhaps be initiated by persons encountering a normal animal which they believe to be something out of the ordinary – a puma perhaps. As the details of the report are publicized by the media, people think about the animal and form a picture of it in their minds. As they do this they literally create the beast, which continues to draw on their mental powers. As people begin to lose interest in the animal, their attention being perhaps distracted by another news story, it begins to fade and lose its substance, and the reports cease. The initial reports might genuinely refer to an escaped puma, but the mass subconscious creates replicas of it, like carbon copies, which are imprinted on the landscape and continue to be seen after the original animal has been caught or has died, and in areas where it never roamed in the first place. There could be an element of wish-fulfilment in such a process. In an age when many people feel threatened by technology and the rapid social changes it can bring about, and when the environment seems increasingly threatened by pollution and urban sprawl, there is something appealing about the concept of a big-cat at large. It adds an element of mystery and wildness to the homely British countryside, a pleasant distraction from ordinary, uneventful daily life. There is also an element of humour in the situation, indeed in the very names of the mystery animals – the Nottingham Lion, the Surrey Puma – with their incongruous juxtaposition of the familiar with the alien.

The power of the human mind may be greater when 'boosted' by other factors – electrical energy for example. (We saw earlier how Black Dogs sometimes displayed an affinity with electrical phenomena.) Stormy weather may facilitate the creation of other paranormal entities and the numerous sources of electromagnetic radiation scattered over the British Isles, generating stations, microwave towers, nuclear power plants and overhead power lines may all play their part in supplying the human mind with all or some of the energy needed for the calling up of paranormal animals.

Hilary Evans cites two cases which are perhaps relevant here.

The first incident reportedly occurred in the laboratory of the Rhodes Electrical Company in London some years prior to 1951. The chief engineer, Mr Eastman, was working on high tension wires forming a magnetic field in a dark room. Suddenly he saw a glowing blue sphere forming over a revolving dynamo. The light grew brighter and a shape resembling a human hand appeared in the sphere. The image was watched by Eastman and his assistant, Harold Woodew, for several minutes before it faded away. The men, after trying for four days, managed to recreate the conditions, and obtained the image of a human head, white and with indistinct features which slowly revolved.

The second case occurred in the United States:

> Fay Clark told Brad Steiger that one evening in 1931, at the Northern State Power Company in La Crosse, Wisconsin, a standby boiler had just been put on line at maximum power, when a cloud began to form over the turbine. Fearing overheating, the men checked and found that the machine was operating normally. They then saw appear in the cloud 'as clearly as could be, the image of a woman lying on a couch. One of her arms was covered with jewels, and there were rings on her fingers'.

Location may be an important factor. As mentioned earlier, events involving violence and strong emotions may leave some sort of trace on their surroundings, a form of energy which may later be picked up by the minds of witnesses. Certain topographical features seem to recur in Black Dog cases, and the Bords suggest that alien animal sightings might occur along ley-lines. The concept of leys was originated in the 1920s by Alfred Watkins. He believed that in the distant past, the British countryside was covered by a network of straight trackways. The trackways themselves had been covered over or obliterated but their paths could still be plotted by such features as standing stones, hillforts, old churches, prominent hills, holy wells and ancient earthworks. Watkins called these alignments 'leys'. Later researchers, notably John Michell, suggested that leys were not merely old route ways but indicated the flow of some sort of force or energy. This energy could perhaps be utilized by the witnesses' minds in the creation of paranormal animals.

A witness's subconscious mind may delve into the collective unconscious to give the phantom its form, but the creature is not merely an hallucination, as it is visible to others, perhaps having enough solidity to be touched, and even photographed. The creature may reflect its creator's desires. A lonely night-time traveller wishes for some form of companion and might provide himself with one – a friendly Black Dog, perhaps. On the other hand the wayfarer might be fearful of what the darkness conceals, and his fears are realized when some hideous creature, a man-monkey, for example, appears.

Of course, the theories discussed in this chapter are highly speculative, and attempt to provide answers to questions which may be unanswerable. One thing seems certain, sightings of mystery animals, whether flesh and blood or paraphysical beings, will continue. We react in our individual ways: with credulity or incredulity; with amusement or amazement, but perhaps in most of us there is a tiny rebel spark, which surreptitiously rejoices in the discomfiture of reason – and, if only one of the sum total of strange happenings is proved true, then any or all may be possible.

APPENDIX ONE

Sighting of Morgawr by Sheila Bird

This report is reproduced exactly as it was given to the author by Sheila Bird.

(See Chapter 2 for Sheila Bird's letter of 31 August 1985, to the *Falmouth Packet*)

Date: Wednesday, 10 July 1985
Time: Approx 8.00p.m.
Conditions: It had been misty and warm during the day, but the sun broke through in the late afternoon and it was warm with bright sunlight and very clear visibility in the evening. The sea was exceptionally calm, virtually rippleless with a glassy, silvery surface. It was still and quiet.
Scene: Writer Sheila Bird, who had just met her brother Dr Eric Bird, a coastal geomorphologist from Melbourne University, off the train at Truro, was relaxing with him on the clifftop at Pencabe, Portscatho. Suddenly Dr Bird caught sight of 'a large marine animal swimming slowly northward, about 200 metres offshore'.
Dr B: Whatever's that?
S.B. Good heavens! I've never seen anything like that before; whatever can it be?
(Dr B. called to a man and a woman who had just walked past carrying binoculars and said that there was something unusual and interesting worthy of closer inspection.)
S.B. (Suddenly realizing the significance of what she had seen, exclaimed excitedly) It's Morgawr! It's Morgawr!
Dr B. Who?
S.B. Morgawr!
Man: Is it a sea lion?
S.B. It's nothing like a sea lion. A sea lion doesn't have a head like that, a neck like that or a whacking great hump like that. It's the monster of Falmouth Bay generally known as Morgawr.
Other Three: Eh? Well, it's certainly very unusual . . .
Someone: I can imagine that sightings like this could give rise to such stories . . .
S.B. There have been reported sightings for about 100 years and on one occasion I think one was caught and landed by fishermen. My friend George Vinnicombe has seen it and his drawing of it appears in my book.

(There were two or three small boats probably fishing offshore and gulls were wheeling in the sky. S.B. who was observing points very closely, noticed that the skin of the neck was grey and had darker markings like folds or pockets of saggy skin, rather than scales. She noticed the unaccustomed speed and smooth, gliding motion which appeared not to disturb the still waters. The apparent swiftness was accentuated as a gull swooped low, skimming the surface of the water passing close to the creature in the opposite direction, then gained height and disappeared from the scene.)

Man: It's grey and slightly mottled.

Someone: There's a second hump.

Someone else: Yes, there are two humps.

S.B. Look. There's a tail just below the surface of the water.

(As the creature drew level with them, all four observers looking down through the clear waters were aware of this at the same moment. And then they realized that it was much longer than it appeared to be at first sight.)

S.B. Just look at the length of the tail; if you look carefully you can see the end of it just below the surface of the water.

Others: Oh yes, so you can.

Man: Well, that must be quite a size. It's big from here . . . just imagine what it must be like when you get close to it! What would you say, about seventeen feet?

Dr B. I'd say about seventeen feet.

S.B. Allowing for distance I'd say more like twenty.

Others: Difficult to assess at a distance.

Someone: Would you think about 200 metres offshore?

Someone else: About that; but it's difficult to judge. It's certainly a terrific size.

S.B. (to her brother) I've been out with 'Doc' Shiels and David Clarke, editor of *Cornish Life*, hoping to get a sighting of this monster, but without success. They've both seen it. And now I've seen it when I was least expecting to do so. I'm glad that you – a scientist who had never heard of it before – saw it first. If you hadn't pointed it out I would never have noticed it.

(All four watched the unfamiliar, unlikely creature in fascination until it suddenly submerged. It dropped vertically, like a stone, with head held high and disappeared beneath the glassy surface without leaving a ripple or any trace of where it had been just an instant before. The man and woman made their thoughtful way onwards, while Sheila Bird and her brother waited hopefully for about twenty minutes for it to put in another appearance.)

S.B. How do you explain it disappearing like that and not re-emerging for air, for most creatures of that size would surely have resurfaced again by this time. Anyone looking for Morgawr now would have little idea he is around the area. Perhaps his ability to stay submerged for so long accounts for his being so seldom seen.

Copy of report made by Eric Bird regarding the sighting of an unidentified marine animal off Pencabe, Portscatho, on 10 July 1985.

I endorse the report made by my sister.

On the evening of 10 July 1985, I was on the top of the cliff at Pencabe, near Portscatho, with my sister, looking out over the calm waters of Gerrans Bay. At about 8.00p.m., I noticed a marine animal swimming slowly northward, about 200 metres offshore. Its head projected about a metre from the water, and there was a curved back about two to three metres behind. As it moved, it caused a slight ripple of the otherwise calm sea. I drew my sister's attention to it, and also that of two passing holidaymakers, one of whom saw it through binoculars and said it was grey in colour. It appeared rather darker to me, but as he passed me the binoculars the animal sank quickly and quietly from view, and although we waited about twenty minutes there was no further sign of it.

I was surprised by its size. I am an earth scientist (coastal geomorphologist) rather than a biologist, and I have little knowledge of marine animals. It did not look like a seal or porpoise, and was not a whale: I could not identify it.

I had only just arrived that day in Cornwall, having flown in from Australia a few days before. I had not heard of the Morgawr story which my sister explained to me immediately after we had seen the animal. It seemed to me that sightings such as ours would have easily led to such a local tradition. I hope the animal will soon be identified, and its role in the ecology of the Falmouth/Veryan Bay area clarified.

(Signed) ERIC C. F. BIRD, MSc (Lond & Melb) PhD (ANU)
August 1985

APPENDIX TWO

Note regarding photograph of monster in Lough Leane, County Kerry, taken by Pat Kelly in August 1981

So far as I know, this photograph (*see* Plate 23) has not been published before. It was sent to Anthony Shiels, who, with the author has some reservations about this photograph. It certainly bears a great likeness to the Mary F. pictures of Morgawr, but, it could be pointed out, also resembles the descriptions of two-humped creatures seen in Loughs Fadda, Mask, Nahooin and Bran.

Kelly asserts that he is a direct descendant of Edward Kelly, assistant to the Elizabethan necromancer Dr Dee, and claims himself to have psychic powers. His father (Laurence O'Talbot Kelly) was acquainted with Aleister Crowley and claimed that the latter, whilst at Boleskine House, actually succeeded in his attempts to raise the monster from Loch Ness early in the century.

APPENDIX THREE

Land Sightings of Loch Ness Monster – Chronological Order

Date	Witnesses	Description
1879	Group of children near graveyard on North Shore	See p. 96
1880	E. H. Bright and cousin near Drumnadrochit	See p. 97
During 1890s	Gypsy woman near Dores	Animal was apparently seen by the woman lying by the road. According to Jock Forbes, himself a witness, the incident was quite well known in the area.
1909	Margaret MacGruer, Elizabeth MacGruer and others at Inchnacardoch Bay	See p. 97
1919	Jock Forbes and his father, two miles north of Inverfarigaig	See p. 99
April 1923	Alfred Cruickshank, two miles north of Invermoriston	See p. 99
During 1930s	Alec Muir, near Inverfarigaig	Capt Alistair MacIntosh described in his memoirs, *No Alibi*, published in London in 1961, how during the 1930s he met Alec Muir, a carpenter at the Foyers aluminium works, on the Dores road. Muir stated that he had just seen the monster cross the road in front of his car. Capt MacIntosh described how he and Muir followed a trail of crushed undergrowth through the

Date	Witnesses	Description
		woods to a clearing where, 'Showing in the moss was an immense depression where the monster had obviously lain down to rest.'
During 1930s	Schoolchildren at Drumnadrochit	According to Constance Whyte, some time during the 1930s, the children at Drumnadrochit School told their master that they had seen 'a most peculiar and horrifying animal' in a swamp near Urquhart Bay. Children picked out a drawing of a plesiosaurus as similar to what they had seen.
1933	Mrs Eleanor Price-Hughes, in scrub near Drumnadrochit	Monster was seen to emerge from bushes and vanish into lake, carrying something pink in its mouth. Commander Gould regarded this incident as a hoax.
1933 22 July	Mr and Mrs G. Spicer. Dores – Inverfarigaig road	The Spicers saw the animal cross the road about 200 yards in front of their car. It had a bulky body and a long thin neck which undulated up and down. It was a dirty-greyish colour and about twenty-five feet long. (The Spicers' original estimate of length was six to eight feet, but they revised this after measuring the road.) Commander Gould interviewed the Spicers shortly after their encounter. He considered their report to be entirely genuine.
1933 August	Mrs T. McLennan, near Whitefield	The animal was seen lying on a small beach at the edge of the water. Described by witness as about twenty-five feet long, with short, thick legs, with a back resembling that of an elephant, being ridged and grey in colour.
1933 December	Mrs Reid, near Inverness	Animal seen lying in glade on wooded slope, partly hidden by undergrowth. Described as dark, hairy, short thick legs and large head, about six to seven feet long.

Date	Witnesses	Description
		Roy Mackal suggests this is a misidentification of a Highland cow.
1934 5/6 January	Arthur Grant, near Abriachan	Animal seen about 1.00a.m. in bright moonlight at roadside. Described as fifteen to twenty feet long, with a small eel-like head, long neck, bulky body, two humps and four flippers. Re-entered loch in two great bounds, in a motion resembling that of a sea-lion.
1934 February	Patricia Harvey and Jean MacDonald, near Inchnacardoch Bay	Seen in moonlight at distance of about twenty feet. Described as about six feet tall, between eight and ten feet long, with four short legs. Underside of neck white. Possible misidentification of deer or cow.
1934 June	Margaret Munro at Kilchumein Lodge	Seen at a distance of about 300 yards from window of Kilchumein Lodge. Animal seen on loch shore. Described as dark grey, with long neck, 'absurdly small' head and pair of front flippers. Watched through binoculars for twenty-five minutes; animal rolled about and arched its back into large humps as if enjoying sunshine. Cyril Dieckhoff, who knew witness's father and employers, considered sighting genuine.
1960 28 February	Torquil Macleod, observed beast on beach opposite Invermoriston	Observed at 3.30p.m. in rainy conditions, at distance of 1700 yards. Creature observed through binoculars for over ten minutes, showing what seemed to be front half of body above water, with two large paddles and long neck. Dark grey or black. Animal remained still for eight or nine minutes, then moved neck in circular manner as though scanning shore. It finally lurched to left and flopped off bank into loch. Using graticulations of binoculars and almanac, witness

Date	Witnesses	Description
		estimated length to be a minimum forty-five feet.
1963 6 June	Members of the Loch Ness Phenomena Investigation Bureau at Achnahanat	A large dark object was filmed at water's edge on beach two and a half miles from the Achnahanat Camera Rig. The RAF's Joint Air Reconnaissance Intelligence Centre estimated the creature's length at between seven and seventeen feet. Obviously little can be deduced from this incident because of great distance.

APPENDIX FOUR

Dinoteuthis proboscideus

In an article in *Fortean Times* (No. 42, autumn 1984), Anthony 'Doc' Shiels suggested that the Loch Ness Monster could be a form of cephalopod, one of a group that comprises the squids, cuttlefish and octopuses. He postulates a cephalopod with a long and flexible proboscis which would resemble a neck if held out of the water, and calls his hypothetical creature *Dinoteuthis proboscideus.*

This, he suggests, could have several inflatable humps on its back, shaped by the animal's buoyancy mechanism – a series of gas-filled cavities. (Several of the known species of cephalopod have gas-operated buoyancy devices.) Thus the animal would have a varying back contour, showing a different number of humps according to the displacement of the gas. The animal has a muscular tail with a pair of horizontal lobes, which would be used for swimming and act as stabilizers, six small tentacles and a pair of larger arms which could be used for crawling. The most distinctive feature of the animal is the long and flexible proboscis which could be used for catching prey and bringing it towards the mouth. Doc points out that, according to Professor J. E. Morton in his book *Molluscs* (London: Hutchinson, 1979) some of the early cephalopods may have had such a feature. Dinoteuthis, like some known species of cephalopod, could have the ability to change its colour and skin texture and, like the octopuses, the ability to crawl about on land for short periods.

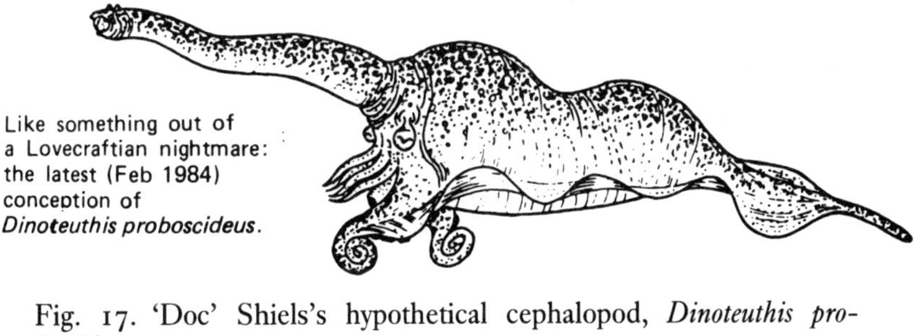

Fig. 17. 'Doc' Shiels's hypothetical cephalopod, *Dinoteuthis proboscideus.*

There is nothing inherently impossible about a beast such as Dinoteuthis. The known cephalpods have evolved into a fantastic variety of creatures. Some, like the cuttlefish, are only a few inches long, while the giant squid is known to attain a length of sixty feet. Some of the deep-sea cephalopods, trawled up by scientific expeditions appear almost nightmarishly grotesque. Although all the known species of cephalopod are marine, a fresh-water form could have evolved.

Doc admits that his theory is highly speculative but points out that a creature such as Dinoteuthis would account for the varying characteristics that have been reported of the Loch Ness Monster over the years, such as the difference in the number of humps, varying colouration and different skin textures. The theory might also explain the reactions of fear and loathing by those witnesses, such as the Spicers, who have seen the Loch Ness Monster at close range.

APPENDIX FIVE

Sightings by County

Mysterious Big Cats

England

County	Location
DEVON	Bishop's Nympton
	Bovey Tracey
	Drewstone
	Hacche Moor
	Haytor Vale
	Moretonhampstead
	North Molton
	Parracombe
	South Molton
	Tedburn St Mary
	West Buckland
	Wistlandpound Reservoir Track
HAMPSHIRE	Crondall
	Ewshot
	Farnborough
	Froyle
	Heathy Park Reservoir
	Hurtwood Common
	New Forest
	Preston Candover
HERTFORD	Cuffley
KENT	Canterbury
LONDON	Shooter's Hill
NOTTINGHAM	Nottingham Airport
SOMERSET	Seven Ash
STAFFORDSHIRE	Wolverhampton
SURREY	Abinger Hammer
	Aldershot
	Chiddingfold
	Cranleigh
	Dunsfold

	Ewhurst
	Farnham
	Godalming
	Guildford
	Hale Common
	Hascombe
	Hindhead
	Hog's Back
	Munstead
	Runfold
	Shackleford
	Tweezledown Racecourse
	Waverley Abbey
	Woldingham
	Worplesdon
SUSSEX	South Downs, Belle Tout area
	Tilgate Forest

Scotland

AYRSHIRE	Kilmarnock
CAITHNESS	Berriedale Brae
INVERNESS	Balloch
	Cannich
	Castle Urquhart
	Garve
KIRKCUDBRIGHTSHIRE	Borgue
LANARKSHIRE	Biggar
MIDLOTHIAN	Fountainhall
	Garvald
	Penicuik
	Rosewell
	Roslin
MORAY	Advie
	Dufftown
	Grantown-on-Spey
	Kellas
PERTH	Ochil Hills
ROSS	Cononbridge
SUTHERLAND	Achiltibuie
	Embo
WEST LOTHIAN	Whitburn

Sea Serpents

England

County	Location
CORNWALL	Carrick Roads, River Fal
	Durgan, Helford River
	East Looe
	Falmouth, three miles south of Gerrans Bay
	Grebe Beach, Helford River
	Gyllyngvase, Falmouth
	Lizard Point, 25 miles south of
	Mawnan, Helford River
	Parson's Beach, Helford River
	Pendennis Point, Falmouth
	Portscatho
	Restronguet Point, River Fal
	Rosemullion Head, Falmouth Bay
	Trefusis Point
	Between Cornwall and Brittany
DEVON	Prawle Point
LINCOLN	Chapel St Leonards
	Trusthorpe
SCILLY, Isles of	30 miles north-north-west of
SUFFOLK	Thorpeness
THAMES ESTUARY	Black Deep
YORKSHIRE	Filey
ISLE OF MAN	Off coast of

Ireland

CLARE	Off coast of
CORK	Queenstown (now Cobh)
LIMERICK	River Shannon

Scotland

ARGYLL	Kilchoan
DUMBARTON	Helensburgh
INVERNESS	Loch Hourn
ORKNEY ISLANDS	Hoy, off the coast of
	Pentland Skerries
	Skerries of Work
ISLAND OF SKYE	Sound of Sleat
WESTER ROSS	Kyle of Lochalsh

Wales

CARDIGAN	New Quay
GLAMORGAN	Gower Peninsula

Lake Monsters

Ireland

County	Location
CLARE	Lough Graney
CORK	Lough Attariff
DONEGAL	Lough Muck
GALWAY	Lough Abisdealy
	Lough Auna
	Ballynahinch Lake
	Between Loughs Crolan and Derrylea
	Dhulough
	Lough Dubh
	Lough Fadda
	Lough Mask
	Lough Nahooin
	Shanakeever Lough
KERRY	Lough Bran
	Lackagh Lake
MAYO	Sraheens Lough, Achill Island
ROSCOMMON	Lough Ree
WICKLOW	Lough Bray

Scotland

ARGYLL	Loch Fyne
HEBRIDES	Loch Urabhal, Isle of Lewis
INVERNESS	Loch Arkaig
	Loch Eil
	Loch Lochy
	Loch Morar
	Loch Ness
SUTHERLAND	Loch Assynt

The Black Dog

England

County	Location
CAMBRIDGE	Balsham
	Peterborough
	West Wratting

CORNWALL	Whiteborough Tumulus, Nr Launceston
CUMBRIA	Thirlmere
DERBY	Upper Booth
	Lea
	Edale
DEVON	Allen's Week
	Black Dog
	Bow
	Braunton Burrows
	Copplestone
	Dartmoor
	Dean Combe
	Down St Mary
	Hollocombe
	Lydford
	Molland
	St Giles-in-the-Wood
	Tamar, River
	Thelbridge
	Tiverton
	Torridge, River
	Torrington
	Uplyme
	Week Hill
	Wembworthy
ESSEX	Hatfield Peverell
	Hockley
HEREFORD	Hergest Court
HERTFORD	Six Hills, Nr Stevenage
	Tring
LANCASHIRE	Burnley
	Thackergate
LEICESTER	Birstall
LINCOLN	Alford
	Algarkirk
	Blyborough
	Brigg
	Crosby
	Horncastle
	Kirton
	Leverton
	Manton
	Moortown
	Northorpe

	Scotter
	Till, River
	Willoughton
	Wrangle
NORFOLK	Buxton Lamas
	Coltishall
	Ditchingham
	East Dereham
	Geldeston
	Gorleston
	Hilgey
	Markey Hole
	Overstrand
	Peddars Way
	Rockland
	Sheringham
SOMERSET	Wambarrows, Nr Winsford
SUFFOLK	Barham
	Blythburgh
	Bungay
	Great Bealings
	Leiston
WILTSHIRE	Chippenham
	Doghill Barrow
	West Kennet, burial mound
WORCESTER	Bewdley-on-Severn
	Bredon
YORKSHIRE	Kettleness

Ireland

DUBLIN	Knocklyon
	Pussy's Leap
	Templeogue
GALWAY	Ballygar
MAYO	Area around Loughs Conn and Cullen
ROSCOMMON	Ballaghadereen
WICKLOW	Redcross

Scotland

ARGYLL	Craignish
	Knapdale
ISLE OF MULL	Ardura
	Lochbuie
SUTHERLAND	Creag an Ordain
OUTER HEBRIDES	Dun Borbe

Wales

ANGLESEY	Nr Amlwch
CARMARTHEN	Laugharne
PEMBROKESHIRE	Camrose
	Cot Moor
	Haverfordwest
	Pembroke Ferry

Bibliography

Chapter One: Mystery Cats

Beer, Trevor, *The Beast of Exmoor* (Countryside Productions, Barnstaple, 1984)
Bowen, Charles, 'Mystery Animals', *Flying Saucer Review* (Nov/Dec 1964)
Briggs, Katherine, *A Dictionary of Fairies* (Allen Lane, London, 1976)
Burton, Maurice, 'Is this the Surrey Puma?', *Wildlife* (no. 260 Nov 1966)
Chard, Judy, *Devon Mysteries* (Bossiney Books, Bodmin, 1979)
Clair, Colin, *Unnatural History* (Abelard-Schuman, London, 1967)
Cobbett, William, *Rural Rides* cited by Janet and Colin Bord in *Alien Animals*
Dunne, John J., *Haunted Ireland* (Appletree Press, Dublin, 1977)
Fort, Charles, *The Complete Books of Charles Fort* (Dover Publications, New York, 1974)
Francis, Di, *Cat Country: The Quest for the British Big Cat* (David & Charles, Newton Abbot, 1983)
Hall, Chris, 'Stalking the Surrey Puma', *The Unexplained* (no. 29)
Head, Victor, 'Trailing the Surrey Puma', *The Field* (8 April, 1965)
Rickard R. J. M., 'If you go down to the woods today . . .', *Info Journal* (vol. IV no. 1 May, 1974); 'The Surrey Puma and Friends: More Mystery Animals', *The News* (now *Fortean Times*) (no. 14, January, 1976); 'Out of Place', *Fortean Times* (no. 18, October 1976; no. 19, December 1976; no. 20, February 1977; no. 25, Spring 1978; no. 26, Summer 1978; no. 30, Autumn 1979; no. 32, Summer 1980; no. 34, Winter 1981; no. 35, Summer 1981); 'The Exmoor Beast and Others', *Fortean Times* (no. 40, Summer 1983)
Tabori, Paul and Underwood, Peter, *The Ghosts of Borley* (David & Charles, Newton Abbot, 1973)
Young, Stanley P. and Goldman Edward A., *The Puma: Mysterious American Cat* (Dover Publications, New York, 1964)

Chapter Two: Sea Serpents

Campbell, Elizabeth M., with Soloman, David, B.SC. PH.D., *The Search for Morag* (Tom Stacey, London, 1972)

Clarke, David, 'The Myth and Mystery of Morgawr, the Helford Monster', *Cornish Life* (vol. 4, no. 1, 1977); 'Morgawr – Myth or Mystery', *West Country Mysteries* (Bossiney Books, Bodmin, 1985)

Dinsdale, Tim, *The Leviathans* (Routledge & Kegan Paul, London, 1966 and revised edition Futura Publications, London, 1976); *The Loch Ness Monster* (Routledge & Kegan Paul, London, 1961 and revised edition, 1976)

Gould, Rupert T., *The Loch Ness Monster and Others* (Geoffrey Bles, London, 1934)

Heuvelmans, Bernard, *In the Wake of the Sea Serpents* (Rupert Hart-Davis, London, 1968)

Maxwell, Gavin, *Harpoon at a Venture* (Rupert Hart-Davis, London, 1955)

Rickard, R. J. M., 'The Durgan Dragon', *The News* (now *Fortean Times*) (no. 15, April 1976); 'More Cornish Unidentifieds', *Fortean Times* (no. 16, June 1976); 'Morgawr Update', *Fortean Times* (no. 19, December 1976); 'The Monstermind Experiment', *Fortean Times* (no. 21, Spring 1977)

Rostron, Arthur, *Home from the Sea* (Cassell & Co., London, 1931)

Shiels, Anthony Nichol, 'Words from the Wizard', *Fortean Times* (no. 35, Summer 1981)

T. T. and Buckland, Frank, 'The Sea Serpent in a Highland Loch', *Land and Water* (7 September 1872)

Thompson, A. G., *Gower Journey* (published by the author, Swansea, 1950)

Chapter Three: Lake Monsters

Alexander, Marc, *To Anger the Devil* (Neville Spearman, Sudbury, 1978)

B. B., *September Road to Caithness* (Nicholas Kaye, London, 1962)

Binns, Ronald with Bell, R. J., *The Loch Ness Mystery Solved* (Open Books Publishing, Somerset, 1983)

Bord, Janet and Colin, *Alien Animals* (Granada Publishing, London, 1980); 'Creatures of the Irish Lakes', *The Unexplained* (no. 38) and 'The Perplexing Irish Peiste', *The Unexplained* (no. 39)

Campbell, Elizabeth M., with Soloman, David, B.SC. PH.D., *The Search for Morag* (Tom Stacey, London, 1972)

Costello, Peter, *In Search of Lake Monsters* (Garnstone Press, London, 1974)

Dinsdale, Tim, *The Loch Ness Monster* (Routledge & Kegan Paul, London, 1961 and revised edition, 1976); *The Leviathans* (Routledge & Kegan Paul, London, 1966 and revised edition Futura Publications, London, 1976); *Project Water Horse: The True Story of the Monster Quest at Loch Ness* (Routledge & Kegan Paul, London, 1975)

Gould, Rupert T., *The Loch Ness Monster and Others* (Geoffrey Bles, London, 1934)
Gregory, Augusta Lady, *Visions and Beliefs in the West of Ireland* (Putnam & Sons, London, 1920)
Holiday, F. W., *The Great Orm of Loch Ness* (Faber & Faber, London, 1968); *The Dragon and the Disc* (Sidgwick & Jackson, London, 1973)
Mackal, Roy P., *The Monsters of Loch Ness* (MacDonald & James, London, 1976)
Malmesbury, Lord, *Memoirs of an Ex-Minister* (Longmans, Green & Co., London, 1857)
Meredith, Dennis L., *Search at Loch Ness: The Expedition of the New York Times and the Academy of Applied Science* (New York, 1977)
Rice, H. J., *Thanks for the Memory* (Athlone Press, Athlone, 1953)
Rickard, R. J. M., 'Nessie: the Shiels 1977 Photos', *Fortean Times* (no. 29, Summer 1979)
Shiels, Anthony Nichol, 'Words from the Wizard', *Fortean Times* (no. 23, Autumn 1977); 'Words from the Wizard', *Fortean Times* (no. 34, Winter 1981)
Smith, J. L. B., *Old Fourlegs – The Story of the Coelacanth* (Longmans, Green & Co., London, 1956)
Somerville, Edith, *The Smile and the Tear* (Methuen & Co., London, 1933)
Sundberg, Jan-Ove, 'The Monster of Sraheens Lough', *Info Journal* (March 1977)
Whyte, Constance, *More Than a Legend* (Hamish Hamilton, London, 1957)
Witchell, Nicholas, *The Loch Ness Story* (Terence Dalton, Suffolk, 1974)

Chapter Four: The Black Dog

Alexander, Marc, *To Anger the Devil* (Neville Spearman, Sudbury, 1978)
Beer, Trevor, *The Beast of Exmoor* (Countryside Productions, Barnstaple, 1984)
Bord, Janet and Colin, *Alien Animals* (Granada Publishing, London, 1980)
Briggs, Katherine, *A Dictionary of Fairies* (Allen Lane, London, 1976)
Brown, Theo, 'The Black Dog', *Folk-Lore* (vol. 69, 1958)
Chambers, R., *The Book of Days* (vol. ii) (W & R Chambers, London, 1888)
Cade, C. Maxwell and Davies, Delphine, *The Taming of the Thunderbolts* (Abelard-Schuman, London, 1969)
Clark, Jerome and Coleman, Loren, *Creatures of the Outer Edge* (Warner Books, New York, 1978)
Dale-Green, Patricia, *Dog* (Rupert Hart-Davis, London, 1966)
Day, J. Wentworth, *Portrait of the Broads* (Robert Hale, London,

1967); *The Ghost Hunter's Game Book* (Frederick Muller, London, 1958)

Deane, Tony and Shaw, Tony, *The Folklore of Cornwall* (B. T. Batsford, London, 1975)

Dunne, John J., *Haunted Ireland* (Appletree Press, Dublin, 1977)

Fleming, Abraham, *A Straunge and Terrible Wonder* (Francis Godly, London, 1577), quoted in William Hone's *Everyday Book* (vol. 1) (Hunt and Clarke, London, 1826)

Garmonsway, G. N., *The Anglo-Saxon Chronicle* (J. M. Dent & Sons, London, 1972)

Grinsell, Leslie V., *Folklore of Prehistoric Sites in Britain* (David & Charles, Newton Abbot, 1976)

Hamel, Frank, *Human Animals* (The Aquarian Press, Wellingborough, new ed, 1973)

Harland, John and Wilkinson, T. T., *Lancashire Folk-Lore* (John Heywood, Manchester and London, 1882 and E. P. Publishing, Wakefield, 1973)

Harries, John, *The Ghost Hunter's Road Book* (Frederick Muller, London, 1968)

Hippisley-Coxe, Anthony D., *Haunted Britain* (Hutchinson & Co., London, 1973)

Hole, Christina, *English Folklore* (B. T. Batsford, London, 1940)

Innes, Simon, 'Beware of the Dog', *The Unexplained* (no. 86) and 'Tracking down Black Dogs', *The Unexplained* (no. 87)

Jefferies, Richard, *Wild Life in a Southern County* (Moonraker Press, London, 1879)

Jenkins, Stephen, *The Undiscovered Country* (Neville Spearman, Sudbury, 1977)

Jones, Edmund, *A Relation of Apparitions of Spirits, In the County of Monmouth and the Principality of Wales* (Newport, 1813) cited in Bords, Janet and Colin, *Alien Animals*

Killip, Margaret, *The Folklore of the Isle of Man* (B. T. Batsford, London, 1975)

Lane, Frank, *The Elements Rage* (Country Life, London, 1948)

Lofthouse, Jessica, *North Country Folklore* (Robert Hale, London, 1976)

MacGregor, Alasdair Alpin, *The Ghost Book* (Robert Hale, London, 1955)

MacManus, Dermot, *The Middle Kingdom: The Faerie World of Ireland* (Colin Smythe, Gerrards Cross, 1972)

Maple, Eric, *The Realm of Ghosts* (Robert Hale, London, 1964)

Page, J. L. W., *An Exploration of Dartmoor* (Seeley & Co., London, 1889)

Palmer, Roy, *The Folklore of Warwickshire* (B. T. Batsford, London, 1976)

Porter, Enid, *The Folklore of East Anglia* (B. T. Batsford, London, 1974)

Rudkin, Ethel H., 'The Black Dog', *Folk-Lore* (vol. 49, 1938)

Tongue, R. L., *Somerset Folklore* (The Folk-Lore Society, London, 1965)
Underwood, Peter, *Ghosts of Wales* (Christopher Davies, Swansea, 1978)
Whitlock, Ralph, *The Folklore of Devon* (B. T. Batsford, London, 1977)
Wiltshire, Kathleen, *Ghosts and Legends of the Wiltshire Countryside* (Compton Russell, Salisbury, 1973)

Chapter Five: Many Kinds of Life

Bord, Janet and Colin, *Alien Animals* (Granada Publishing, London, 1980)
Briggs, Katherine, *A Dictionary of Fairies* (Allen Lane, London, 1976)
Burne, Charlotte S., *Shropshire Folklore* (Trübner & Co., London, 1883 and E. P. Publishing, Wakefield, 1974)
Cavendish, Richard, *The Powers of Evil* (Routledge & Kegan Paul, London, 1975)
Collins, Andrew, *The Brentford Griffin: The Truth Behind the Tales* (Earthquest Books, Wickford, 1985)
Curle, Richard, *Caravansary and Conversation* cited in Grey, Affleck, *The Big Grey Man of Ben MacDhui* (see below)
Dunne, John J., *Haunted Ireland* (Appletree Press, Dublin, 1977)
Forman, Joan, *The Haunted South* (Robert Hale, London, 1978)
Gardner, E. L., *Fairies: The Cottingley Photographs and their Sequel* (Theosophical Publishing House, London, 1945)
Grey, Affleck, *The Big Grey Man of Ben MacDhui* (Impulse Books, Aberdeen, 1970)
Haining, Peter, *A Dictionary of Ghosts* (Robert Hale, London, 1982)
Harland, John and Wilkinson, T. T., *Lancashire Folk-Lore* (John Heywood, Manchester and London, 1882 and E. P. Publishing, Wakefield, 1973)
Jobson, Allan, *Portrait of Suffolk* (Robert Hale, London, 1973)
MacManus, Dermot, *The Middle Kingdom: The Faerie World of Ireland* (Colin Smythe, Gerrards Cross, 1972)
Maple, Eric, *The Realm of Ghosts* (Robert Hale, London, 1964)
Marwick, Ernest W., *The Folklore of Orkney and Shetland* (B. T. Batsford, London, 1975)
O'Donnell, Elliott, *Great Ghost Stories* (including *A Casebook of Ghosts*) (W. Foulsham & Co., London, 1983)
Price, Harry, *The Most Haunted House in England* (Longmans, Green & Co., London, 1940)
Rickard, R. J. M., 'A Celtic Werewolf?', *The News* (now *Fortean Times*) (no. 15, April 1976)
Robins, Don, 'The Hexham Heads', *Alpha* (no. 8, May/June 1980)
Rogo, D. Scott, *Phantoms* (David & Charles, Newton Abbot, 1976)

Sanderson, Ivan T., *Things* (Pyramid Publications, New York, 1967)
Saxby, Jesse, *Shetland Traditional Lore* (first published: 1932) Cited in Briggs, Katherine, *A Dictionary of Fairies*
Screeton, Paul, 'Curse of the Hexham Heads', *The Unexplained* (no. 117)
Summers, Montague, *The Werewolf* (Kegan Paul, Trench, Trubner & Co., London, 1933)
Vallee, Jacques, *Passport to Magonia: From Folklore to Flying Saucers* (Neville Spearman, London 1970)
Wentz, W. Y. Evans, *The Fairy Faith in Celtic Countries* (Oxford University Press, Oxford, 1911 and Colin Smythe, Gerrards Cross, 1977)
Wilkins, Harold T., *Mysteries, Solved and Unsolved* (Odhams Press, London, 1959)
Woodward, Ian, *The Werewolf Delusion* (Paddington Press, London, 1979)

Chapter Six: Thoughts

Bord, Janet and Colin, *Alien Animals* (Granada Publishing, London, 1980)
Cavendish, Richard, *The Powers of Evil* (Routledge & Kegan Paul, London, 1975)
Clark, Jerome and Coleman, Loren, *Creatures of the Outer Edge* (Warner Books, New York, 1978)
Evans, Hilary, *Visions, Apparitions, Alien Visitors: A Comparative Study of Entity Enigma* (Thorsons/Aquarian Press, Wellingborough, 1984)
Fortune, Dion, *Psychic Self-Defence* (The Aquarian Press, London, 1930)
Keel, John A., *UFOs: Operation Trojan Horse* (G. P. Putnam & Sons, New York, 1970)
Mamontoff, Nicholas, 'Can thoughts have forms?', *Fate* (June 1960)
Michell, John and Rickard, R. J. M., *Phenomena: A Book of Wonders* (Thames & Hudson, London, 1977)
Rogo, D. Scott, *Phantoms* (David & Charles, Newton Abbot, 1976)
Shiels, Anthony Nichol, 'Words from the Wizard', *Fortean Times* (no. 34, Winter 1981)
Watkins, Leslie, *The Real Exorcists* (Methuen & Co., London, 1983)
Wiltshire, Kathleen, *Ghosts and Legends of the Wiltshire Countryside* (Compton Russell, Salisbury, 1973)

Index

FOR:

NIC–YOU HELPED ME TAKE
THE BIGGEST OF STEPS

HOPE AND HARRISON–
GROW UP TO DO WHAT YOU LOVE